Politics of Symbolization Across Central and Eastern Europe

Studies in Sociology: Symbols, Theory and Society

Edited by Elżbieta Hałas and Paolo Terenzi

Volume 11

PETER LANG

Elżbieta Hałas / Nicolas Maslowski (eds.)

Politics of Symbolization Across Central and Eastern Europe

PETER LANG

Bibliographic Information published by the Deutsche Nationalbibliothek
The Deutsche Nationalbibliothek lists this publication in the Deutsche
Nationalbibliografie; detailed bibliographic data is available online at
http://dnb.d-nb.de.

Library of Congress Cataloging-in-Publication Data
A CIP catalog record for this book has been applied for at the
Library of Congress.

This publication was financially supported by the Faculty of Sociology and the
Centre de Civilisation Française, University of Warsaw.

Reviewer: Dennis Smith
(Loughborough University, Emeritus Professor of Sociology).

ISSN 1618-775X
ISBN 978-3-631-84285-0 (Print)
E-ISBN 978-3-631-84537-0 (E-PDF)
E-ISBN 978-3-631-84538-7 (EPUB)
E-ISBN 978-3-631-84539-4 (MOBI)
DOI 10.3726/b17961

© Peter Lang GmbH
Internationaler Verlag der Wissenschaften
Berlin 2021
All rights reserved.

Peter Lang – Berlin · Bern · Bruxelles · New York · Oxford · Warszawa · Wien

This publication has been peer reviewed.

www.peterlang.com

Contents

6 Contents

Symbolic Construction of Communities: New Beginnings and New Divides

The Symbolic Politics of European (Dis)unification

Introduction: European Space, Semiosis and Politics of Symbolization

On semiosis, symbolic power and politics

The issue of meaning is unquestionably pivotal for shaping the social world and learning about it. There can also be no doubt that the most fundamental social process is communication, which reveals the social genesis and variability of meanings and their symbolic vehicles. To be communicated, meaning needs an objectifying form of expression: externalization, which is sensorially available to the communicating person. Signs and symbols serve this purpose.

Communication, as shown already by the founders of modern semiotics, Ferdinand de Saussure, Charles S. Peirce and George H. Mead, is not a simple process determined by a code. It consists of communicative acts and is therefore an active achievement which generates understandable text, the interpretation of signs and symbols by other signs and symbols, or a meaningful conversation of gestures and symbols. The social world is constantly rife with active processes of semiosis: creating, expressing and symbolically objectifying meanings. As symbols created in the social process of interactions become established, they may define the forms of social life, stabilizing the underlying meanings in the form of obvious typifications, normal forms, commonsense knowledge, doxa, or ideology supported by the authority of power and symbols of power. After discovering the symbolic constitution of society (like Émile Durkheim and Alfred Schütz, who both pointed out the existence of symbolism-based structures of socially shared knowledge, or symbolic interactionists, who drew attention to the emergence of a meaningful order of collective actions and their symbolic framework), the next step was to study the problems of symbolic power and the politics of symbolization. One of the scholars who studied these issues was Pierre Bourdieu. He criticized the dominant symbolic orders and analyzed symbolic struggles. However, symbolic power does not lie in symbolism itself, but in the social relations of power that make use of this symbolism. Representatives of national authorities, i.e. those who manage the dominant classifications, occupy a privileged position in the space of social relations (Bourdieu 1989: 21, 109).

Because the processes of semiosis are constitutive for the social world, symbolism represents an integral dimension of social relations. The issue of power in relations remains a central issue, hence the importance of politics of symbolization. In other words, it is necessary to study the relationship between power and symbolic actions in society (Edelman 1985, Geertz 1973, Kertzer 1988). *Homo politicus* is simultaneously *homo symbolicus* (Cohen 1976).

Symbolic representations of the norms and values on which social practices are based are examined as social images, following the French tradition of the Durkheim school. However, it is not the symbols themselves, but acts of symbolization and the pragmatic use of symbolism that are of paramount importance for the constitution of society. Words, in particular, designate real objects, but also signify ideas by expressing their meanings, which are mental images. Thus, symbolism is constitutive both for the orders of cultural knowledge (i.e. visions of the world) and for the orders of social relations and interactions. Pierre Bourdieu characterized this as a complex social symbolic system (Bourdieu 1991: 237).

Social crises, catastrophes and radical social changes expose the symbolic construction of the social order. Furthermore, collective actions directed towards change are not possible without a symbolic framing of their meanings. Of key importance is the issue of social identity and its semantics, usually based on a binary code, i.e. on the definition of that identity and its confirmation by emphasizing differences. Competition for the meaning of social reality, along with symbolic struggles, shows that politics of symbolization are an integral part of the social processes of semiosis.

One of the key issues is the control of historicity (Touraine 1981: 31) through the strategic use of symbolism in the politics of remembering and forgetting various aspects of collective historical experience. European nation-states are historical formations. Their symbolic identities emerged in the course of the historical process, where the modern era brought a plethora of symbolic inventions, such as the construction of traditions, institutionalization of symbols and symbolic practices (flags, hymns, national holidays) by symbolic elites (Hobsbawm, Ranger 1983). Legitimation of the nation-state and the shaping of civic loyalty occur through a game of memory and history, which is always a problematic construct of what is remembered and commemorated.

Politics of symbolization are not under the state's sole control; at any rate, democracy makes freedom possible also as regards the range of symbols that function in a society and the symbolic representations of its identity. Similarly, politics of symbolization do not have to focus primarily on the meaning of the past, as various temporal orientations of these politics (wherein either the present or the future predominates) are possible. However, an orientation towards the past (either recent or distant) makes it possible to give meaning to both the present and the future.

In the communication process, signs and symbols express meanings. Semiosis means creating meanings, as well as using objects and events as signs or symbols that relate to something other than themselves. The interchangeable use of the terms "sign" and "symbol" is possible when symbols are broadly understood as conventional signs, i.e. signs intentionally used to signify or symbolize. At this point, it should be noted that when talking about semiosis, we refer loosely to its concept introduced by Peirce, who considered its various forms to be the subject of semiotics, including instances of unintentional semiosis where something becomes a sign, i.e. stands for something else. Semiosis is a continuous process, a flow or chain of formation of meaning structures, the basis of which is the sign as a relation between the initial sign, its object and the new sign that arises; in other words, between the representamen, the object and the interpretant:

> by 'semiosis' I mean ... an action, or influence, which is, or involves, a cooperation of *three* subjects, such as a sign, its object, and its interpretant, this tri-relative influence not being in any way resolvable into actions between pairs. (Peirce 1935: 484 after: Heiskala 2003: 212)

The relationship between a symbol's meaning and the thing symbolized is arbitrary. Symbols in language (natural language as a symbolic system) are, to quote semioticians of culture from the Tartu-Moscow school, the primary system that models reality, because the meanings expressed by other types of symbolism (i.e. the symbolism of objects, the symbolism of performative actions) can be communicated discursively. It should be noted that ideologies, as symbolic systems, not only provide meaningful ideas that model reality, but also supply patterns or programs of action: i.e. the "of" models and the "for" models (Geertz 1973). Viewed from this angle, the symbolic system of language is a set of images that represent the world. As an instrument (the Platonic *Organon*) of communication and mutual understanding, it also has other functions. Roman Jakobson expanded their basic triad, i.e. the model presented in the 1930s by Karl Bühler in his *Sprachtheorie* (representational function, expressive function, appellative/conative function), adding the following functions: metalingual, poetic and phatic (Jakobson 1971: 239–259). When interest in the functioning of language and symbolism is focused on the situation and context of use, a broader spectrum of functions comes into play as regards social relations and social order, i.e. the constitutive, conservative and transformative function; all of them result from strategies of using symbolism (Hałas 2008).

Significantly, language as a symbolic system is not autonomous; it does not stand for itself (this is true for all other symbolic systems as well). It develops and changes in the context of social relations and interactions, as well as in the cultural context. Discourse linguistics and discourse analysis (the latter is currently very popular) take this into account. Symbolic power exercised through language, but also through other symbolic systems, has its sources in various forms of social power relations. A politics of symbolization is the active exercise of this power.

As symbolic universes that transcend empirically available reality, religious systems hold a special position among symbolic modeling systems, and symbols of holiness, which embody sublime feelings of reverence and fear, occupy a central place within them. The symbols of the sacred and the profane, as Émile Durkheim noted when discussing quasi-religious systems, may represent other things besides the transcendent reality, since they can refer to collective entities, such as the nation, and their metonymic representatives, such as national heroes. Sacralization still remains an important strategy in politics of symbolization despite ongoing secularization processes in contemporary societies, especially European ones.

It can be interesting here to notice the added value of the so called tournant critique – a critical turn, presupposing convergence with French pragmatic sociology, which should lead to the constitution of "pragmatic social history." The actors, equipped with competencies, are, during processes of regular negotiations and hierarchizations, focusing on the conditions of the social agreements or new conventions (Lepetit 1995). It is about opening up and approaching the pragmatic sociology of Luc Boltanski and Laurent Thévenot (2006). This sociology, which surprisingly failed in the historical contextualization of its model, as evidenced by Boltanski's and Thévenot work *De la justification: les économies de la grandeur*, represents an opportunity to find a new way of thinking about the structurizations of the meanings. Actors, their identities, beliefs and strategies are dependent on cultural norms and conventions, which are the result of social interactions. Interpretation is not the result of a purely individual reasoning process; structures of interpretations are part of social reality. On the other hand, even the actors are not determined by the structures as they can variously use their cultural competences.

This approach has a larger support, generally within a less structuralist perspective than that Boltanski and Thévenot (2006). It is the case of the Jeffrey C. Alexander cultural sociology (2004; Alexander Mast, 2006).

Within this line, Jane Erik Lane and Svante Ersson (2002), relying upon the hypothesis of a relative autonomy of the culture towards institutions and structures, show the cultural and social conditions of emerging politics. It is generally difficult to define conditionalities. It is even more the case, if we limit our reflection to symbols. But it reminds us that strategic-centrist models explaining the political action based on symbols has limits. The actors are only playing with the cards that they have received.

As argued by Dominik Bartmanski and Jeffrey C. Alexander (2012: 3), the actors have specific competencies – the iconic ones. The authors put into relief iconic power and iconic consciousness. They make a direct link with the French pragmatic sociology, taking into consideration the competencies to criticize applied by actors.

In such an approach, like for the existentialists, essence precedes existence for objects. But the autonomy of culture does not imply automatically the autonomy of neither a political culture – like for, Paul Lichterman and Daniel Cefraï (2006) nor of a symbolic politics sphere.

For Alison Brysk

> symbolic politics achieve social changes through a two-stage process: first, the projection or performance of narratives opens hearts and changes minds, and then changes in consciousness produce changes in political behavior (Brysk 1995: 574).

What makes persuasive a new story about politics?

> Firstly, symbolic politics must speak to the heart: successful symbols must be culturally appropriate, have historical precedent, be reinforced by other symbols, and signal a call for action (Brysk 1995: 576).

And the power of those symbols depends on the cultural, historical, political and social background. Therefore, it becomes necessary to study them within a regional context.

Central and Eastern Europe as a space of semiosis

One of the aims of this book is to promote reflection on the problems posed by politics of symbolization in Central and Eastern Europe. As outlined above, symbolization in a broad sense means assigning meanings to all objects, including ideas, allowing individual and collective actions to be directed in an uncertain and contingent environment. Thus, politics of symbolization entail intentional meaning-making and strategically using those meanings. In other words, these politics involve exercising symbolic power in its various forms, ranging from the ability to influence social practices and actions to coercion or symbolic violence. As such, politics of symbolization refer to the symbolization of identity and the establishment of relationships where power is a significant dimension.

Analyzing social processes from the angle of the processes of semiosis taking place within them, i.e. assigning meanings and the use of symbolism, allows us to trace the symbolic construction of communities, the identity of nations and states, as well as the part played by symbolism in the mobilization of social movements, i.e. its significance for the politics of contention, as well as for "polite politics," which are always based on symbolic power and need symbols of power (Tilly, Wood 2009).

A look from this perspective at the social space of Central and Eastern Europe as a space of semiosis allows us to better understand the mechanisms of sym-bolization processes that maintain the continuity of socio-cultural formations rooted in this space or initiate changes in those formations. The term "space" is fraught with semantic ambivalence, because on the one hand we are dealing with physical space as something objective and unchanging, and on the other hand with the relative space of changing social relations, including interna-tional relations. This ambivalence is visible in the notion of European space, where space can be viewed as a territory and as places, but also as a social space defined by networks of relations, connections and divisions, identities and differences of entities who enter relations of varying complexity and of different duration, on the micro and macro scale. In fact, "territory" in a geographical sense is not unproblematic either, as it is also subject to the processes of semi-osis. The unity and multiplicity of the European space, both in the geographical or territorial sense and as a social space within which a symbolic culture forms, poses an intriguing problem for thinkers and researchers. It is also a significant issue for political practices occurring within this space.

We utilize a concept that questions the dichotomous division into Western Europe and Eastern Europe, hence the notion of Central and Eastern Europe: the region that once separated the empires of tsars and sultans from those of the Habsburgs and Hohenzollerns (Delanty 1995: 48). This space is not uniform either. It encompasses the countries of Central Europe: Poland, the Baltic states, the Czech Republic, Slovakia and Hungary, as well as the south-eastern region: the Balkans. Even the singling out of these different Europes lies in the sphere of semiosis. It is a symbolic construct whose meaning is subject to various interpretations.

As a project, the European Union has enlivened discussions and continues to generate disputes regarding the concept of European unity, as well as new ideologies of the East (Zarycki 2014). Like the borders of European countries throughout history, the European space as a territory has also undergone changes. The border changes and divisions within Europe, both geographical and historical (Halecki 1950), took a particularly dramatic turn after World War II, as a result of which Western Europe became separated from the Soviet Eastern Bloc by the Berlin Wall. This division, lasting almost half a century, meant that even after its abolition and the accession to the European Union of many post-communist countries that regained their sovereignty, the historical effects of this division are still being reproduced in the European social space. The incessant conflicts between "nationalisers" and "Europeanisers" (Hedetoft 1998: 1–19) can be regarded as, in a sense, internalization of this division among the nation-states which have become members of the European Union or aspire to membership. European history, which is also the history of European nations (Halecki 1950), is the source of a divided memory of trauma as a history of perpetrators and victims. There are attempts to address this through a symbolic politics that strives for reconciliation. At the same time, the universal symbolism of the Holocaust serves as a constant reminder that the issue of guilt remains timeless, in a metaphysical sense as well (Jaspers 2000), and requires transcending the boundaries of politicalness as such. The social space of the former Soviet bloc also sees constant symbolic conflicts related to demands for settling accounts with the communist regime.

Politics of symbolization extend to the social meaning of space, time and history, and thus encompass various modalities of collective memory. The processes of semiosis and politics of symbolization take place in the present, the perception of which may be more or less extensive, i.e. in "the specious present". This present is determined by boundary determinants of the imaginable past and the projected future, situated closer or farther in relation to the current activities and events. Everything that has been removed beyond these boundaries is no longer, or not yet, relevant.

Thus understood, politics of symbolization not only give meaning to constitutive elements of the social world, categorizing and classifying them (including entities involved in social interactions and relations), but also give them temporal meanings in the process of making history. Namely, politics of symbolization also include various strategies of referring to collective experiences in the past in view of images and representations of the future. The prospective-retrospective orientation of politics of symbolization from the present point of view makes control over social and collective memory extremely important in the process of making history (Hałas 2017).

The book proposes reflection on the processes of semiosis and politics of symbolization located in the space of Central and Eastern Europe, which is highly complex as a result of symbolically diverse cultural geography and differing historical experiences. Past historical experiences in Central and Eastern Europe include global catastrophes (two world wars, the Holocaust, the rule of totalitarian systems: fascism and communism) as well as regional ones with global consequences, such as social movements, especially the phenomenon of the Solidarity movement in Poland (Kubik 1994), post-communist transformations, a symbolic example of which is the fall of the Berlin Wall, military conflicts and humanitarian crises in the Balkans. The European migration crisis (2015/2016) and the Covid-19 pandemic seem to mark a new era with its global challenges, into which Central and Eastern Europe is also entering. As a result of these historical events and accelerated processes of change, in a relatively short period of time, many radical reconfigurations and symbolic rearticulations of identities and relationships have occurred and are still occurring on many levels: local, national or state, in international and transnational relations.

Although the issue of different interpretations of various events and processes that occurred in the past and are taking place today in Central and Eastern Europe is undoubtedly important from the perspective of history and political science, the perspective proposed here assumes a more abstract view of Central and Eastern Europe as a diverse space of semiosis and politics of symbolization. The book represents an attempt to search for more general patterns as regards politics of symbolization: different ways of using symbolism that can ignite conflicts as well as resolve them – and assume both reproduced and innovative forms (the latter ones in the form of symbolic innovations).

The Central and Eastern European space of semiosis, or rather spaces of semiosis, are full of similarities and differences, continuities and discontinuities of meaning structures and symbolic forms relating to identity, mutual relations, symbolic boundaries, places of memory and the meaning of time, especially those constitutive for nation-states. This diverse space overlaps with the space of the European Union, within which various ideas of Europe compete. The European Union's politics of symbolization is occasionally at odds with the symbolic politics of national states, particularly those of Central European states that have regained their sovereignty.

The similarities and differences between the created and utilized symbolism and its functions serve here as grounds for reflection. The book also makes it possible to survey different approaches to studying the processes of semiosis as pragmatic meaning-making in the context of changing social life. Numerous studies of symbolism and symbolization practices are based on various theoretical and methodological perspectives, although the semiotic traditions started by Ferdinand de Saussure, Charles S. Peirce and George H. Mead are clearly visible. However, the differences resulting from the local specificity of the processes of semiosis taking place in different parts of a culturally, socially and politically diverse Europe obviously prove significant. Reflection on the patterns of creating and using symbolism, on different politics of symbolization at different times, along with meta-reflection on the various ways of understanding and interpreting these patterns, should contribute to a better understanding of the inherently relational symbolic constitution of the social world. Examining the problems of politics of symbolization in Central and Eastern Europe, necessarily with a closer focus on some of the manifestations of those politics, should bring us closer to this goal.

Explorations in politics of symbolization

The book's twelve chapters are divided into four interrelated topics. In the first part, "Spaces of Semiosis and Politics of Symbolization," the fundamental issues of social space, communication and politics of symbolization are discussed by scientists who conduct research based on their own theoretical concepts, which fit into the broadly understood semiotic approach. In other words, the main focus is on processes of communication. Hubert Knoblauch proposes his own theory of communicative construction of reality, Peeter Selg develops political semiotics on the basis of the theory of communication, whereas Paul Blokker analyzes the instrumental and symbolic dimensions of constitutionalism.

In the opening text, Hubert Knoblauch addresses the extremely important problem of groundbreaking changes in the constitution of social space associated with the rapid expansion of virtual space and the shrinking space of the natural order of face-to-face interactions. This spatial reconfiguration is being thrown into especially stark relief by the "corona crisis" and the consequent restrictions regarding movement in space, both locally and globally: from everyday life to international travel. The crisis caused by the coronavirus pandemic is being analyzed from the perspective of the applied politics of symbolization under conditions of risk and asymmetric relations between state authorities and expert knowledge.

Peeter Selg tackles a broad category of new problems termed "wicked problems"and analyzes them, using the example of the unprecedented European migration crisis and employing conceptual tools of political semiotics.

Paul Blokker reveals the symbolic dimension of polities, showing the constitution as a symbolic-integrative framework for society. He analyzes constitutions as meta-symbols that are objects of competing interpretations in political conflicts, as exemplified by the Polish case.

The second part of the book, "Time and Semiosis of History: Symbolic Conflicts Over Remembering and Forgetting," also consists of three chapters. In this section, attention shifts to the politics of memory as politics of symbolization. Here, strategies of meaning-making include time and the past in the present.

Luba Jurgenson focuses on the use of the anthropologically rich symbolism of the tree in commemorative practices in various countries. She critically analyzes the ambiguities and contradictory features of practices commemorating fighters, victims, witnesses and the righteous, wherein tension is present between the universal and particular, i.e. national, meanings of the symbol used.

Joanna Nowicki, in turn, characterizes the problems arising from politics of symbolization in Poland after the fall of communism in relation to the difficult past of World War II and memory in international relations. On the one hand, there exists a politics of memory focused on reconciliation and forgiveness; on the other hand, a new emerging vision described as historical politics is provoking controversy and disputes regarding the master narrative of the history of World War II.

Elżbieta Hałas discusses politics of symbolization as a constitutive dimension of systemic transformation in Poland, during which managing the meanings of ongoing changes, the emerging meanings of events, was as important as representing historical continuities and discontinuities. In this chapter, systemic transformation is presented as the complex nature or polymorphism of transformation time, which is a correlate of many fields of social practice. These fields also included symbolic practices relating to the past.

The third section, "Symbolic Construction of Communities: New Beginnings and New Divides," focuses on issues of civic culture and the articulation of national identity after communism. Ulf Hedetoft tracks the similarities and differences between symbolic politics related to national identity in Poland and Hungary. These politics utilize religious symbolism. The author attempts to explain the mechanisms behind the current populist configuration of history, religion and politics in both countries.

The analysis presented by Anna Pless and Dick Houtman echoes Hedetoft's diagnosis, while also providing a broader context regarding value changes and cultural cleavages in European societies. Pless and Houtman show value divides on the axes of moral traditionalism and progressivism on the one hand, and authoritarianism and libertarianism on the other hand, emphasizing the influence of the secularization factor. In a broad comparative context, they analyze moral traditionalism and authoritarianism in post-communist countries as different cultural and political dimensions.

Nicolas Maslowski presents the Central European region as a space of post-dissent political conflicts over the meaning of the past. He claims that the post-1989 transformation should be viewed as a period of post-dissent, when the symbolic capital of former dissidents plays a significant role. He shows the logic of distinction of post-dissent groups and their discourses.

A multifaceted exploration of the politics of symbolization that can be observed in Central and Eastern Europe inevitably must include the issue of the European Union, both as a space for the realization of these politics and as their actor, and finally also as a symbol. The chapters contained in the fourth section of the book, "Symbolic Politics of European (Dis)Unification," discuss the demands and expectations of post-communist and post-conflict countries regarding the symbolic recognition of their specificity.

Laure Neumayer takes up the important problem of a common historical narrative for Europe as a whole and analyzes the challenges posed on the forum of European institutions by symbolic actions that aim to equate communist crimes with Nazi crimes. He follows the mobilization initiated by Central European members of European assemblies and anti-communist memory entrepreneurs.

Adopting a transnational perspective and examining the flows of ideas in the transnational networks of conservative intellectuals, Valentin Behr highlights the role of Polish representatives of this orientation in shaping a governmental political program that is presented as an alternative to the liberal European values. He analyzes the ideology shaped by Polish conservative intellectuals who are transforming the anti-communist doctrine of the pre-1989 opposition into an anti-liberal doctrine, also contributing to the reconfiguration of the European Right, and the discursive symbolism of that ideology.

The book's final chapter shows the symbolism of the European Union from the Balkan perspective on the example of Bosnia-Herzegovina. Adopting Pierre Bourdieu's assumptions, on the basis of extensive field research, Rok Zupančič, Faris Kočan and Iris Ivanič show the ambivalence of the symbolic power of the European Union, which on the one hand symbolizes a threat to ethnic identity, but on the other hand still remains the dominant power symbol of all freedoms in post-conflict and post-communist countries.

Although the picture of the social spaces of semiosis in Central and Eastern Europe presented in this book remains fragmentary, it hopefully sheds a new light on them and shows these spaces from a new angle in many ways. The book's leitmotif is the conviction that politics of symbolization deserve the in-depth attention of researchers. This is especially true as regards the development and transformations of these politics in Central and Eastern Europe, where the liberating and dominating powers of symbols have clashed in the past and continue to do so.

References

Alexander, Jeffrey C. (2004) "Cultural Pragmatics: Social Performance Between Ritual and Strategy," *Sociological Theory* 22 (4): 527–573.

Alexander Jeffrey C. and Jason L. Mast (2006) "Symbolic Action in Theory and Practice: The Cultural Pragmatics of Symbolic Action" in Alexander, Jeffrey C., Bernhard Giesen, Jason L. Mast (eds.) *Social Performance: Symbolic Action, Cultural Pragmatics, and Ritual*, pp. 1–28. Cambridge: Cambridge University Press.

Bartmanski, Dominik and Jeffrey C. Alexander (2012) "Introduction: Materiality and Meaning in Social Life: Toward an Iconic Turn in Cultural Sociolgy" in Jeffrey C. Alexander, Dominik Bartmanski, Bernard Giesen (ed.), *Iconic Power: Materiality and Meaning in Social Life*, pp. 1–14. London: Palgrave.

Boltanski, Luc and Laurent Thévenot (2006) *On Justification: Economies of Worth*. Princeton: Princeton University Press.

Bourdieu, Pierre (1989) "Social Space and Symbolic Power," *Social Theory* 7: 14–25.

_____(1991) *Language and Symbolic Power*, John B. Thompson (ed.), Cambridge, Mass.: Harvard University Press.

Brysk Alison (1995) "Hearts and Minds": Bringing Symbolic Politics Back In," *Polity* 27(4): 559–585.

Cohen, Abner (1976) *Two-Dimensional Man. An Essay on the Anthropology of Power and Symbolism in Complex Society*. Berkeley: University of California Press.

Delanty, Gerard (1995) *Inventing Europe. Idea, Identity, Reality*. London: MacMillan Press.

Edelman, Murray (1985) *The Symbolic Uses of Politics*. Urbana, Ill.: University of Illinois Press.

Geertz, Clifford (1973) *The Interpretations of Cultures*. New York: Basic Books.

Halecki, Oskar (1950) *The Limits and Divisions of European History*. London and New York: Sheed & Ward.

Hałas, Elżbieta (2008) "Social Symbolism: Forms and Functions – a Pragmatist Perspective," *Studies in Symbolic Interaction* 30: 131–149.

_____ (2017) "The Future Orientation of Culture and the Memory of the Past in the Making of History," *Sign Systems Studies*, 45(3/4): 361–379.

Hedetoft, Ulf (1998) "On Nationalisers and Europeanisers in Contemporary Europe – an Introduction" in Ulf Hedetoft (ed.) *Political Symbols, Symbolic Politics. European Identities in Transformation*, pp. 1–22. Aldershot: Ashgate.

Heiskala, Risto (2003) *Society as Semiosis*. Frankfurt am Main: Peter Lang.

Hobsbawm, Erie and Terence Ranger (eds.) (1983) *The Invention of Tradition*, Cambridge: Cambridge University Press.

Jakobson, Roman (1971) *Selected Writings* (Vol. 2). Berlin: Walter de Gruyter.

Jaspers, Karl (2000) *The Question of German Guilt*, transl. by E. B. Ashton, New York: Fordham University Press.

Kertzer, David (1988) *Ritual, Politics and Power*. New Haven: Yale University Press.

Kubik, Jan (1994) *The Power of Symbols against the Symbols of Power: The Rise of Solidarity and the Fall of State Socialism in Poland*. University Park: Pennsylvania State University Press.

Lane, Jane E. and Svante Ersson (2002) *Culture and Politics. A Comparative Approach*. Aldershot: Ashgate.

Lepetit, Bernard (1995) "Histoire des pratiques, pratique de l'histoire." in Bernard Lepetit (ed.) *Les Formes de l'expérience: une autre histoire sociale*, pp. 9–22 Paris: Albin Michel.

Lichterman, Paul and Daniel Cefraï (2006) "The Idea of Political Culture" in Robert Edward Goodin, Robert E. Goodin, Charles Tilly, Joseph L. Buttenwieser (eds.), *The Oxford Handbook of Contextual Political Analysis*, Vol. 5, pp. 392–414. Oxford: Oxford University Press.

Peirce, Charles S. (1935) *Collected Papers*, vol 5. Cambridge, Mass.: Harvard University Press.

Tilly, Charles and Lesley J. Wood (2009) *Social Movements 1768–2008*. London: Paradigm Publishers.

Touraine, Alain (1981) *The Voice and the Eye. An Analysis of Social Movements*. Cambridge: Cambridge University Press.

Zarycki, Tomasz (2014) *Ideologies of Eastness in Central and Eastern Europe*. London: Routledge.

Elżbieta Hałas and Nicolas Maslowski

SPACES OF SEMIOSIS AND POLITICS OF SYMBOLIZATION

Hubert Knoblauch

Symbols and Spaces: Sociological Reflections from Inside the Corona Crisis

Abstract: Based on the thesis that the corona crisis can be explained as a conflict between two spacial figurations, this chapter is devoted to the question of whether and to what extent precisely the massive closures can be understood as a kind of symbolic politics. Indeed, the massive space closures serve the communication between a government now in an equally massive asymmetric leadership position and a society degraded to a "population." However, this asymmetric communication must not be seen as a legitimizing superstructure phenomenon, as is the case in conspiracy theory approaches. Just as symbolic communication with spaces draws very material boundaries that extend from state borders to the doors of apartments, it serves to communicate a risk that is anchored in physical communication. It can be accessed only by knowledge in a way which extends the asymmetries of knowledge between lays and experts.

Because the spaces of interaction are increasingly digitalized, mediatized and thus brought into a network logic, the "crisis" is characterized by a dramatization of the tension between the special configuration of closed containers and unbounded networks. This pattern may appear in its radicality as an antistructure (which suspends basic rights of co-determination, habitual work activities, etc.), but according to the thesis of this contribution, it does not represent a break, but rather follows and intensifies the developments that we describe as the refiguration of spaces.

Keywords: communicative constructivism, corona crisis, refiguration, sociology of knowledge, sociology of space

From events to the historical event of the corona crisis

While preparing for the conference, which was to be the place where this paper would be presented and discussed in real life, my original intention was to address the visit of pope Benedict to Germany. The first German pope visiting for the first time the German capital, I assume, is such a striking fusion of two symbols and symbolic spheres, i.e. religion (the Catholic Church) and politics (Germany as a nation state and Berlin as its capital) that would have been worthwhile to be analyzed when asking for the politics of symbolism. In my study, I would have focused particularly on the pope's mass in the Olympic Stadium; more specifically I would have framed the mass as communicative event which is communicating its symbolic meaning by way of its performance, arguing for the role of the embodied, material the spatial aspects of communication by which its symbolic meaning is constructed. The fact that we had access to data on the first visit of the Polish pope John Paul II. in Berlin and to studies on John Paul's sensational first visit to Poland would have allowed for a comparison between central and Eastern Europe.

Now (late spring 2020) things have changed fundamentally. The conference has been cancelled due to the corona crisis as have most other conferences at least until late summer 2020. Universities have been closed already in early March, as have private companies. Many public spaces are locked materially so that one cannot enter hotels, restaurants, theatres and cinemas. In addition, large parts of populations of an increasing number of states are subject to quarantine or at least severe restrictions on movement outside of their own private space.

Sociologists are faced with a most challenging topic: Society has changed so dramatically in recent weeks and will continue to do so in ways which may be unprecedented. Due to the lockdown of public life, a new "emergency state" is being established in more and more countries, affecting all spheres of social life, including economy, culture and politics in such a way that the lives and the life-worlds of more and more people have changed fundamentally. At least for the time being, while the pandemic is still spreading to new countries and numbers of infected and death are still rising in most countries, most of us live most of the time (since weeks) in some form of quarantine, the form of which is not only dependent on the severity of the crisis but just as much on the politics of the respective governments. These politics differ quite clearly on the national level (from early ignorance particularly by populist governments and liberal openness to rigid closures and political authoritarianism), yet it was certainly the ruling parts of the political system which have been in charge worldwide for the lockdown and consequently the dramatic changes in the social order. In many ways, these changes, still referred to as "corona crises" are linked to the title of this volume, the "politics of symbolization and the spaces of symbols."

The changes are so dramatic, so fast and their beginnings can be roughly identified (and an end can be expected, even if no one knows when) so that the corona crisis may be said to constitute an event – yet in a quite different sense than the event I had planned to study. This latter kind of events are specific social occasions which usually include some kind of performance (or presentation of objects) with respect to an audience witnessing this performance of objectivations (which is usually participating in some way). Events of this kind are locally and spatially bounded, yet not separated. Events may last weeks, such as the Olympic games (in this case they usually consist of a series of minor events) and they are mediatized across space, in modern times with the use of electronical and digital media, even simultaneously. However, these kinds of events which are structured no matter how small they may be (ranging from an anniversary dinner of a married couple to the global celebration of New Year's Eve or the landing of Apollo 13 on the moon, which could be witnessed by anyone) differ from the kind of event we are talking about here probably by one major feature. While the first kind of events are constituted by actors, expected (often linked with positive affectivity) and organized in such a way as to move something which is intentionally set into the focus of the audience, events like the Corona pandemic, the Spanish flu or the Tsunami are unexpected, unintended and dangerous, often linked with negative affectivity. They are what we call historic events (Clemens 2007). While the former kind of events is co-produced by the actors in an expected way, historical events like the corona crisis seem to be "imposed" as if nature, fate or another ontological power breaks into the social order which is made to transform it (Badiou 2007).

Despite the tendencies of some conspiracy theories to debunk hidden intentionalities of the crisis, there are good reasons to believe that the corona crisis has not been created on purpose. Nevertheless, the crisis is also not an event that is just happening to us. Instead, I want to support the argument that the corona crisis is a communicative construction (Knoblauch 2020). This does not mean that the crisis is made up, but rather it means that it results from actions (crisis scripts) and institutions (e.g. of the national governments), and it depends on structures already established (such as the respective state of medical systems). Although actors are constructing the crisis, the idea of communicative construction also means that the material object of the virus appears in the crisis as part of a very basic process of transmission. As basic as this object may be, it ultimately affects the symbolic order of society.

It is this symbolic order of society we want to address in this paper. More specifically, we want to focus on the way how the symbolic order of society is expressed in and produced by space.[1] In fact, it is our thesis that the corona crisis is, first of all, a crisis in and of social space. Space is the medium in which these changes occur. It is still open if these changes are transient or permanent, space exhibits a symbolic dimension or, to be more exact, social space is symbolizing

---

1   We follow here a relational concept of social space as suggested by Löw (2018); the theory of communicative construction is elaborated in Knoblauch (2020).

the order, "nomos" or, as we would like to call it, following Elias (2012), the figuration of society in ways which includes the materiality of built spaces, bodies, media and the technological mediation of action. If we understand space in this materialist sense, we can start to see that the changes expressed in space enforce a pattern which we have called the refiguration of spaces. The tensions between two spatial logics of centralized territoriality and decentered transgressive networking, which has been built up in the last decades, has increased massively by the corona crisis and, we believe, will leave their traits for a long time.

Before we sketch the temporal order of the corona crisis in rough terms, a word on the methodology is necessary. It is certainly a challenge to observe the change from the eye of the cyclone while it is still on the move. Things are changing continuously, so that many statements may become obsolete while the text is being published. Yet, as we can witness the changes currently more clearly, it may be an additional value to reflect them at the present time. As sociologists it is certainly a task to focus on society at any time. Particularly during rapid social changes and crises, such as revolutions or epidemics, it is the sociologist's task to make sense of them by using the analytical tools we have cultivated. The analysis may contribute to the ways how the society can handle these changes – a contribution now left to some selected sociologists who are close to actors in power, by identifying what these changes are. It is this task which we (Knoblauch 2020) call "sociological diagnosis" (which should be distinguished from more practical tasks of advising the various mostly political crisis management committees on various levels). Diagnosis is not only due to its actuality; diagnosis also accounts for the selected focus of what seems to be relevant at the time being; and finally, diagnosis means that analysis can lack sufficient empirical data and thus empirical foundation, as the collection of data would require much longer than most events tend to last. On these restricted grounds, the status of this diagnosis cannot really be called sociological analysis but rather, analytical reflections, as the validity of the analytical statements depend on the question if and which observations can be confirmed as holding generally, holding over (which) time or holding to which extent.

The temporality of the corona crisis: liminal anti-structure or refiguration?

The ubiquity of Quarantine and other severe spatial restrictions is the most obvious phenomenon which, I gather, is unprecedented in history. Before I turn to the spatiality of the corona crisis, we need to reflect at least some basic temporal aspects of the crisis. Although we sit in the eye of the tiger who is still on the move, the corona crisis already now seems to exhibit some temporal sequences known from similar events.[2] Although the crisis has not been labelled pervasively a catastrophe in administrational and legal terms, it exhibits some traces of what a catastrophe means to sociology: the latency phases of a disaster is followed by an identification phase, which took quite different routes in different nations and government settings,[3] including denial, and a phase of definition, before the major actors and victims could be identified for the action phase (Dombrowsky 1987).[4]

While being in the midst of catastrophes' action phase while writing this article, a more specific distinction has been proposed which comes close to the policies of many governments, their legitimations in public and the public discourses relating to them. It is the distinction between the "hammer" phase (Pueyo 2020) in which very severe restrictions on mobility are implemented to the vast majority of the population, and the phase of loosening these severe measures, Pueyo calls "dancing." In the city first hit, Wuhan in China, it took more than 70 days that the boundaries of households, most city areas and the city itself (e.g. train stations) opened. Journalists reporting from Wuhan had been surprised by the discrepancies between the small steps ("dancing") of opening the city (witnessing severe controls all over the city, long queues at the stations, areas fenced off from the public) on the one hand and the tremendous celebration of the opening: the whole skyline of the city was illuminated, and pictures were sent all over the world (often questioned as to whether it was merely "propaganda")

This celebrative transition from the "hammer" to the "dance" reminds of another temporal sequence which is very common in the study of simple culture. It is the "rites de passage" (Gennep 1909), a typically tripartite sequence of rituals which (a) mark off the departure from an ordinary state of affairs, (b) indicate a transitory state, and (c) allow to move back to the state of ordinary affairs, indicate it or the re-transition of it. To the study of symbols these rituals are most relevant since they do not only relate directly to the kind of social order; this order may be highly individualized, as in the case of a status

---

2   As I am not an epidemiologist, I would compare it to more general phenomena such as catastrophes rather than epidemics, and, due to the speed how the pandemic has spread across the globe, there are good reasons not to liken it to the earlier pandemics.

3   Some states are reacting very quickly by harsh measures, some starting with very liberal methods – both depending on the political position of the governments and, it seems, on the position of the advising experts, epidemiologists and virologists.

4   As to the various authority linked to quarantine regulation cf. Ding 2014.

Photo 1:
https://theglobalherald.com/wp-content/uploads/2020/04/X15yfPr5auY.jpg

passage (from child to adult); or it may be collective, as in the case of carnival or warfare. In this sense, the symbol is one of the means by which the social order is established, changed and restituted.

Before we turn to the question how symbols accomplish this task, how they relate to order and (our thesis) how they contribute to the (communicative) construction of order, we should at least hint at one extension of Gennep's theory: In his study of tribal societies, Victor Turner (1986) suggested that the rites de passage not only allow for changes in the social order; the transitory or what he called "liminal" phase itself is characterized by something like an counter-order, or, as he called it, an "anti-structure" of the (relevant) ordinary social structure. Those who are subordinate would rule, humans become animals or men become women and vice versa. As much as this anti-structure may be an archaic model, in all states in the corona crises there is a narrative by the governments which is up until now quite frankly believed by most of the population: that the severe restrictions will only hold for what we call the hammer phase or the state of "emergency," while after some time of loosening in the dancing phase, "we" will go back to normal. In this sense, the temporal model shares the idea of a retransition; the adaptation to the crises which took various steps may be understood as the transition. One of the most important questions (which unluckily can only be answered retrospectively) would be if the emergency state we are in can be understood as an "anti-structure" leading back to normal, or if the changing order is establishing a path on its own or what we call the refiguration of society (Knoblauch/Löw 2020)?

Corona and the refiguration of space

As the corona virus exists in the relations between people and ranges from microsocial to macro-social relations, the notion of figuration by Elias (2012) may be quite useful. It designates the interdependencies between people in society so that even the encompassing "figurations of figurations" (Couldry & Hepp 2016) is connected to the social relations between subjects, their bodily constitution and even their affectivity. As is well known, Elias (2006) has been studying the historical constitution of the (French) nation state as a centralized figuration and its monopoly on bodily violence which allowed the king to control the aristocracy and was accompanied by the disciplining of the subject's affectivity. Corona however is not about affectivity but about health, the human and its interaction. Or, as the virologists' concern for the length and distance of social contacts and the relevance of "social distancing" indicates, it is about the space between persons bodily interaction. Thus, as in Elias figuration, the global pandemic is directly linked to the micro-social space of interaction. Space plays a role across most aspects of corona: Quarantine is as much a spatial phenomenon as is its soft variant, social distancing, the spatial lockdown of the public sphere as well as the demand to "stay at home." Likewise, the reaffirmation of the nation underlines the national territory and even its subdivisions as contained and bound off from the rest of the world, which includes border controls (even in Schengen Europe) and the "bringing back" of the traveling citizens into the country.

While some observers only recognize the "de-globalization," we should not ignore the maintenance and even strengthening of global principles. Thus, while logistical chains are partly re-nationalized, global economic exchange is still at work; not to forget the quite relevant activities by the WHO or the EU. Most importantly, however, the restrictions on embodied co-presence in public space are compensated in an exponential way by digital mediatization. Instead of flying to their conferences across the world, people now get used to tele-conferencing; instead of traveling across the city to meet at offices, people work at their home office, and even cultural, religious and sports events are transferred to the net on all spatial scales.

However, the corona crisis is not only spatial, but also shows conflictual dynamics between different spatial principles. There are particularly two spatial principles or logics which seem to be most relevant (Knoblauch/Löw 2020). On the one hand, we have territorial closure. Countries, residential areas, homes as well as gated communities or quarantines (Turner 2007) are treated as "containers" that contain the virus or are isolated against it. On the other hand, we see the uncontained, global spread of bodies infected with the virus, the densification of digital networking and a massive opening up of communication networks which are fulfilling new functions in the crisis. The same tension between two basic spatial logics is expressed in the figuration of the centralized territorial state on the one hand and globalization across borders on the other, as well as in the sharp top-down hierarchies and logical-conceptual analyzes versus flat network formation or "rhizome" and ontological metaphors. Territorial spaces follow the logic of placing and arranging (Löw 2001/engl 2018) with clearly drawn boundaries (externally) and restrictions on diversity (internally). In contrast, network spaces follow the logic of relationizing the heterogeneous. In network spaces, distant elements are put into relation and differences between the elements are the basic characteristics.

Refiguration explains the simultaneity and tension of different spatial logics in the corona crisis. However, refiguration is only a general thesis claim, independent of the corona crisis. Therefore, we want to focus on some spatial phenomena which allow us to address the symbolic role of space and the way how space is refigured in the corona crisis

Population, social distancing and symbolic communication

National, regional and urban governments seized a range of measures which were essentially spatial. Among those, the shutdown of public space has been probably the most visible. As opposed to some emergency states when governments would seize control for all means of (mass) communication, the sphere of media discourse remained untouched by most governments. Instead, it was the public places which had been closed. Concert halls, theatres, restaurants, shops and many other places where people interact in professional ways, but also schools, playgrounds, or sports areas where they would interact in private matters had been barred from access in a most conspicuous way. Spatially, the closure of the public places has been paralleled by the restriction of "staying at home" in ones' own household with only the persons living there.

There have certainly been differences to the degree in which public places had been closed and the nature of the compulsion to stay in ones' home, even if one accounts for the different temporal phases of the crisis. While in some countries people can leave home only with few exceptions (food, medicine) so that they entered a state of private quarantine, in other countries rules had been much more liberal so that people were in addition allowed to go walking, jogging or even buy and sell books or flowers. It is not very clear to which degree the rigidity of policies depends on the political positions of the government (and their medical advisers), yet it is most noteworthy to what degree governments in general took control over their citizen's liberty of movement even in the most democratic societies. In fact, one of the most striking features of the corona crisis is the role of national, regional government with respect to their constituency.

Although it seems taken for granted that political institutions would seize special power in a state of emergency, it was Foucault (2004) who had characterized this figuration by the notion of governmentality. In contrast to the earlier "pastoral" power, it is characterized by the government as apparatus and ensemble of practices arising in early modernity particularly during epidemics. These practices include security technologies and control strategies regulating institutions, such as the police and other law enforcement agencies. The innovation of governmentality is directly connected to and constitutive of the population. Populations are not just any people, but those people are in a "land," a territorial container to be governed. Populations are basically generated by the fact that space is (de)limited to create forms of territory – state, province, cities. And finally, the new kind of governmentality is characterized by what we may call social technology: Governmentality is based on information about the population, which is collected in and objectified by diagrams, figures and statistics, the government vows to take care of the security and safety of the country's "population." Now, during the crisis, we are quite familiar to be addressed as "population" by government as well as by experts; moreover, we are facing a huge range of numbers, statistical data and visualizations, most prominent the Johns Hopkins Coronavirus Resource Center comparing the numbers of infected, recovered and dead by country.[5]

One could wonder if the transmission of this expert knowledge to the "population" is typical of contemporary knowledge societies (or knowledge classes) and the role of its subjectivation for self-control, but here I would like to focus on another aspect which seems, in its extension, to be specific to the worldwide corona crisis: social distancing (Valdez et al., 2018). Already in the identification phase of the crisis, but also when it came to the question of shifting to the

---

5   https://coronavirus.jhu.edu/map.html.

Photo 2: Park in Berlin during the Corona Lockdown
Foto: Nina Baur

dance phase, there have been debates about whether the "population" would take the regulations seriously and if they would actually keep social distance.

There were scandalous reports in the press, and there were indignant comments on other assemblies on the net, labelled as "corona parties." It is noteworthy that here the media themselves used images of public space to interpret the attitude of the population. In public discourse such images served as justification for "unreasonableness" in the public, which then led to the tightening of the rules on 22 March 2020, closing further public spaces, reducing interaction units to two and sending police into the public space to emphasize and enforce the regulation.

It is noteworthy that here the interactions in public space are not simply interpreted. Rather, the way how bodies are located in the public space itself serves as an indication or, rather, as a symptom for how the population deals with and "understands" the regulations of cities, regional and national governments. As opposed to the situation described by Foucault, it is important to note that the information about the population is not restricted to the government.[6] As most other information it is part of and accessible by public discourse. This accessibility in discourse is certainly one reason for the high acceptance of these measures; following Foucault, one could say that this discourse contributes to the subjectivation of this knowledge into the selves who, in a way, become reduced to and part of the population addressed by the government.

In the corona crisis however, space is not only a discursive phenomenon. On the contrary, the lockdown of public space has been expressed in very material terms: shops have been closed, police enforced the shutdown of bars and clubs, and even gatherings in parks have been prohibited by state power. It is this kind of prohibitions on bodily access to built spaces as well as to open public spaces (playgrounds, beaches, sport fields), but also offices, factories and anything accessible to a larger ground (with notable exceptions) which made Pueyo (2020) talk about a "hammer:" people could not get to work, they could not meet in leisure time, etc. Again, as this prohibition has been enforced by police and other authorities, the exclusion from these spaces has also been a *sign* in itself. It was intended to demonstrate to the people the severity of the situation; in addition to the mild or harsh forms of quarantine at home it should prevent many people from meeting one another, and it should remind those who do meet in public to keep social distance.

Although the exclusion of people from these spaces may reduce them to encounter one another, the hammer is quite ambivalent. On the one hand, single offices where no one would sit with others had been closed as well as buildings in which access would have been easily regulated in terms of social distancing and hygiene. On the other hand, those public places which have remained open often constituted dangerous places in terms of the virus: service encounters at the supermarket, the medical care in hospitals and care homes (where the toll of people dying from the virus has been quite significant) and even in many public places which remained open to access. Despite these ambivalences, it was not only the discursive dissemination of the concept of shutdown but the very inaccessibility, exclusion of and material closure of spaces (some locked, others marked symbolically) which constituted in itself a sign or, to be more exact, a symbol: it did not only indicate something else but represented a part of the new emergency order.

---

6 It was Giddens (1985) who took this governmentality to information and thus allowed to identify the continuity into the era of information systems.

Symbolization includes, of course, rituals, such as the social distancing queues, and performances, such as the presence of police in parks. In addition to the idea that symbols are enacted meaning (Halas 2002) or performances (Alexander et al., 2006) as part of a cultural system, the focus on space adds three additional aspects to the idea of symbolization which have become particularly relevant in the corona crisis: Symbols are part of communication and communicative actions; symbols are material and exhibit some sense in their materiality; and the meaning structure is not a closed culture but dependent on the (socially distributed) meaning of actors (cf. Knoblauch 2020: Ch. III).

The materiality of space as a symbol becomes quite obvious in the re-erection of frontiers during the corona crises. In order to "signal" the material boundaries of the nation state, fences had been erected even in urban settings, such as in the Swiss-German twin towns Konstanz and Kreuzlingen. The symbolic role of material frontiers has become a global icon, e.g. in Berlin, but also the embodied performance of border control (as in the UK after Brexit, or as during the migration crisis within Europe) quite obviously takes a symbolic role for the "sovereignty" of the particular nation state. In the corona crisis, materiality plays an even more crucial role on a spatial level which ranges from biological nano-level to the sociological micro-level. In fact, the corona crisis is basically a crisis located in the very locus of interaction or, to be more precise (and since interaction can be realized e.g. on the phone) in the embodied face-to-face interaction. As it seems now, the infection by the virus is almost exclusively linked to the bodily exchange of humans who are in "close contact." If people are facing each other, sneezing or coughing in front of each other or touching each other, the virus can be easily transmitted. In social theory, the face-to-situation is the paradigm of the social situation, here even more, as the contagion is linked to some kind of action of the body. As opposed to SARS which is located deep in the lungs, the corona virus can travel on the invisible waves of exhalation, sit on the skin of someone who has touched his mouth, or be swallowed by using the same spoon (Roloff 2007). As the infection is based in a social relation of co-presence, enacted bodily, and transmitted from sender to receiver, it not only metaphorically compares to communicative action in terms of communicative constructivism: sneezing may not be a verbal form of action, yet it "makes sense" in a very material and embodied form. In the very material sense of communicative constructivism, the virus is the kind of material objectification characterizing any communicative action within a social relation as a performative working act: it is a thing which is transmitted and effects the other in a physical way as an illness.

As much as the emphasis on this social and communicative nature of the virus may sound irritating, it allows to reassess the process of infection with respect to the spatial contexts of interaction.[7] One reason for the irritation lies certainly in the fact that we can neither experience the objectivation nor its effect in temporal or spatial co-presence: the symptoms only appear after days, and the virus itself cannot be seen nor sensed in any life-worldly way. We may make guesses about the potential forms of action (sneezing, coughing), yet in principle the virus remains invisible. We do not perceive the virus, we only know about the virus. Moreover, expert knowledge about the virus is not be acquired by everyone, but translated into general knowledge, sometimes transformed into rules (keep distance) which are to be obeyed, and people who have no access to internet may not even be aware of the concept. The knowledge about the virus is a feature of a culture (even if some cultures are better prepared for the virus), it is an achievement of medical technology and medical knowledge. In this sense, the virus is what Beck (1999) has called a risk. The fact that this knowledge is generated by scientific experts and managed and communicated by specialized institutions easily calls up conspiracy theories nowadays. Because the knowledge about the virus, which can have such severe consequences, is conveyed through science, we are dealing with a risk (Beck 1986). The corona epidemic is a risk that, in obvious ways, requires scientific expertise, not just to cure the disease but also to define it.[8] The sheer distinction of Covid-19 (*Coronavirus SARS-CoV-2*) from an "ordinary" influenza, takes, as we painfully experience now, a great deal of technical and scientific effort. Moreover, the danger itself is in large parts a "scientifically" determined one. In addition, the estimated number of unreported cases is a topic which receives much attention in the discourse concerning the spread of the virus.

The meaning of the virus, its risk and its very existence are therefore subject to an unequal social distribution of knowledge: Experts and their systems such as virologists are not only required to identify the virus; as epidemiologists they are also the ones who identify the social dissemination of the virus in the population. It is certainly no accident that the medical profession is addressing society also by the notion of "population," as, according to Foucault, the political idea

---

7   As important as the epidemiological stress on the duration and distance of contacts between infected and non-infected may be, it would be very useful to know about e.g. the specific spatio-material settings, forms of exchange and body formations facilitating or preventing infection. Cf. Goffman 1963; 1981.

8   There are even some speculations about the virus being the unintended result of scientific research which seem to be part of conspiration theories.

of population seems do go back to the biopolitics of epidemics. The asymmetry of knowledge on the virus and its relevance to the actors certainly contributes to the construction of the sudden power of these experts by the symbol of the virus. Or, to say it in another way, *the invisibility of the virus in the interaction between people is made visible and symbolized by the radical closure of spaces in which interactions could occur.* Of course, public spaces and interactions are located on a different scale so that it appears as an oversized instrument. That is what makes it the "hammer;" yet, it is by way of this oversize that the closure of space became a symbol: communicating to the people some meaning and at the same time establishing, performing and materializing a spatial order which became part of the social order for the time being.

When talking about asymmetry, we should not only focus on the knowledge of experts but also on the asymmetry of power. Although particularly the massive increase in the role of digital media allowed for a public discourse, the well accepted emergency order provided governments with additional power. In fact, governments started to decide without consulting parliaments on the restrictions of basic rights (freedom to move, to assemble, to practice religion etc.). Although we drew on Foucault, the government's power cannot just be considered a (discursive) "practice." As opposed to anti-subjectivist social theories one must stress that policies, such as the closure of public spaces, have to be understood as strategically intended actions initiated by governments, oriented and communicated to the population so that they not only be "understood" in meaning but also translated into embodied action. The virus may be a (more or less natural) object, yet the corona crisis is not "caused" by the virus but by the actions of governments, the knowledge of experts as well as by the fact that society became partly reduced to a territorially bounded population.

These actions, we should be reminded, are mainly targeted not at preventing the virus, which is expected to be passed to the majority of the people (some 60–70 %) anyway, as is common with most influenza viruses. The strategic goal consists mainly in preventing the overstress on the medical system. As earlier waves of influenza have been linked with a certain amount of mortality which mostly pass unnoticed in public discourse, the corona virus seems to affect a much larger proportion of infected persons so that they need intensive care, and the mortality rate also seems to be higher. The explicit goal of the government's action therefore is to keep the increasing numbers of people low who need to be provided with intensive medical care and all it needs. Epidemiological calculations of the potential exponential numbers of infected, the numbers of those in need of intensive care and the numbers of dead, have been disseminated in public particularly in the beginning of the pandemic in order to legitimize the form of actions. At least in Europe, which is unfamiliar with these kinds of pandemics, the case of Italy seemed to provide strong additional legitimation not only for the curfews but also for the enormous investment in the intensive care sectors (and later, in other sectors of care and medical equipment).

As trivial it may be, we should note that the corona crisis is a result of human actions, mostly of state regulations, but also of the consent by almost all parts of the population, at last in many countries. It is in this sense that the temporary or transient order of society resulting from these regulations is a communicative construction: it is performed by the powerful actions of political actors, executed by their administration, legitimated by the media and accepted by most parts of the society who, at least in liberal nations, in quite explicit discourses had consented in a public discourse to these measures. The difference to the classical social construction consists in that the social and spatial order is not just produced by meanings; as much as order is produced by human actors, it also includes the virus, and its consequences, the people infected, coughing, getting to hospitals and dying.

Conclusion

Being in the thick of events, the analytical question of what we can learn about symbols from the corona crisis seems not to be of prior importance. Suffice it to say here, that the symbolic order created by the spaces in the corona crisis very much support the idea that social "meaning" of symbols is highly dependent on their embodied, material and mediated character realized in and performed by communicative actions oriented towards a collectivity of actors.

As this paper is diagnostic in character, it focuses on the question if the corona crisis will enforce the course of the refiguration processes or if it will remain an exceptional state which will lead back to the structures known from the situation before. When arguing that, the refiguration thesis is supported by the symbolism of the spatial order, one has certainly to contend that the crisis implies quite some elements which will remain transient and will disappear with the crisis: Thus, the overarching role of the state which takes care of the provision of medical aid, food provisions and the economic situation of a large part of the population, employees and companies for example reminds of war economy unlikely to lead into a permanent form of state socialism. There is no doubt that the restrictions on the public space and the restraints on individual liberties will not be kept up for a longer period of time. As a consequence, we will live to see the resurgence of public life, events and the various forms of collectives in co-presence (audiences, demonstrations and other aggregations of bodies in public).

As much as the exceptionality of the situation will be expected to normalize, the way how the crisis has been constructed and managed reinforces patterns visible already before the crisis and possibly extended into the phase of "dance:" the phase of transition with its continuing risk will certainly affect the interaction order and interaction rituals. On a macro-scale, the unquestioned competence of the nation state and territorially based authorities follow the path of turning spaces into closed containers; although we will live to see the attempts to reaffirm trans-local entities, the obvious need for the self-provision of "necessary" goods and "systems relevant" services will strengthen the role of "local" (national, regional) economic production. The differences between the various countries are likely to extend the role of border control and quarantine so that international tourism, international trade and even migration will be affected. Territorialization is, of course, no one way road. The massive intensification of digital mediatization allows for an enormous increase of professional and private trans-local communication and, consequently, synthetic situations (Knorr 2009), while at the same time supporting the transformation of the interaction order by the diminution of local shops, meetings, conferences and other forms of embodied encounters. This may not only affect the role of urban life but probably transverse the relation between urban and rural regions.

The refiguration of society is, however, not fate; it builds on communicative actions. While actions may anticipate and prevent, some tendencies have been sketched here, the solution to the problem lies in the materiality of communicative action: be it in the distancing of actors and the protection of their bodies (e.g. by face masks) or be it in the medical manipulation of the virus and its effects, which simultaneously means the deconstruction of its symbolism.

References

Alexander, Jeffrey, Bernhard Giesen, Jason L. Mast (eds.) (2006) *Social Performance. Symbolic Action, Cultural Pragmatics and Ritual*. Cambridge: Cambridge University Press.

Beck, Ulrich (1992) *Risk Society: Towards a New Modernity*. New Delhi: Sage.

_____ (1999) *World Risk Society*. London: Polity.

Clemens, Elisabeth S. (2007) "Toward a historicized sociology: theorizing events, processes, and emergency," *Annual Review of Sociology* 33: 527–549.

Couldry, Nick, Andreas Hepp 2016. *The Mediated Construction of Reality*. London: Polity.

Ding, Huiling (2014) "Transnational Quarantine Rhetorics: Public Mobilization in SARS and in H1N1 Flu," *J Med Humanit* 35: 191–210. https://doi.org/10.1007/s10912-014-9282-8

Dombrowsky, Wolf R. (1987) "Critical Theory in Sociological Disaster Research" in R. Russel Dynes, Bruna de Marchi, Carlo Pelanda (eds.): *Sociology of Disasters. Contribution of Sociology to Disaster Research, pp. 331–356*. Milan: Franco Angeli.

Elias, Norbert (2006) *The Court Society*. Dublin: UCD Press.

_____ (2012) *On the Process of Civilisation*. Dublin: UCD Press.

Foucault, Michel (2009) *Security, Territory, Population: Lectures at the College De Frane, 1977–78*. New York: Palgrave MacMillan.

Gennep, Arnold van (1909) *Les rites de passage*. Paris: É. Nourry.

Giddens, Anthony (1985) *Profiles and Critiques in Social Theory. Power, the Dialectic of Control and Class Structuration*. London: Polity.

Goffman, Erving (1963) *Behavior in public places: Notes on the social organization of gatherings*. New York: The Free Press.

_____ (1981) "The Interaction Order," *American Sociological Revue* 48: 1–17.

Hałas, Elżbieta (2002) "Symbolic politics of public time and collective memory: The Polish Case" *European Review* 19 (1): 115–129.

Hall, Edward T. (1982) *The Hidden Dimension*. New York: Anchor Books.

Knoblauch, Hubert (2020) *The Communicative Construction of Reality*. London/New York: Routledge.

Knoblauch, Hubert, Martina Löw (2020) "The Re-Figuration of Spaces and Refigured Modernity – Concept and Diagnosis," *Historical Social Research* 45: 2, doi: 10.12759/hsr.45.2020.2.263-292.

Knorr-Cetina, K. (2009). "The Synthetic Situation: Interactionism for a Global World," *Symbolic Interaction* 32 (1): 61–87.

Löw, Martina (2018) *The Sociology of Space. Materiality, Social Structures, and Action*. New York: Palgrave Macmillan.

Pueyo, Tomas (2020) *Coronavirus: The Hammer and the Dance. What the Next 18 Months Can Look Like, if Leaders Buy Us Time*. https://medium.com/@tomaspueyo/coronavirus-the-hammer-and-the-dance-be9337092b56.

Roloff, Evelyn, Lu Yen (2007) *Die SARS-Krise in Hong Kong. Zur Regierung von Sicherheit in der Global City*. Bielefeld: transcript.

Turner, Bryan S. (2007) "The Enclave Society: Towards a Sociology of Immobility," *European Journal of Social Theory* 10 (2): 287–304 https://doi.org/10.1177/1368431007077807.

Turner, Victor (1969) *The Ritual Process: Structure and Anti-Structure*. Aldine Transaction.

Valdez Lucas D., Camila Buono, Pablo A. Macri and Lidia A. Braunstein (2018): "Social Distancing Strategies Against Disease Spreading," "WSPC – Proceedings" 19/8, September 26: 1–28.

Peeter Selg

A Political-Semiotic Explanation of Wicked Problems

Abstract: In this chapter the focus is on political semiotics as a form of relational political analysis that the author has developed in numerous publications over the past decade. Political semiotics' potential for explaining wicked problems of governance is analyzed. Wicked problems are distinguished from simple and complex problems on the one hand and from de-problematized problems on the other. The notion of political semiotic explanation with its concrete categories for conducting such explanation is developed and its application illustrated by analyzing the constitution of wickedness of the European Migrant Crisis that started in 2015.

Keywords: governance, political semiotics, power, relational political analysis, wicked problems

Introduction

This chapter uses the notion of political semiotics I have developed within the framework of relational social science in a book *Introducing Relational Political Analysis: Political Semiotics as a Theory and Method* (Selg and Ventsel 2020). Among other topics wicked problems and their governance is analyzed in the book (see especially chapters 3, 8 and 9). In this chapter I will make the connection between wicked problems and political semiotics more explicit than in the book. Before I proceed, a brief explication is needed on why we characterize the approach to political analysis in our work as "relational."

For semioticians, "relational" approach is something to be presumed by default: the very notions of sign, semiosis, semiosphere, etc. refer to networks of dynamic relations that constitute the very elements they are composed of. Sign, for instance, in the Saussurean outlook is a relation between the signifier and the signified. And even more so: this relation is constitutive, meaning that the signifier *as* signifier and the signified *as* signified are not pregiven outside this relation. Thus, "relational" approach has informed semiotics since its inception in the works of Saussure and Peirce. In the social sciences, however, the usual research strategy has been "the art of separation" (Selg and Ventsel 2020, chapter 7): elements and their relations are analyzed in a piecemeal manner as separate units. What we propose, following the tradition of relational sociology (Emirbayer 1997; Dépelteau 2008; 2018) and our earlier attempts at bringing it to bear on political analysis (Selg 2016a; 2016b; 2018; 2019; Selg and Peiker 2019) is the dictum originating from Norbert Elias, a relational sociologist par excellence. The dictum states that elements and their relations should be "considered *separately*, but *not as being* separate" (1978: 85). This is the core of relational social sciences. The details and the relevance of relational and non-relational approaches cannot be untangled here. For that, the reader should consult the book in total, but especially chapters 2 and 7 where both the ontological foundations and the methodological consequences of both of the approaches are analyzed. In this chapter I focus mostly on political semiotics, a more specific version of relational political analysis, and open its potential for explaining the wickedness of problems of governance. I start with a brief characterization of the later, by distinguishing them from simple and complex problems and from what we call de-problematized problems. Then I move straight on to the notion of political semiotic explanation and offer concrete categories for conducting such explanation. Finally, I offer an illustration of a political semiotic explanation by analyzing the constitution of wickedness of the European migrant crisis that started in 2015.

What are wicked problems of governance?

Wicked problems have features that Peters (2017: 388) has put in an abbreviated mode, based on one of the foundational texts on the notion (Rittel and Webber 1973):

(1) Wicked problems are difficult to define. There is no definite formulation.
(2) Wicked problems have no stopping rule.
(3) Solutions to wicked problems are not true or false but good or bad.
(4) There is no immediate or ultimate test for solutions.
(5) All attempts to solutions have effects that may not be reversible or forgettable.
(6) These problems have no clear solution, and perhaps not even a set of possible solutions.
(7) Every wicked problem is essentially unique.
(8) Every wicked problem may be a symptom of another problem.
(9) There are multiple explanations for the wicked problem.
(10) The planner (policymaker) has no right to be wrong.

Following various eminent treatments of the topic (e. g. Roberts 2000; Turnbull and Hoppe 2018; Van Bueren et al., 2003) we can initially classify all problems of governance into three categories: simple, complex and wicked problems. Later we will add the fourth type (de-problematized problem), which is usually ignored in governance literature.

Many, if not most of the problems of governance are simple and technical. In their case, both the problem as well as its possible solution is clear for the affected parties. Solving simple problems requires specialists. All the routine activities of executive power ranging from delivering pensions to regular activities of border control are simple problems.

Complex problems differ from simple problems by the following aspect: although there is an agreement among the affected parties on the meaning and definition of the problem, there is a substantial disagreement over its possible solutions. This could be a considerable hindrance to reaching a successful solution to the problem. Nevertheless, we can say that complex problems are by their nature solvable and their difference from simple problems is quantitative, not qualitative. Solving complex problems requires cooperation among specialist. Implementing the priorities of educational policy could be an example of a complex problem. Although the government, the opposition, the educational researchers, parents, teachers and other affected parties, might agree that the quality of education needs to be increased, there could be huge disagreements over how to achieve this goal.

Wicked problems differ from both simple and complex problems qualitatively: there is no agreement among the affected parties on neither the definition of the problem at hand nor about its possible solutions. There cannot be any experts or specialists in the strict sense here, and often rigorous method-based approach to their solution can be futile. Wicked problems have constantly changing background conditions; they are often comprehended retroactively after a particular solution has been implemented; they bring along other problems (often wicked too) whenever there is an attempt to solve them. Consequently, we could say that although wicked problems are not solvable, they might be governable.

There is an additional possibility: a situation where there is a *disagreement* about the nature of the *problem* but at the same time an *agreement* about its *solution*. Although never discussed in governance literature it is a potentially fruitful research topic. Drawing parallels with various discussions on "depoliticization" (see Hay 2007) "as the set of processes (including varied tactics, strategies, and tools) that remove or displace the potential for choice, collective agency, and deliberation around a particular political issue" (Fawcett et al.,

2017: 5) we can call them "deproblematized" problems that are "solved" by *displacing* them through ready-made ideological responses that are presented as universal solutions to whatever social issues. Often the tactics of this *displacement* means treating wicked problems as basically simple, solvable problems. Besides, various techniques to "cover up" or "spin" unsolved societal problems might turn them into wicked problems. This form of governance has certain semiotic form. In fact, what we call "political semiotics" presumes "the political" and its dimensions of power, governance and democracy to have all certain semiotic forms whose relational constitution is an important part of political analysis. I move next to these issues.

What is political semiotic explanation?

The main task of semiotics is studying meaning in terms of translation as the main mechanism of communication through which meaning systems or discourses are constituted. The notion of translation in terms of discrete/continuous coding from the Tartu-Moscow school and the notion of hegemony in terms of the logic of difference and equivalence of the Essex school form the basis for the theory of political semiotics outlined in my writings on political semiotics (besides Selg and Ventsel 2020, see Selg and Ventsel 2008; 2010; 2012; 2019; Selg 2010; 2011; 2013; Selg and Ruutsoo 2014). In other words, the ways through which discrete elements are translated into a more or less continuous whole (system) of meaning is the research object of semiotic explanation as I understand it. It is important that the mechanism of the constitution of meaning is *rhetorical* translation that works at the foundation of every meaning-system. This is because the coding systems – the discrete and the continuous – are *not directly* translatable, but are so only *figuratively*. That, in turn, entails that studying rhetorical figures or tropes that are present in our surrounding world is not just a matter of studying how the world is "expressed" through meanings (in speeches, literature, art and the like) – it is studying the *constitution* of the surrounding world *itself* (tacitly I, of course, presume this world to be what is usually referred to as *social* world or reality). The world cannot be made sense of outside some rhetorically constituted system of meanings. That is why the political, which I propose to analyze as hegemony with its dimensions of power, governance, and democracy (Selg and Ventsel 2020, chapter 3) is first and foremost an issue of different rhetorical translation strategies that are realized in communication (*public* communication as I specify below).

Since the dawn of rhetorical studies, there is a distinction between metaphor and metonymy as two opposing rhetorical strategies: the first is presenting constituent elements of meaning as belonging together based on their similarity; the second is doing the same based on their contiguity. The more *metaphoric* a system of meaning is the more it is prevailed by the logic of *equivalence* (Laclau 1996) or *continuous* coding (Lotman 2001). The more *metonymic* a system of meaning is, the more it is prevailed by the logic of *difference* (Laclau 1996) or *discrete* coding (Lotman 2001). In actual meaning making there cannot be final victory of metaphoric or metonymic principles, but there is always a tendency towards either of them. We could still imagine two opposite world views where either the principle of metaphor or that of metonymy is stretched to its extreme. A "purely" metaphoric world view would be akin to what in cultural semiotics has been described as pre-literate mythological consciousness: "The main feature of such a world is universal resemblance of everything to everything; the main organizing structural relation that of homomorphism" (Lotman 2004: 570). This worldview "makes one see manifestations of the One phenomenon in the various phenomena of the real world and observe the One Object behind the diversity of objects of the same type" (Ibid, 571). Although origins of such a world view go back to pre-literate period, as a cultural layer it is still with us in various forms of stereotypes, myths and conspiracy theories that guide our thinking. A "purely" metonymic worldview would the one in which everything belongs together with everything as different singular or unique entities. Now, but what lies between those (theoretically imaginable) extremes? Can we even provide some methods for identifying different configurations of meaning between metaphoric and metonymic rhetorical translations? And how are these related to the political, that is, power, governance and democracy? In the next section we take up these issues.

The semiotic logic of power, governance and democracy

An important link for moving from general emphasis of the constitutive role played by rhetorical figures or tropes in meaning-making to concrete framework of analysis is Roman Jakobson's model of communication. Bringing in Jakobson is a useful step for at least two reasons. First, as is a common knowledge among semioticians, Jakobson (1971: 239–259) explicitly identified *metaphoric*, and *metonymic* poles of language. This helps us to bring Laclau and Mouffe's theory of democracy into a substantial dialogue with semiotics. To recap what I have argued elsewhere, Laclau and Mouffe see democratic discourses as articulated between the tension towards metaphoric and metonymic tendencies (Laclau and Mouffe 1985; 1987; Laclau 2001). The issue here is roughly this: in one extreme we could imagine democracy as articulated in purely metaphoric terms where basically the mythological consciousness in Lotman's sense with its perception of universal resemblance of everything with everything prevails. There is a total unity and homogeneity in society and, simply put, people act as one. This is a totalitarian extreme of democratic logic. The other extreme would be a totally metonymic discourse where plurality and difference prevails, and the contingency of each link between elements consti-tuting the discourse is actively acknowledged. But what types of democracy are there between the purely theoretical extremes of totalitarian social order and the order that is completely aware of its contingency and the differences con-stitutive of it? In Lotman's terms: what forms of democracy are there between completely continuous-mythological and completely discrete-analytic demo-cratic texts or semiospheres? Jakobson's view of language functions combined with general insights from political scientific research on different public com-munication could provide us with a coherent response. The guiding insight about the "extremes" of democratic discourse in terms of *plurality* and *homoge-neity* is well captured by Laclau:

> the attempts at *homogenizing* the social space within which democracy operates (the universal class in Marx, the dissolution of social diversity in a unified public sphere in Jacobinism) necessarily produce a *democratic deficit*. Democracy faces the challenge of having to unify collective wills in political spaces of universal representation, while making such universality compatible with a *plurality of social spaces* dominated by particularism and difference (Laclau 2001: 13, italics added).

Jakobson, as is well known, has distinguished six dimensions of communication that are articulated in meaning-making process: addresser, addressee, contact, context, message, and code. Depending on different orientations of communi-cation we could say that in their "pure" form there could be a communication oriented to each of those dimensions. He also refers to those orientations as "language functions."

The *emotive* function, an orientation toward the ADDRESSER is discernable in the "direct expression of the speaker's attitude toward what he is speaking about" (Jakobson 1960: 354). The *phatic* function is a "set for CONTACT" that "may be displayed by a profuse exchange of ritualized formulas" (ibid, 355) like appeals to common places or stereotypes. The *metalingual* function, orienta-tion toward the CODE (Ibid, 356), is exemplified most clearly in definitions or question about the language/code being used like in "*Mare is the female of horse*" (Ibid, 358) answered to the metalingual question: "What is *mare*?" The *poetic* function, "promoting the palpability of signs," is first an orientation "toward the MESSAGE as such" (Ibid, 356). Second, it is the primary verbal means for *building* metaphoric chains of equivalences between disparate linguistic elements and this way it is in a diametrical opposition to metalingual function: "in metalanguage the sequence is used to build an equation, whereas in poetry the equation is used to build a sequence" (ibid, 358). The *conative* function "the orientation toward ADRESSEE... finds its purest grammatical expression in the vocative and imperative" (*Ibid*, 355). Finally, the *referential* function is "an orientation toward the CONTEXT" (Ibid, 353), exemplified most clearly in descriptive sentences, discussions of matters of fact, and logical arguments. It is important to stress that the "verbal structure of a message depends primarily on the *predominant* function" (Jakobson 1960: 353, italics added), and hence those "pure" forms never exist in actual communication. But we can speak of different hierarchies of those orientations or prevalence of certain orientations, making each communicative act, and in turn, each meaningful whole thoroughly relational. When translated into the problematic of studying the political, we should first point to Jakobson's general remark that those functions of communication are not restricted to verbal language only but "must lead mutatis mutandis to an analogous study of the other semiotic systems" (1998: 703). Semiotics is thus a general study of communication. (Jakobson 1998: 666). But if our aim is to delineate possibilities for *political* semiotics then our focus is not on *general*, but *political* communication, that is, *public* communication in relation to *power, governance, and democracy* as different dimensions or moments of the political as *hegemony* (Selg and Ventsel 2020, chapter 3). Political semiotic model proposed below deals with conceptualizing different types of hegemony established in public communication. As we have insisted via Laclau and Mouffe, the practico-political continuum of democratic institution of the social lies in between those two extremes that they characterize as "totalitarian" and "radical democratic" imaginary: "while the radical democratic imaginary presupposes openness and pluralism and processes of argumentation which never lead to an ultimate foundation, totalitarian societies are constituted through their claim to master the foundation" (Laclau and Mouffe 1987: 105–106). By connecting the insights of democratic hegemony and Jakobson's six-fold model of communication we could provide a model of the political by distinguishing different forms of political communication depending on which language function prevails in the system of meaning (ranging from a singular micro-level communicative act to, in principle, macro-level configurations of political culture, period, or era). This would entail semiotic redefinition of power, governance and democracy in terms of six functions of language (or semiotic system more generally).

As already mentioned, Jakobson never deemed the language functions he distinguished as possible in their *pure* form. So, when I speak of phatic and metalingual communication, we could in practice intelligibly speak of tendencies only. Nevertheless, analytically speaking, we could say that the constitution of the political can have tendencies ranging from phatic, emotive, poetic, conative, referential and metalingual form as proposed by Jakobson.

In what follows, I will propose six ideal types for conceptualizing power, governance and democracy in terms of prevalent language function in *public* communication, and the respective forms of power and governance.

Semiotic categories for explaining the political

In each of the categories outlined below the general label (like "authoritarian populism" or "authoritarian deproblematization") refers to an ideal type in which a certain logic of translation or articulation is overwhelmingly prevalent. A crucial notion for me especially for conceptualizing democracy is "public communication." Of course, there is an important strand of research lining up under the banner "Personal is political." But we restrict the following presentation to more traditional understanding of power, governance and democracy – or the political more generally – that views these as public phenomena.[1] The stress on *public* communication should not be overlooked, since I would not want to claim below that *phatic* communication, for instance, necessarily implies authoritarian personality. Phatic dialogues between lovers for example, are not signs of authoritarianism *per se*. What I do want to insist, however, is that the *publics* among which there is an overwhelming tendency to address issues only for the sake of contact (the phatic function of language) itself – in terms of stereotypes or "common places" – renders a good ground for suspecting deficiency in effective democratic participation in the corresponding social formation, as it is characteristic of authoritarian societies.

All the adjective markers in the following exposition ("totalitarian," "authoritarian," "democratic," "clientelist," "deliberative," "radical") point to the *form* of political *articulation*, not their (ideological) content (like, liberal, socialist etc.). Thus, one can be "deliberative" about "fascist" contents as well as "totalitarian" about "liberal" contents. Political semiotic explanation is none other than explaining how certain political forms are constituted within relations to

---

1   We discuss this in more detail at the end of chapter 3 of Selg and Ventsel 2020, referring to the historical extensions of these terms.

other forms and how they in turn constitute political contents. Both form and content are, of course relational That is why we call this explanation "political form analysis" (Selg and Ventsel 2020, chapter 8). In practice, there is in principle infinite array of variations on the *content* level, which, of course can be analyzed separately, but not as being separate from the *form*, since both form and content are relational phenomena.

Radical/agonistic democracy, power and governance (metalingual public communication)

Laclau and Mouffe defend what they call "radical plural democracy" conceived "in a form of politics which is founded not upon dogmatic postulation of any 'essence of the social,' but, on the contrary, on affirmation of the contingency and ambiguity of every 'essence'" (Laclau and Mouffe 1985: 193). We could interpret this ideal of **democracy** in terms of prevalence of metalingual messages in the public discourse, characterized by questioning and explicating the public *code* of, for instance, the underlying values and aims of the political community as a whole.

It is no coincidence that the form of **governance** that can be associated with the prevalence of metalingual public communication is termed "metagovernance" in the governance studies literature. Metagovernance or "governance of governance" as it is sometimes described is often associated exactly with questioning and specifying not even the underlying rules or norms of governance, but the very values from which those norms are derived (Kooiman 2003; Kooiman and Jentoft 2009). The principles of "requisite variety," "reflexive orientation," and "self-reflexive irony" that Jessop (2011) discusses in relation to a suitable ethos of metagovernance all boil down to questioning the foundations of governance practices, including why they and not others have become dominant, hegemonic or just taken-for-granted.

The metalingual notion of **power** could be associated with Giddens' (1984: 41–45) differentiation between practical and discursive consciousness knowledge. Practical consciousness knowledge according to Giddens is the tacit knowledge that is not put into question and usually not even realized: it is the taken-for-granted knowledge based on which everyday conduct is carried out more or less automatically. Discursive consciousness knowledge is the knowledge that is put into explicit reflective form: into words, arguments and questions. Metalingual power is present in the transformation of practical consciousness knowledge into discursive consciousness knowledge.

Deliberative power, governance and democracy (referential public communication)

If we presume the public code to be given, unquestioned and fixed, but have the focus on the *context* of its realization we could link this form of public discourse to the ideal of "deliberative **democracy**" originating from different works of Habermas (1996a; 1996b) and famously summarized by Cohen (2005: 347–348). Crucial here is the view that the ideal of "deliberative procedure" ought to be 1) *free*; 2) *reasoned*, roughly in the sense that "no force except that of the better argument is exercised" (Habermas 1975: 108, quoted in Cohen 2005: 347); 3) the parties involved are *equal* both formally and substantially in a sense that no distribution of power affects the deliberation; 4) the ideal deliberation "aims to arrive at a rationally motivated *consensus*" (Ibid, 348). We could interpret this in terms of prevalence of *referential* messages in the public discourse.

Deliberative form of **governance** is usually associated with networks or the so-called "heterarchy" – it is a form of governance that lies between the anarchy of the market and the hierarchy of the state. The form of communication in network governance is dialogue which "depends on continuing commitment to generate and share information (thereby reducing, without ever eliminating, the problem of bounded rationality)" (Jessop 2016: 169). This is what we can conceptualize as the constitution of public through referential communication.

It is understandably hard to conceptualize deliberative **power**, since as we already saw, in an ideal deliberative procedure no power relation should affect the deliberation. Nevertheless, the genealogy of the referential notion of power might be traced back to at least Weber's conception of legal-rational *domination* (1978: 217–226), that is, rationally legitimate *power over*. However, as it is argued in several normative models, this form of power might also be considered as *power to* in the sense of springing from people's ability to act in concert (Arendt 1970: 52) or as "the formation of *common* will in a communication directed to reaching agreement (Habermas 1986: 76). Consequently, in its ideal-typical form, this is the power in the form of the (unforced) force of a better argument (Habermas 1975: 108).

Clientelism in power, governance and democracy (conative public communication)

When moving to a form of *conative* language function and imagining a public discourse in which it is prevalent, we could relate this picture of **democracy** with what is described as "clientelism." This is the form of politics characterized by a "non-horizontal," "particularistic" and "asymmetric" communication, which, among other things "places a premium on public demonstrations of loyalty to the patron" (Hallin and Papathanassopoulos 2002: 185–189). Thus, we conceive it as a form of politics in which the patron (the political elite) is the active addresser and focuses directly to the people, a passive addressee who receives an order or is being called to order.

Governance that manifests itself mainly through vocative and imperative – that is through the conative function of language – is referred to as hierarchy in governance literature. The main mechanism of hierarchy is command in the broadest sense, including bureaucratic directives, performance measurements, and direct orders in rank-based branches of executive power. Command in general "involves *ex ante* imperative coordination in pursuit of substantive collective goals set from above (hierarchical command in the firm, organization, or state). It prioritizes the 'effective' pursuit of successive policy goals" (Jessop 2016: 167).

Of course, this is related to the most classical understanding of **power**. And its roots lead back to at least Hobbes's *Leviathan*. From more contemporary times, it is again Weber who lies behind this view when he distinguishes "two diametrically contrasting types of domination, viz., domination by virtue of a constellation of interests (in particular: by virtue of a position of monopoly), and domination by virtue of authority, i.e. power to command and duty to obey" (1978: 943). The former is "based upon influence derived exclusively from the possession of goods or marketable skills guaranteed in some way and acting upon the conduct of those dominated, who remain, however, formally free and are motivated simply by the pursuit of their own interests" (Ibid.). This could be conceptualized as a pure form of conative power. The classical pluralist (Dahl 1957) and elitist (Mills 1956) views of power that inform the bulk of mainstream political science are also relevant here since they revolve around either actual decision-making or the potential to force through decisions.

Democratic populism in power, governance and democracy (poetic public communication)

The prevalence of *poetic* language in public communication, indicates to form of **democracy** that could be called "democratic populism" or "petty demagogy" in Laclau's (2005: 191) sense. This is the populist rhetoric in a "highly institutionalized society" (Ibid). Western countries are familiar with this, since it is provided in abundance during party campaigns characterized by attempts to construct through disrupting metaphors the poetic chains of equivalences opposing "us" and "them" or "right" and "wrong" policies. Due to firm institutional framework of these societies the "equivalential logics have less terrain on which to operate" (Ibid) and this way these constructed oppositions rarely succeed in "equivalentially dividing the social field into two *antagonistic* camps" (Ibid, 189, italics added).

When it comes to **governance**, democratic populism is a form of deproblematization of policy problems (see Selg and Ventsel 2020, chapter 3). It is not widely discussed in governance literature. Jessop discusses "cynicism" as a reaction to governance failure: "Cynicism is the realm of symbolic politics, accelerated policy churning (to give the impression of doing something about intractable problems), and the 'spin doctor' – the realm of 'words that work and policies that fail.' This is particularly evident in the highly mediatized world of contemporary politics" (2011: 118). This is basically governance that displaces policy issues without addressing them by constructing them as problems for which a readymade solution is at hand.

In terms of **power**, Bourdieu points out that "there are always, in any society, conflicts between symbolic powers that aim at imposing the vision of legitimate divisions, that is, at *constructing* groups. Symbolic power, in this sense, is a power of "world-making" (1989: 22, italics added). Referring to Nelson Goodman (1978) he specifies that this "'world-making' consists 'in separating and reuniting, often in the same operation,' in carrying out a decomposition, an analysis, and a composition, a synthesis, often by the use of labels" (Ibid.). That is why creating poetic equivalences is often key to this type of power strategy.

Authoritarian populism in power, governance and democracy (phatic public communication)

The form of **democracy** I label "authoritarian populism" is characterized by the prevalence of *phatic* messages in the public discourse resulting in public appeals to stereotypes and common places. In practice the latter's function is akin to *myths* in Barthes' sense. A myth "abolishes the complexity of human acts" and "gives them simplicity of essences" (Barthes 1993: 143). In political psychology Lifton used the term "thought-terminating cliché" for characterizing "the language of the totalist environment:" "the most far-reaching and complex of human problems are compressed into brief, highly reductive, definitive-sounding phrases, easily memorized and easily expressed" (Lifton 1989: 429). The prevalence of myth and thought-terminating cliché lead to phatic communication characterized by Baudrillard as follows: "Contact for contact's sake becomes the empty form with which language seduces itself when it no longer has anything to say" (Baudrillard 1991: 164). Thus, the prevalence of appealing to perceived common places, stereotypes or other ritualized formulas in the public discourse is characteristic of "authoritarian populism" in our framework.

In terms of **governance**, this "authoritarian populism" would include various strategies of deproblematization of policy issues (Selg and Ventsel 2020, chapter 3). In fact, in the governance literature, this phatic form of communication is not discussed very much as a form of governance in its own right. What we can, of course, point to is a form of reactions to governance failure that Jessop discusses: "stoicism" that "rests on passive resignation in the pursuit of familiar routines" (2011: 118). This is basically an appeal to commonplaces that would take the problematic issues off the agenda.

More than in governance literature, the topic of agenda-setting which always involves taking issues *off* the agenda, is discussed in the literature on **power**. The founding arguments for *phatic* power could be found already in Weber's notion of traditional domination (1978: 216), Marx's notion of fetishism (1982: 163–177) developed into a more general framework by Lukacs' notion of "reification" (1971: 83–110). Contemporary conceptualizations of *phatic* power include the theories that relate power with the reproduction of tacit social knowledge: Bourdieu's habitus (1998: 7–8; 1989: 18–19), Giddens' "practical consciousness knowledge" (1984: 41–45), Foucault's episteme (2002) (applied not only to scientific but everyday discourses as well) and disciplinary power (1978; 1979), Lukes' "false consciousness" (2005), Bachrach and Baratz's "mobilization of bias" (1962: 949–952) or Clegg's (1997: 207) and Haugaard's reification (2006: 60) in the form of "appeal to nature" (Ibid.) could be conceptualized in terms of Jakobson's phatic communication. In general: authoritarian populism with a prevalence of phatic communication is oriented to presenting given social reality as fixed, unproblematic and uncontested.

Totalitarian populism in power, dovernance and democracy (emotive public communication)

Finally, when there is what Laclau described as "the *Jacobin* conception of democracy, with its concomitant ideal of a transparent community unified – if necessary – by terror" (Laclau 2001: 250), then the appeal to emotions through exacerbating the antagonism between "us" and "them" in the public discourse is inevitable. Hence, I label "totalitarian populism" the form of **democracy** articulated prevailingly through *emotive* messages in public communication.

In terms of **governance**, this is a form of deproblematization of policy problems that appeals to general and often abstract threats to the public, through depicting the enemy that is identifiable but not containable and hinders through its vicious activities the very foundation of the public (be it embodied in a nation, state or group). The view that "totalitarianism" should not be conflated with ancient form of governance usually referred to as despotism or tyranny, since it is a specifically modern and "democratic" phenomenon or even one emerging not until the 20th century "mass society," has gained much support since Arendt (see Arendt 1962; cf Sartori 1987: 193–203; Marchart 2007: 101; Lefort 1988).

Drawing on Lefort we could characterize totalitarian populist governance as one in which "social division, in all its modes, is denied, and at the same time all signs of differences of opinion, belief or mores are condemned" (1988: 13). This might point to phatic communication that we attributed to "authoritarian populism." Yet, as Marchart is quick to explain:

> since that division can never be completely erased as an ontological dimension and will continue to surface in the form of disturbances of the imaginary concealment, it has to be displaced. In order for the 'People-as-One' to be presented as a totality, as full identity, a relation to some sort of *outside* is inevitable. What acts as the new outside is a series of internal substitutes representing the 'enemy within:' the kulaks, the bourgeoisie, the Jews, spies, and saboteurs (2007: 102).

The paradox of totalitarianism is thus the following: "division is denied . . . and, at the same time as this denial, a division is being affirmed, on the level of phantasy, between the People-as-One and the Other" (Lefort 1988: 298). This points to the fact that "totalitarianism needs the enemy as a reference point and thus relies on division at the very moment when the latter is decried" (Marchart 2007: 103). And the role of it is a populist cohesion: "Precisely because totalitarianism presents itself as an entirely rational order, it has to adopt the form of an uncontaminated purity, and that which is excluded has, conversely, to be essentially impure" (Laclau 1990: 90).

The roots of what could be called emotive **power** are, again, pretty traditional. It was among the central concerns of Machiavelli's *Prince* in its discussions on the role of fear and love as instruments of *power over* especially in the phase of nascent rule. We can also see them in Weber's notion of charismatic authority (1978: 241–245) in the sense of *power to*. All the models of power that conceptualize the latter in terms of, for instance, manipulating emotions or the need to "constantly short-circuit all thought and decision" (Ellul 1973: 27) could be articulated into the emotive notion of power. Of course, the appeal to emotive power is present at least latently in all the conceptions that grasp it in terms of "*threat* of violence" in the roughly Weberian sense. Of course, as the purely "emotive communication" would amount to non-communication (in the form of unarticulated interjections), the pure *"threat* of violence" could be conceived to fuse into the very "violence" itself. And this is the moment when, for many significant theorists – both normative (Arendt 1970) and analytical (Foucault 1982; Luhmann 1979; Haugaard 2010: 434–5) – power ceases to function. Thus "physical power is not the ultimate form of power. Quite the contrary, its use represents the failure of social power" (Haugaard 2003: 108). The point, however, is that "in most complex social orders violence is blended with social power and then we get coercion" (Ibid.). Similarly, the purely emotive power is, in practice, usually blended with other forms of power – and this, of course, in a way, holds regarding all the six forms of power discussed here

We have now covered the six categories for semiotic explanation of the political. Table 1 summarizes these categories in a discrete/deductive manner.

But as we argue the categories in fact are not meant to be readymade deductive categories under which we can subsume reality. Political semiotic explanation as a form of constitutive not causal explanation is *abductive* in principle (Selg and Ventsel 2020, chapter 7), meaning that the categories used do not come off without a remainder: what counts as phatic message, for instance, is dependent on the network of relations with other messages in the discourse, text or semiosphere under scrutiny. Therefore, a more accurate depiction of these categories would be something along the lines of Figure 1.

This should be taken into account when we analyze the constitution of wickedness in the next section through the categories just outlined.

An example: European migrant crisis and the constitution of wickedness

The example considers the European Migrant Crisis.[2] On August 31, 2015, German Chancellor Angela Merkel uttered the words: "Wir haben so vieles geschafft – wir schaffen das," which could be translated roughly as "We have managed so many things – we can manage this too." Given that the words we spoken after the chancellor's visit to a German refugee camp near Dresden where she was met with hostile reactions by anti-refugee activists we could say that at this very communicative context Merkel's words constituted a *metalingual* communication: it addressed the rising sentiment of being unable to manage the flow of migrants and refugees from the third world countries and it was also

---

2   The example is partly based on Selg and Ventsel 2020, chapter 8, and Klasche and
    Selg 2020.

Tab. 1. Deductive presentation of the semiotic categories for explaining the political. Source: Selg and Ventsel 2020, chapter 6

Form of democracy	Form of power	Form of governance	Dominant orientation in public communication			
Totalitarian populism	Emotive power (threat, fear charisma, agitative propaganda)	Governance as de-problematization through constructing threats (securitization, war, apocalypse)	Emotive: orientation toward addresser	**DE-DEMOCRATIZATION**	**DE-PROBLEMATIZATION** **NON-DISCRETE**	**METAPHORIC**
Authoritarian populism	Phatic power (reification, mobilization of bias, tacit knowledge, rituals, myths, stereotypes)	Governance as de-problematization through stoicism (passive resignation, familiar routines)	Phatic: orientation toward contact			
Democratic populism	Poetic power ("world-making")	Governance as de-problematization through cynicism ('spin doctor', displacement)	Poetic: orientation toward message			
Clientelist democracy	Conative power (command, directive, order)	Governance as hierarchy (administration, bureaucracy)	Conative: orientation toward addressee	**DEMOCRATIZATION**	**PROBLEMATIZATION** **DISCRETE**	**METONYMIC**
Deliberative democracy	Referential-rational power ('force of a better argument')	Governance as network	Referential: orientation toward context			
Agonistic/radical democracy	Metalingual power (power to make practical knowledge into discursive knowledge)	Metagovernance ('self-reflective irony')	Metalingual: orientation toward code.			

questioning the increasingly influential anti-immigration movement. However, the initially metalingual communication ended up being an *emotive* common place. The reason for that could partly be seen in that taken out of context, the second part of Merkel's statement – "wir schaffen das" – could also be translated as just "we can do it." This part of her utterance became a slogan (essentially *emotive/phatic* form of communication). It became a slogan for those positively minded about the welcoming of refugees from East Asia and Africa – resonated by Merkel herself by repeating it – as well as for those who vehemently opposed it – the latter using it in an ironic or disdainful sense. Consequently, a year later, in September 2016, Merkel reflecting in an interview to a financial

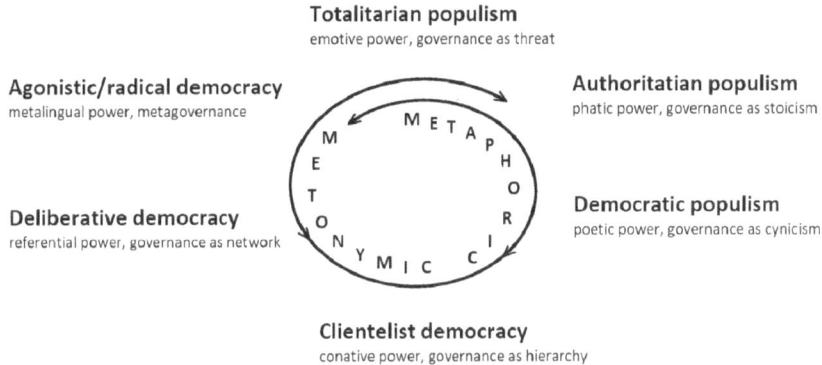

Totalitarian populism
emotive power, governance as threat

Agonistic/radical democracy
metalingual power, metagovernance

Authoritatian populism
phatic power, governance as stoicism

Deliberative democracy
referential power, governance as network

Democratic populism
poetic power, governance as cynicism

Clientelist democracy
conative power, governance as hierarchy

Fig. 1. Abductive presentation of the semiotic categories for constitutive explanation of the political. *Note*: metaphoric or non-discrete pole is also the de-problematization and de-democratization pole; metonymic or discrete pole is also the problematization and democratization pole. Source: Selg and Ventsel 2020, chapter 7.

newspaper *Wirtschaftswoche* said: "I sometimes think this phrase was a little overstated, that too much store was set by it — to the extent that I'd prefer not to repeat it," and adding: "It's become a simple slogan, an almost meaningless formula." (quoted in Livingstone 2016). "Wir schaffen das" was said in the latter part of 2015, a year when we saw movement upwards of 28 million people displaced due to conflict, violence and disaster, joining the 244 million international migrants already moving throughout the globe (Kaundert and Masys 2018: 73). During 2015 the major referent object regarding the European Migrant Crisis among top politicians in the EU was that the crisis is first and foremost about an issue of an overflow of migrants to Europe and the humanitarian crisis related to that. Representing the crisis as a humanitarian crisis meant *referential*-deliberative communication – "sticking to the point," talking of facts and figures and organizing means for dealing with concrete people and their problems. There is, however, a catch in this representation.

Already more than 3 years ago it was conceptualized as a " 'wicked problem' – one characterized by: (1) multiple, potentially conflicting values, (2) strong political passions on different sides of the issue, (3) substantive uncertainty on how best to solve the problem, and (4) multiple independent arenas for social deliberation and action" (Geuijen et al., 2017: 622). The quoted publication, in a leading academic journal *Public Management Review*, which was made available online already in 2016, is telling in many ways. Given the time academic publishing takes (with its rounds of reviews and lingering editorial decisions and production), it can be presumed to be composed roughly around 2015, the year of "Wir schaffen das." According to the authors the "wickedness" of the European Migrant Crisis is related to the multiplicity of interdependent and mutually constitutive crises, conflicts and threats both at the local and global level.

In the following, I want to demonstrate the usefulness of political semiotic explanation when analyzing this wickedness of the crisis. I start with the actions taken by Germany during the European Migrant Crisis. My focus at this moment will be put on the apparent shift in governance to address the crisis in 2015–2016. In terms of the above-proposed methodology, one should say that the dominant form of communication has been replaced with another one. Even though my aim here is not to conduct a fully developed empirical study, but to illustrate the methodology of political semiotics, I use the Jakobsonian categories outlined above to understand the initial discourse (2015) and the workings of the superseding one (since 2016).

Initially, one can track an overarching *metalingual* discourse that leads to the original offer of support to arriving refugees (see Lichtenstein et al., 2017: 108). It is metalingual in the sense of appealing to empathy – ability to perceive the contingency of social positions, including one's own. From the semiotic point of view, it is appealing to the contingency of the code that defines "us" and "them" as being in a "natural," "fixed" position. This relates the initial metalingual discourse to the ideas of radical democracy and metagovernance. At the center of radical democracy, as we argued in chapter 3 of Selg and Ventsel 2020 lies "the ethos of contingency" (see also Selg 2012). And above I explicitly tied the idea of radical democracy to the prevalence of metalingual public communication. In 2015, the support to help the refugees had also been expressed by the media, the government and even the opposition in Germany. Why such a metalingual discourse? The constitution of such a discourse can be traced down to the so-called "*Willkommenskultur*" (*welcoming culture*) which finds its historical roots in the events in and after the Second World War, such as Germany's collective memory of the crimes performed in the War, and the fact that many Germans were refugees themselves after the war had ended (Holmes and Castañeda 2016: 14–16) – pointing again to the contingency of social positions. In Germany, specifically, we can find some more historical junctures that strengthened this discourse. The cruelties of the Second World War have been mostly concealed in the direct aftermath of the War and have been only introduced into the public discourse once the following generation asked the question of collective guilt of the German people. This public debate erupted anew in the mid-1980s when a sense of collective memory, centering around the holocaust, started to affect political outcomes in the German Federal Republic and has been for instance used as an argument for expanding the EU eastwards (Langenbacher 2003: 46–47). A debate of the historians (*Historikerstreit*) about the Nazi regime was held for years in the leading German news outlets and actively followed by many Germans. The continuous recapturing of the attention and recall of the past kept the discourse in its dominant position and in a way buttressed the welcoming culture. Up until this day, it is part of Germany's identity to carry the guilt and the responsibilities (remembering and preventing) deriving from it. Additionally, migration waves of the last 50 years emanating from Southern Europe but also the Muslim World (Caglar and Soysal 2003) created a multi-ethnic society that has sensitized the population to accept the arrival of people with different cultural backgrounds.

Thus, the *metalingual* welcoming culture could lie behind the initial open-door governance of migrants. However, this also plays a crucial role in the constitution of "wickedness" of the problems to come. By autumn 2016 the open border had been suspended and completely turned around. Germany, like many of its neighboring countries, shut down the unconstrained flow of migrants and installed border controls to control the flow. It appears that the *metalingual* discourse has lost its dominant position and taken a back seat. A discourse that considers refugees and migration a security issue has taken hold. Securitization is a dominantly *emotive* discourse, which entails certain hierarchical action (*conative* communication) (Selg and Ventsel 2020, chapter 6). *Security* discourse emerged in the post-Cold War world which saw a change in the security paradigm from simple military threats to a broad definition of threats to human security. (Paris 2001) In this new paradigm, refugees were seen as a potential threat to international and domestic stability and therefore, states grew reluctant to host them. This led to the eventual state in which the Global North viewed asylum as a problem of South from which most refugees emanated. (Betts 2011) The discourse was already active in the 1990s when the dissolution of Yugoslavia created masses of refugees to EU countries and the paths to asylum have been narrowed. (Suhrke 1998: 406) However, at least in Germany, it went in and out of the dominant position. This frame is very attractive for political use since avoiding the short-term costs of hosting asylum-seekers by making them stay in the region was easily politicized. With this, the discourse focused on the economic, social and terrorist threats that could originate from asylum-seekers, not on their human needs. Most parts of the Western World swiftly felt comfortable in this new discourse, adopted this way of thinking and viewed the flow of migrants immediately as a threat.

This was not directly the case in Germany where, due to the strong presence of the *metalingual* discourse for several generations, the crisis was viewed dominantly as a humanitarian and not a political one. Politicizing the humanitarian issue through *emotive* discourse of security was noticeable in other European countries. These countries have seen the awakening and rise of mostly right-wing populist parties or rhetoric after the recession of 2010 and the resulting austerity politics. (Taggart 2017: 256) Later populists would also willingly connect migration with questions of security. Germany had proven to be somewhat immune to the populist movement by stigmatizing every new right-wing party as heirs of National Socialism. This turned with the events around the Cologne Central Station at New Year's Eve 2015–2016 and the growing number of terrorist attacks in Europe like in Nice, Reutlingen, and Berlin–that were partly committed by individuals getting into Europe seeking for protection (Trauner and Turton 2017: 39) – which has captured the attention of the Germans. This gave the AfD (Alternative for Germany) – Germany's right-wing populist party – and the PEGIDA (Patriotic Europeans Against the Islamization of the Occident) protest movement new breeding ground which they used to penetrate the public discourse with their ideas on migration. The receptivity of the German people to this type of *emotive* discourse derives from the electoral success similar parties had in other Western European countries – most notably Austria, France, and the United Kingdom – which molded it into an acceptable opinion to have. Given these developments, the *emotive* discourse was eventually picked up and propagated by the German mainstream parties (Trauner and Turton 2017: 40). The change in the public discourse, together with the attention that the terror attacks demand, sedimented the new emotive *security* discourse.

We have seen the shift in Germany from *metalingual* metagovernance to a form of *emotive* de-problematization of the humanitarian crisis: in essence there is a movement from empathy-based perception of the contingency of social positions of "us" and "them" to an antagonistic fear-based emotive discourse that constitutes "them" as a "natural" enemy. But what makes European Migrant Crisis a wicked problem from the political semiotic point of view? A simple answer would be: miscommunication. It is the miscommunication between problematization and de-problematization, democratic and authoritarian discourses – or in most general terms: between metonymic and metaphoric coding. Miscommunication from the political semiotic point of view is none other than extreme untranslatability between coding systems. The latter are none other than political *forms*. It is crucial to stress that again: the conflict is not so much about the contents of the issue – which would be central if conflicting parties would have a metalingual or, more generally, metonymic form of communication. It is exactly the untranslatability of *political forms* that constitutes the wickedness of the issue: the untranslatability of metonymic and metaphoric discourses. We can only touch very general contours of this constitution of wickedness here.

Wicked problems are often symptoms of other problems and attempted solutions can never be right or wrong but only *good* or *bad* (Rittel and Webber 1973; Peters 2017). On top of that, solution attempts will have consequences that may not be reversible. We can see all those aspects here. Various attempts at solution created other crises: *metalingual-democratic* "wir schaffen das" became essentially *emotive-totalitarian* "wir schaffen das," for instance. These might have even more drastic impact on the European population and the decision-makers themselves. In other words, "[m]any wicked problems seem to lurch from crisis to crisis" (Head 2019: 189). To show this we will point out the different crises of which the European Migrant Crisis is comprised of and how they constitute each other. In more detail we will look at the *humanitarian*, the *political/legitimacy* and the *geopolitical* crisis which interdependently ground the wicked problem we call European Migrant Crisis.

Humanitarian Crisis. The humanitarian issues lay within a complex system which makes successful intervention especially problematic. In fact, approaching a problem in such a complex system with "a linear mindset can lead to interventions that result in unintended consequences" (Kaunert and Masys 2018: 81) and "the failure to understand or ... acknowledge the non-linear and highly complex nature of global linkages on every level of governance leads to growing weakness and can paralyze decision-making" (Goldin and Mariathasan 2014: 3). In a sense the initial *metalingual* addressing of the very crisis as "merely" a humanitarian crisis can be considered a source of this paralysis of decision-making constituting among other things the political crisis the EU and many of the national governments of its member states face, and mostly in the form of *emotive* discourse of right-wing populism.

Political Crisis. Analytically we can discern two mutually constitutive processes of the political crisis in the EU. One of them is a *crisis of democracy* as a result of which we can trace a demise of general democratic tendencies in Europe allowing for anti-democratic and anti-establishment parties to gain confidence. The other part must be considered a *legitimacy crisis* which is leading to growing mistrust in the EU institutions, the idea of the EU itself or even the nation-state. This got expressed by voters in national and European elections in which anti-establishment and anti-EU parties recorded great results, but also by national governments and politicians who actively seek more (economic) freedom and independence for their states, with Brexit being the most significant example. When the Commission's majority decisions to relocate 120.000 refugees in 2015 was objected and ignored by Poland, Hungary and Czech Republic (European Commission 2017) it indicates for many a clear lack of resonance of the EU's values (Murray and Longo 2018: 575). Murray and Longo conclude that this "rebellion by member states … is unprecedented in its breadth and depth, given that i[t] constitutes not only contestation but direct opposition to the EU's authority and legal framework" (2018: 575). There seems to be a mistrust by national governments that EU-wide solutions can govern the problem. Nicola Phillips goes even a step further and states that the "migration crisis represents one of the most notable and consequential episodes of political failure in the history of European cooperation, which, many worry, retains the capacity to challenge the core of the European project" (2018: 62).

The legitimacy crisis of the EU is born out of the latter's responses towards the humanitarian crisis, which has "witnessed contestation by the government of states, by opposition parties and by citizens" (Murray and Longo 2018: 571). At its ground, the issues relate to the governing of the humanitarian crisis and the differences in practices that various actors are promoting (Murray and Longo 2018: 571). Here, we can start to see the constitutive relations among the crises. The political crisis is beginning to be inextricably linked with the humanitarian crisis, being part of its very identity. The intense politicization through emotive de-problematization of the (initially) referential – or even technical – issue of handling the flows of refugees and other migrants – makes it an issue that cannot be contained safely in the sphere of expert knowledge anymore: it has become a "people's" issue, that mostly but not exclusively have been put on the table by right-wing populist parties all over Europe. Therefore, it makes little sense to claim that the Migrant Crisis is over, even though the flows of migrants at the borders of the EU are (relatively) under control. It has become a wicked problem that is constantly fluctuating between different crises, political being one of them. Responses to one crisis – especially attempts to "solve" it in isolation – will inevitably affect the others, since, in case of constitutive relations, the crises are interdependent and cannot be considered as being separate from one another. One literally cannot comprehend or even access the *referential* handling requiring humanitarian crisis without the lens of the *emotive* discourses around threats to nation-states and European national cultures, terrorism, etc. that the populist parties and politicians resonate throughout Europe. Not only does the humanitarian crisis – and more generally the flows of migrants in Europe – constitute a political crisis, but the opposite is true as well: the political crisis frames how it is conceivable to handle the humanitarian crisis. Further, it is unlikely that large migration waves will stop in the future as living conditions in many parts of the world will get worse and migration is for many the answer to this (Castelli 2018). The political crisis is not only a result of the humanitarian crisis. They are intrinsically intertwined. They cannot be seen independent from each other, but as mutually constituting each other. Approaches to govern one of them will have to take into account the consequences of governing another. However, from the semiotic point of view, this would entail reconciling highly metonymic (metalingual, referential) discourse with highly metaphoric (emotive) discourse. Such a situation of extreme untranslatability is a major part of the "wickedness" of the problem. And this has ramifications to the geopolitical level as well.

Geopolitical Crisis. The geopolitical crisis gets fueled by the lack of unity among European countries, but its earliest realization started in 2008 with Russia re-claiming their physical influence on the continent via the Georgian-Russian war and later with the annexation of Crimea in 2014 (Wivel and *Wæver* 2018: 318). This new security environment upset also the geo-economic constellations the EU and its Eastern neighbors were a part of (Youngs 2017). The geopolitical power of the EU is expressed in its unity and it has clearly suffered during the last five years. The dissonance between political camps in most European states has led to unstable societies throughout the continent. This situation is clearly favored by the Russian Federation that feasts on the instability of its competition. Evidence for this type of "Hybrid Warfare" – a subtler approach than plain military one to gain political objectives and retain a certain degree of "plausible deniability" – have been identified in the Crimean Crisis (Lanoszka 2016) and it must be assumed that these methods were executed in other contexts. The tactics include the use of propaganda to initiate insurgencies and divide societies. Germany offers an ideal playing field for the Kremlin's tactics that have already worked during the previous German election (Aaltola 2017) and increased the divide between right and left. This divide is reached through the manipulation of the political discourse that decides on the blame for the situation (political-economic structures, the displaced persons themselves), demarcates the "deserving" migrant from the "undeserving"refugee and generally activates the fear of cultural, religious, and ethnic differences (Holmes and Castañeda 2016: 12).

Taking this brief outline of the constitution of wickedness of the European Migrant Crisis towards some conclusions, we should quote at length the paper we already quoted above. According to the authors, the European Migrant Crisis is

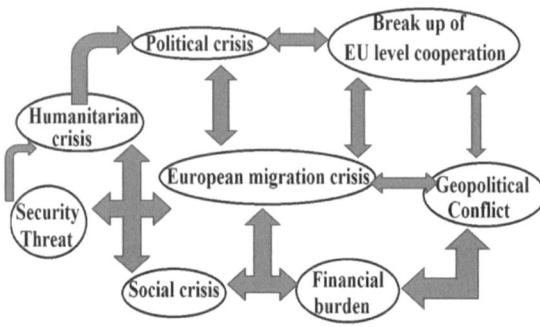

Fig. 2. The "wickedness" of European Migrant Crisis

a problem that could be seen *simultaneously* as: a *humanitarian crisis* based in the suffering of individuals who had abandoned their homes; a *geopolitical conflict* ranging across countries and continents; a *security threat* for both receiving and transit countries; a potentially heavy *financial burden* on already overtaxed states; and the *breakdown of collaboration* in the network of EU member states. Furthermore, the problem would not be addressed in a single political forum where all those with stakes and capacities could together devise a solution, then rely on their common assets to deal with the issue effectively and fairly. The response, instead, would emerge from a disjointed discourse spanning many different polities, government jurisdictions, and even private organizations, who exercised only to lose control over the assets that could help solve the problem (Geuijen et al., 2017: 622, italics added).

All the crises and conflicts mentioned here are in a constitutive relationship and it is not possible to view them as independent entities (see Selg and Ventsel 2020, chapter 8 for more detailed elaboration). They can be viewed "separately, but not as being separate" from both the viewpoint of research and governance. Schematically we can depict the wickedness of the European Migrant Crisis as in Figure 2

Of course, as with static figures on the pages of books, the processual and constantly changing configurations of elements through which the meaning of elements themselves are constituted and reconstituted is somewhat lost. But if we are to conceptualize the crisis as a wicked problem then we have to imagine this scheme in a moving diachronic fashion rather than only as a synchronic snapshot.

Conclusion

Let us recap what makes a governance problem wicked from the political semiotic point of view. Putting it somewhat vernacularly: the main constitutive mechanism of wickedness is the miscommunication between unreconcilable *forms* of communication: problematization and de-problematization, the clash between democratic and authoritarian texts, discourses or semiospheres – or in most general terms: between metonymic and metaphoric coding. Miscommunication from the political semiotic point of view is none other than extreme untranslatability between coding systems. The latter are none other than political *forms*. It is crucial to stress that again: the conflict is not so much about the contents of the issue – which would be central if conflicting parties would have a metalingual-referential or, more generally, metonymic form of communication. It is exactly the untranslatability of *political forms* that constitutes the wickedness of the issue: the untranslatability of metonymic and metaphoric discourses. In this chapter I have articulated the political semiotic categories for explaining the political based on semiotic theory of communication and the conceptualizations of power, governance and democracy found in political theory, political science and political psychology. I have also highlighted that political semiotics is not merely a (re)description of political phenomena, but a constitutive *explanation* of them. Therefore, political semiotics can be considered an important supplement for political analysis in general, especially to those approaches that take seriously the "relational turn" in the social sciences. Bringing out its potential for explaining wicked problems needs, of course, much further conceptual as well as empirical work.

Acknowledgments

Writing this chapter was supported by the Estonian Research Council with the personal research grant "PUT1485 A Relational Approach to Governing Wicked Problems."

References

Aaltola, Mika (2017) "Democracy's Eleventh Hour. Safeguarding Democratic Elections Against Cyber-Enabled Autocratic Meddling," *FIIA Briefing Paper* 226.

Arendt, Hannah (1962) *The Origins of Totalitarianism*. Cleveland and New York: Meridian Books

＿＿＿ (1970). *On Violence*. London: Allen Lane

Bachrach, Peter, Morton Baratz (1962) "Two Faces of Power," *American Political Science Review,* 56 (4): 947–952.

Barthes, Roland (1993) *Mythologies.* London: Vintage

Baudrillard, Jean. (1991) *Seduction.* London: Palgrave Macmillan

Betts, Alexander (2011) "International Cooperation in the Refugee Regime." in Alexander Betts and Gil Loescher (eds.) *Refugees in International Relations,* pp. 53–84. New York: Oxford University Press.

Bourdieu, Pierre (1989) "Social space and symbolic power," *Sociological Theory,* 7(1): 14–25.

_____ (1998) *Practical Reason: On the Theory of Action.* Stanford: Stanford University Press.

Caglar, Ayse & Levent Soysal (2003) "Introduction: Turkish Migration to Germany-Forty Years Afer," *New Perspectives on Turkey* 29: 1–18.

Castelli, Francesco (2018). "Drivers of migration: Why do people move?," *Journal of Travel Medicine,* 25(1), 1–7.

Clegg, Stewart (1997) *Frameworks of Power.* London: Sage.

Cohen, Joshua (2005). "Deliberation and Democratic Legitimacy" in Derek Matravers and Jonathan Pike (eds.) *Debates in Contemporary Political Philosophy: An Anthology,* pp. 342–60. London: Routledge

Dahl, Robert (1957) The Concept of Power. *Behavioural Science,* 2: 201–15.

Dépelteau, François (2008) "Relational Thinking: A Critique of Co-Deterministic Theories of Structure and Agency," *Sociological theory,* 26(1): 51–73.

Dépelteau, François (ed.) (2018) *The Palgrave Handbook of Relational Sociology.* London: Palgrave Macmillan.

Elias, Norbert (1978) *What is sociology?* Columbia University Press.

Ellul, Jacques (1973) *Propaganda: The Formation of Men's Attitudes.* New York: Vintage Books.

Emirbayer, Mustafa (1997) "Manifesto for a Relational Sociology," *American Journal of Sociology,* 103(2): 281–317.

European Commission (2017) European Agenda on Migration: Commission Calls on All Parties to Sustain Progress and Make Further Efforts. Press Release, Strasbourg, 13 June, retrieved from: http://europa.eu/rapid/press-release_IP-17-1587_en.htm. (accessed 6 July 2020)

Fawcett, Paul, Matthew Flinders, Colin Hay, and Matthew Wood (2017) "Anti-politics, Depoliticization, and Governance" in Fawcett, Paul, Matthew Flinders, Colin Hay, and Matthew Wood (eds.) *Anti-politics, Depoliticization, and Governance,* pp. 3–27. Oxford: Oxford University Press.

Foucault, Michel (1977) *Discipline and Punish: The Birth of the Prison*. New York: Vintage.

____ (1978) *The History of Sexuality, Volume I: An Introduction*. New York: Pantheon Books.

____ (1982) "The Subject and Power," *Critical Inquiry*, 8 (4): 777–795.

____ (2002) *The Order of Things: An Archeology of the Human Sciences*. London, New York: Routledge.

Geuijen, Karin, Mark Moore, Andrea Cederquist, Rolf Ronning, and Mark Van Twist (2017) "Creating Public Value in Global Wicked Problems," *Public Management Review*, 19(5): 621–639.

Giddens, Anthony (1984) *The Constitution of Society: Outline of the Theory of Structuration*. Cambridge: Polity Press.

Goldin, Ian, and Mike Mariathasan (2014) *The Butterfly Defect: How Globalization Creates Systemic Risks, and What to Do About It*. Princeton, NJ: Princeton University Press.

Goodman, Nelson (1978) *Ways of Worldmaking*. Indianapolis: Hackett Publishing.

Habermas, Jürgen (1975) *The Legitimation Crisis of Late Capitalism*. Boston: Beacon Press.

____ (1986) "Hannah Arendt's Communication Conception of Power" in Steven Lukes (ed.), *Power*, pp 75–93. Oxford: Blackwell.

____ (1996a) *Between Facts and Norms: Contributions to a Discourse Theory of Law and Democracy*. Cambridge, MA: MIT Press.

____ (1996b) "Three Normative Models of Democracy" in Seyla Benhabib (ed.). *Democracy and Difference: Contesting the Boundaries of the Political* (pp 21–30). Princeton University Press.

Hallin, Daniel, and Stylianos Papathanassopoulos (2002) "Political Clientelism and the Media: Southern Europe and Latin America in Comparative Perspective," *Media, Culture & Society*, 24: 175–195.

Haugaard, Mark (2003) "Reflections on Seven Ways of Creating Power," *European Journal of Social Theory* 6(1): 87–113.

____ (2006) "Power and Hegemony in Social Theory" in Mark Haugaard and Howard Lentner, (eds.), *Hegemony and Power: Consensus and Coercion in Contemporary Politics* (pp. 45–64). London: Lexington Books.

____ 2010 "Power: A 'Family Resemblance' Concept," *European Journal of Cultural Studies* 13: 419–438.

Hay, Colin (2007) *Why We Hate Politics*. Cambridge: Polity.

Head, Brian (2019) "Forty Years of Wicked Problems Literature: Forging Closer Links to Policy Studies," *Policy and Society* 38(2): 180–197.

Holmes, Seth and Heide Castañeda (2016) "Representing the "European Refugee Crisis" in Germany and beyond: Deservingness and Difference, Life and Death," *American Ethnologist* 43(1): 12–24

Jakobson, Roman (1960) "Linguistics and Poetics" in Thomas Sebeok (ed.) *Style in Language*, pp. 350–377. Cambridge, Mass.: MIT Press.

_____ (1971) *Selected Writings* (Vol. 2). Berlin: Walter de Gruyter.

_____ (1998) *On Language*. Linda R. Waugh and Monique Monville-Burstone (eds). Cambridge, Mass.: Harvard

Jessop. Bob (2011) "Metagovernance" in Mark Bevir (ed.). *The Sage Handbook of Governance* (pp. 106–123). London: Sage.

_____ (2016) *The State: Past, Present, Future*. Cambridge: Polity.

Kaundert, Miriam, and Anthony Masys (2018) "Mass Migration, Humanitarian Assistance and Crisis Management: Embracing Social Innovation and Organizational Learning" in Anthony Masys (Ed.) *Security by Design. Innovative Perspectives on Complex Problems*, pp. 73–91. Switzerland: Springer.

Klasche, Benjamin, and Peeter Selg (2020) "A Pragmatist Defence of Rationalism: Towards a Cognitive Frames-Based Methodology in International Relations," *International Relations*. [https://journals.sagepub.com/doi/abs/10.1177/0047117820912519]

Kooiman, Jan (2003) *Governing as Governance*. London: Sage.

Kooiman, Jan and Sven Jentoft (2009) "Meta-governance: Values, Norms and Principles, and the Making of Hard Choices," *Public Administration*, 87(4): 818–836.

Laclau, Ernesto (1990) "Totalitarianism and Moral Indignation," *Diacritics*, 20(3): 88–95.

_____ (1996) *Emancipation(s)*. London: Verso.

_____ (2001a) "Democracy and the Question of Power," *Constellations* 8: 3–14.

_____ (2005) *On Populist Reason*. London: Verso.

Laclau, Ernesto and Chantal Mouffe (1985) *Hegemony and Socialist Strategy: Towards a Radical Democratic Politics*. London: Verso.

Laclau, Ernesto, and Chantal Mouffe (1987) "Post-Marxism Without Apologies," *New Left Review* 1/166, 79–106.

Langenbacher, Eric (2003) "Changing Memory Regimes in Contemporary Germany," *German Politics & Society* 21(2), 46–7.

Lanoszka, Alexander (2016) "Russian Hybrid Warfare and Extended Deterrence in Eastern Europe," *International Affairs* 92(1): 175–195.

Lefort, Claude (1988) *Democracy and Political Theory*. Cambridge: Polity Press.

Lichtenstein, Dennis, Jenny Ritter, and Birte Fahnrich (2017) "The Migrant Crisis in German Public Discourse," in Melani Barlai, Birte Fähnrich, Christina Griessler, and Markus Rhomberg (eds.) *The Migrant Crisis: European Perspectives and National Discourses* Vienna, pp. 107–126. Wien: LIT Verlag

Lifton, Robert (1989) *Thought Reform and the Psychology of Totalism: A Study of Brainwashing in China*. University of N. Carolina Press

Lotman, Yuri M. (2001) *Universe of the Mind: A Semiotic Theory of Culture*. Bloomington and Indianapolis: Indiana University Press.

_____ (2004). |The phenomenon of culture" in *The semiosphere*. Saint Petersburg: Iskusstvo-SPB, 568–580.

Luhmann, Niklas (1979) *Trust and Power*. Chichester: Wiley.

Lukacs, György (1971) *History and Class Consciousness: Studies in Marxist Dialectics*. Cambridge, Mass.: The MIT Press.

Lukes, Steven (2005) *Power: A Radical View*. London: Macmillan.

Marchart, Oliver (2007) *Post-Foundational Political Thought: Political Difference in Nancy, Lefort, Badiou and Laclau*. Edinburgh: Edinburgh University Press.

Marx, Karl (1982) *Capital: A Critique of Political Economy*. Volume One. Penguin Books in association with New Left Review.

Mills, C. Wright (1956) *The Power Elite*. Oxford: Oxford University Press.

Murray, Philomena, and Michael Longo (2018) "Europe's Wicked Legitimacy Crisis: The Case of Refugees," *Journal of European Integration* 40(4), 411–425

Paris, Roland (2001) Human Security: Paradigm Shift or Hot Air? *International Security*, 26(2), 87–102.

Peters, Guy (2017) "What is so Wicked about Wicked Problems? A Conceptual Analysis and a Research Program," *Policy and Society* 36(3), 385–396

Rittel, Horst, and Melvin Webber (1973) "Dilemmas in a General Theory of Planning," *Policy Sciences*, 4(2), 155–169.

Roberts, Nancy (2000) "Wicked Problems and Network Approaches to Resolution," *International Public Management Review*, 1(1): 1–19.

Sartori, Giovanni (1987) *The Theory of Democracy Revisited*. Chatham, New Jersey: Chatham House Publishing.

Selg, Peeter (2011) *An Outline for a Theory of Political Semiotics*. Tallinn: Tallinn University Press.

_____ (2012) "Justice and liberal strategy: Towards a radical democratic reading of Rawls." *Social Theory and Practice*, 38(1): 83–114.

_____ (2013) "A Political-Semiotic Introduction to the Estonian "Bronze-Night" Discourse," *Journal of Language and Politics*, 12(1), 80–100.

_____ (2016a) "Two Faces of the "Relational Turn," *PS: Political Science & Politics* 49 (1): 27–31.

_____ (2016b) "The Fable of the Bs": Between Substantialism and Deep Relational Thinking about Power," *Journal of Political Power*, 9(2), 183–205.

_____ (2018) "Power and Relational Sociology," in Francois Dépelteau (ed.), *The Palgrave Handbook of Relational Sociology*, pp. 539–557. New York: Palgrave Macmillan.

_____ (2019) "Causation Is Not Everything: On Constitution and Trans-Actional View of Social Science Methodology. In Christian Morgner (ed). *John Dewey and the Notion of Trans-Action. A Sociological Reply on Rethinking Relations and Social Processes*, pp. 31–53. London: Palgrave Macmillan.

Selg, Peeter and Piret Peiker (2019) "There Is More to Groups of People Than Just Groups and People: On Trans-Actional Analysis and Nationalism Studies" In Christian Morgner (ed.) *John Dewey and the Notion of Trans-action* (pp. 55–81). London: Palgrave Macmillan.

Selg, Peeter and Rein Ruutsoo (2014) "Teleological historical narrative as a strategy for constructing political antagonism: The example of the narrative of Estonia's regaining of independence," *Semiotica*, 202: 365–393.

Selg, Peeter and Andreas Ventsel (2008) "Towards a Semiotic Theory of Hegemony: Naming as Hegemonic Operation in Lotman and Laclau," *Sign Systems Studies*, 36.1: 167–183.

Selg, Peeter and Andreas Ventsel (2010) "An Outline for a Semiotic Theory of Hegemony," *Semiotica* 182: 443–474.

Selg, Peeter and Andreas Ventsel (2012) "On Semiotic Theory of Hegemony: Conceptual Foundation and a Brief Sketch for Future Research," in Susi Frank, Cornelia Ruhe, and Alexander Schmitz (eds.), *Explosion und Peripherie. Jurij Lotmans Semiotik der Kulturellen Dynamik Revisited*, pp. 41–56. Bielefeld: Transcript Verlag.

Selg, Peeter and Andreas Ventsel (2019) "What is Political Semiotics and Why does it Matter? A Reply to Janar Mihkelsaar," *Semiotica*, 231: 27–37.

Selg, Peeter, and Andreas Ventsel (2020) *Introducing Relational Political Analysis: Political Semiotics as a Theory and Method*. London and New York: Palgrave Macmillan.

Shurke, Astri (1998) "Burden-sharing during Refugee Emergencies: The Logic of Collective versus National Action," *Journal of Refugee Studies* 11 (4): 396–415.

Taggart, Paul (2017) "Populism in Western Europe." In Cristóbal Rovira Kaltwasser, Paul Taggart, Paulina Ochoa Espejo, and Pierre Ostiguy (eds.) *The Oxford Handbook of Populism*, pp. 248–263. Oxford: Oxford University Press.

Trauner, Florian, and Jocelyn Turton (2017) ' "Welcome Culture:" The Emergence and Transformation of a Public Debate on Migration.' *Austrian Journal of Political Science* 46(1): 33–42.

Turnbull, Nick, and Robert Hoppe (2018) "Problematizing "wickedness": A Critique of the Wicked Problems Concept, from Philosophy to Practice," *Policy and Society*, 38.2: 1–23.

Van Bueren Ellen, Erik-Hans Klijn and Joop Koppenjan (2003) "Dealing with Wicked Problems in Networks: Analyzing an Environmental Debate from a Network Perspective," *Journal of Public Administration Research and Theory* 13(2): 193–212.

Weber, Max (1978) *Economy and Society: An Outline of Interpretive Sociology*. Vol. 1. Berkeley: University of California Press.

Wivel, Anders, and Ole Wæver (2018) "The Power of Peaceful Change: The Crisis of the European Union and the Rebalancing of Europe's Regional Order." *International Studies Review*, 20(2): 317–325.

Youngs, Richard (2017) *Europe's Eastern Crisis: The Geopolitics of Asymmetry*. Cambridge: Cambridge University Press.

Paul Blokker

The Constitution as a Symbol

Abstract: Constitutions are a necessary dimension of any modern state. They are frequently approached instrumentally, as providing the "rules of the game," but constitutions ought to be understood as equally comprising a significant symbolic dimension. In fact, the constitution operates as a symbol, a meta-symbol, or a symbolic-integrative framework for society. As such, constitutions carry different symbolic meanings, and are contestable. The Polish case provides a significant example of enduring contestation of constitutional symbolics. The chapter starts with a discussion of the different meta-dimensions – instrumental and symbolic – of constitutions, to subsequently discuss a more fine-grained range of constitutional functions. Subsequently, the Polish case will involve a discussion of the 1997 Constitution, the intense political conflicts around its adoption, to end with a brief discussion of the on-going role of meta-politics since 2015.

Keywords: constitutionalism, conservatism, liberalism, Poland, symbolic dimensions

Introduction

Poland is characterized by intense political, juridical, and cultural conflict since the coming to power of the Law and Justice party (*"Prawo i Sprawiedliwość"*; PiS) at the end of 2015. Many observers understand the political and legal developments since 2015 as "backsliding" and appear to regard the changes since 2015 as having "fallen from the sky" (Wigura 2020: 13). In reality, however, it can be argued, as will be done in this chapter, that the radical changes and the attempts at institutionalizing the conservative political project of PiS have a much longer pedigree, which is closely related to the political and economic transformation of the early 1990s.

In political and legal terms, a crucial dimension is that of the 1997 Constitution and of the constitutional politics around it. In this regard, the on-going conflict over Poland's constitution is of great relevance for socio-legal and socio-cultural studies, in that the Constitution can be understood as a core symbol in ongoing political conflict over the transformation process since 1989. Analyzing the Polish case may hence teach us on the role of constitutions in transformation and democratization processes more generally, and in particular shed light on how constitutions are not merely defining the "rules of the game" and limiting power, but themselves form the core symbolical framework within which, and about which, conflict and political struggle occurs.

The chapter will start with a discussion of the different meta-dimensions – instrumental and symbolic – of constitutions, to subsequently discuss a more fine-grained range of constitutional functions. In the second half of the chapter, the Polish Constitution of 1997 will be discussed in symbolical terms, to be followed by a discussion of the intense political conflicts around the Constitution's adoption in the mid-1990s, the role of the alternative Citizens' Constitution, to end with a brief discussion of the on-going role of meta-politics (cf. Stanley and Bill 2020), with the 1997 Constitution at its heart, since 2015.

The meta-dimensions of constitutions

On one hand, constitutions reflect, in Weberian terms, an instrumental rationality. Constitutions consist in purpose-oriented constructs that bind or limit political power, and that regulate state action as well as interaction with citizens. On the other hand, however, constitutions reflect the Weberian dimension of substantive or value-based rationality: that is, constitutions act as symbolic constructs that perform moral, cultural, integrative and emancipatory roles (cf. Přibáň 2007: x-xi, 91–2; Vorländer 2002: 9–42).

Constitutions express an instrumental language or rationality to the extent that they formulate the functional differentiation of society (for instance, between political and civil society) and the limitation of political power, and it defines the relations between the state and the citizens, as well as between state institutions, and the government and opposition (Přibáň 2007: 20; Scholl 2006: 36). This instrumental rationality can be understood in Weberian terms as rationalizing politics in terms of its purposive rationalization as well as of the political community (Přibáň 2007: 3). Constitutions can however equally be seen as articulating a symbolic language that invokes the substantive, value-based groundings of the political community — that is, the normative principles on which it is based, its collective identity and traditions, and the aspirational and participatory ideals pertaining to that community. In distinctive ways, societies understand themselves through their constitutions (this is, however, true to different extents (cf. Brodocz 2003), that is, some societies – e.g. Germany, the United States – have a more explicit constitutional self understanding than others – e.g. the Netherlands).

From this perspective, the symbolic rationality of constitutions can be observed as reflecting non-legal or "extra-juridical elements" and as accommodating "moral, economic or traditional and religious criteria in the domain of positive law" (Přibáň 2007: 20). Such symbolic rationality invokes ultimate values, extra-societal markers such as natural rights, religious values and ideas, societal traditions and identities which need to be protected and promoted by the constitution. The symbolic dimension of constitutionalism regards the symbolic features of the constitution itself, which ipso facto means it is concerned with the embeddedness of universal values in a local, historical and cultural context (in a similar sense as in Hegel's "absolute spirit," or Montesquieu's "spirit of the laws," cf. Přibáň 2009). In other words, the symbolic dimension creates, or ought to create, explicit lines of interaction between society and the structure of higher legal norms. Martin Krygier aptly speaks of the "spirit of constitutionalism" (Krygier 1996: 22).

On this perspective, constitutions express a "fundamental ethos" of a distinct society. Constitutions express and codify a "characteristic way of life, the national character of a people, their ethos or fundamental nature as a people, a product of their particular history and social conditions" (Pitkin 1987: 167). The symbolic language of a constitution clearly has a collective dimension, which also means that constitutional symbolism "expresses the moral authority of a political collectivity over individuals" (Přibáň 2007: 21). The constitution articulates through its symbolic dimension a (constructed) collective unity, a form of collective self-understanding, and makes the political community visible to itself.

In constitutional practice, the what-might-be-called particularist/ identitarian dimension to constitutions is sometimes portrayed in an extratemporal or essentialist way. This portrayal may take the form of idolatry or veneration (Levinson 1988: 11), in which the constitution becomes an "object of unjustified adoration, as the finest product of human civilization" (Balkin 2011: 11). A particularistic view tends to exalt the role of the constitution as a symbol of unity (Scholl 2006: 38). In this, the symbolic dimension to constitutionalism can be understood as a form of closure or as a means of imposing form onto society. It regards the formation or construction of political meaning-giving and the embedding of an abstract legal language in a sociocultural language. Through the particularist language of a given society and its traditions and history, the constitution gives meaning to legality, the political form, and specific views of justice. The imposed constitutional form includes the expression of normative principles and in particular aspirational values or an "idée directrice" of a (constructed) political community. In this respect, the symbolic dimension is to a large extent concerned with an attempt to integrate modern pluralistic societies (Vorländer 2002: 18 ff).

At the same time, however, the closure or "stabilization" of meaning through constitutionalization can never be complete, as it is in tension with universalistic dimensions of the constitution, for instance in the form of rights, and different interpretations of the constitution's key tenets can be offered. In reality, then, a constitution is always open to contestation and change, as new interpretations of collective identities emerge, or older ones are rearticulated (cf. Balkin 2011: 11). Indeed, constitutions frequently form the object of mobilization and resistance (as is the case in contemporary Poland, cf. Blokker 2020).

Modern constitutions may be understood, to different degrees, as displaying both – instrumental and symbolic – dimensions, and they cannot be reduced to a one-dimensional view. That is to say, instrumental rationality is in need of being paralleled by some kind of socio-cultural embedding and registering of ultimate values, in that individual and collective actors need to be able to relate to constitutional norms and engage in forms of meaning-making on their basis. A purely symbolic constitution, in contrast, would lack a regulatory, ordering language that functionally integrates a political community and creates patterns of foreseeable behavior.

Beyond the two meta-dimensions of instrumental and value-based rationality, the functional dimensions of constitutions can be understood in a more fine-grained manner. Constitutions have a number of dimensions or political meanings that should be taken together if their full significance for democratic regimes is to be understood. First of all, in their political dimension, or what Castiglione refers to as the "functional meaning" (Castiglione 1996), constitutions outline the institutional order, or, in other words, the sphere of politics on which democracy is to be based, as "framing the regular powers of a society and of its political system" (Castiglione 1996: 420). This political dimension or idea of a constitution reflecting the structure of society can be related to the "pragmatic" or "constitutional" imaginary of democracy, that is, the constitution as a regulative principle and as a pacifying and stabilizing force. This regulative idea is often related – although this is not a necessary relationship – with the function of the constitution as a limiting, negative one. Regulation is then perceived predominantly in a negative way in that it sets out – by means of a "set of principles, manners, and institutional arrangements" – to limit government or majority rule in order to prevent the state from subjecting individuals (Sajó 1999: xiv). In this perspective, both the stipulation of the inviolability of a set of rights enjoyed by individuals in the constitution and the idea of separation of powers form the fundamental constitutional principles that prevent political power from being abused or being turned against society in general or against minorities in particular.

The idea of the constitution as a foundational document that "fixes" the institutional "map of political power" for a substantial period of time is strongly related to the liberal-legal vision of democracy, even if its emphasis on negative protection through subjective rights and the limitation of state power, and notions of the rule of law and constitutionalism that are not necessarily compatible with the democratic idea. The political dimensions of constitutions cannot, however, be reduced to the liberal-legal and constitutional visions of a democracy grounded in the *Rechtsstaat*-idea, in that most alternative visions of democracy would accept (a minimal level of) its important regulatory functions, but would endorse more "thick," substantive understandings of democracy and popular sovereignty. One should hence beware of reducing the regulative function to the limitation of state power and citizens' liberty.

Second, constitutions are not only defined by their functional, limitative, and structuring dimension, but, if they are to institute a democratic regime based on the people's sovereignty, also need to meaningfully enable participation or, in other words, to provide for significant forms of political participation and political will formation by the citizens (cf. Gonenc 2002: 12). This participatory dimension or "enabling" dimension of constitutions invokes an "emancipatory" imaginary of democracy, in that it relates to democracy as a project of societal improvement as well as to the idea of self-government. This enabling dimension follows a procedural vision of democracy and the idea of rights and the rule of law when it, for instance, stresses distinctive rights (in terms of civil and political rights, but also comprising social and cultural rights). More substantive or value-based understandings of effective participation tend to stress not merely individual, rights-based opportunities for emancipation, but equally point to collective ones (related to minority groups), including forms of recognition, as well as the creation of spaces or moments of equal participation.

Both the political and rights-based, participatory dimensions can be understood as internal to the formal legal nature or "instrumental rationality" of the constitution. As discussed above, this understanding of the constitution of a legal system based on an instrumental or functional rationality of legality does not exhaust the constitution's nature, as next to its instrumental legal nature constitutions also invoke a substantive or symbolic rationality that is less concerned with the formal institutional order and a set of fundamental rights, and more with the constitution of a political community by means of the founding of a collective identity, the moral values that define such a community, and forms of collective self-understanding (Přibáň 2007: ix, x). The symbolic dimension is, in contrast to the political and participatory dimensions, not concerned with the universal values of constitutionalism and their interpretation within a closed system of law, but rather with the embedment of such universal values in a local, historical, societal, and cultural context.

The symbolic dimension of constitutions cannot, in this, be reduced to a communitarian or even nationalist reading of constitutionalism as the expression of a particular political community. It is equally relevant for any kind of constitutional order in that it entails of a way of giving fundamental meaning to the legal system within a specific historical-cultural context. As argued by Joseph Weiler, the constitution's symbolic function can be implicit, i.e. a constitution's ethos might result indirectly from the political dimension and the stipulation of rights, or this dimension can be explicit, as is often the case when the distinct values and traditions of a specific political community is included in the constitution's preamble (Weiler 2003: 55–6). The symbolic dimension shows that the legal system can be understood as never fully closed off or independent from societal and cultural spheres, and as always permeated by the latter, if not in its norms, then at least in terms of spirit.

The dimensions discussed so far are largely understood in synchronic terms, that is, the way the constitution provides an institutional framework for the present of the democratic regime. However, the constitution clearly also contains important diachronic dimensions, that is, dimensions that explicitly deal with the temporal nature of democratic society. First of all, in some cases, constitutions tend to provide specific interpretations of the past that are meant to create social cohesion and consensus in the present, or, alternatively, to strongly denounce the past. In the case of the former communist states, the illegitimate nature and distortive historical role of the communist regime were an explicit part of the urgency of creating constitutions which could ground the new democracies legally, condemn the recent past, and prevent it from returning. At the same time, the constitutions (in particular but not only through the preambles) invoked the pre-communist past as a historical-cultural basis for the present. A further diachronic dimension to constitutions, also particularly important in the case of the new democracies in East- Central Europe, is the future-oriented invocation of an ideal future society.

Thus, in the case of societies in political transformation, the constitution can provide an aspirational dimension informing a process of societal becoming in that the constitutions drafted in the early 1990s invoked images of democratic rule that were still to be fully institutionalized. Constitutional moments see the outburst of the "politics of enchantment" or the invocation of what may be called the "emancipatory" imaginary of democracy, which is absorbed in the actual creation of a constitution as a legal act. But rather than assuming that such politics of enchantment will necessary end with the formal declaration of a constitution, it needs to be recognized that the emancipatory dimension will always remain latent in the constitution as a text, in that its reinterpretation, or its confrontation with an abstract, radical ideal, can always re-enchant politics again. Constitutional politics hence matters a great deal in understanding the instrumental and symbolic dimensions of constitutions.

Constitutions and symbols

As elaborately discussed above, constitutions have both instrumental and symbolic dimensions. It can, however, equally be argued that the constitution *in toto* operates as a symbol, a meta-symbol, or a symbolic-integrative framework (cf. Brodocz 2003), not least in the sense that constitutions have become a necessary dimension of any modern state. Constitutions have gained a crucial role in modern societies since the late 1700s, but particularly so since 1945 (Thornhill 2011). As argued by Chris Thornhill, the standard account is that

> European societies have inherited a common propensity for constitutional organization and rights-based citizenship that can be traced back to the revolutionary ideals of the Enlightenment. . . These conceptions have been repeatedly invigorated through processes of constitution making in late 20th-century Europe, in which, notably, in the years after 1945, the mid-1970s, and the years after 1989, constitution making has been associated with the overcoming of authoritarianism, and the conscious limiting of state authority (Thornhill 2019: 427).

Indeed, "constitutionalism has become a part of the shared political imagination of European societies" (Thornhill 2019: 427) and provides a common symbolic framework for modern societies. As Thornhill convincingly argues, constitutions have been deeply entwined with the building of the modern state as well as with the emergence of democracy (even if the latter emerged, when understood in an effective manner, only very recently, since ca. 1945).

Larry Baas, with regard to the US Constitution, argued decades ago that the constitution as a symbol regards the way it "aids in the authoritative allocation of values, but [at the same time] represents a creation of the human mind and "an object of popular worship" to which the individual attributes his *own meaning*" (Baas 1980: 237; emphasis added). He continued, "knowledge of the symbolic meaning of the Constitution is important because of the significant role which key symbols can perform in the life of any political system" (Baas 1980: 237). The constitution as a symbol is hence what makes the constitution possible in the first place, in that it needs to be perceived in a distinctive way by political, legal, and social actors, not least as a necessary, fundamental condition for modern society to exist. In Baas' view:

> Depending on personal meaning and affective attachment, a symbol such as the Constitution can be an important resource or reward in the political process, an important facilitator of social integration and change, as well as an important security-providing agent, and a legitimator and rationalizer of public policy and other activities (Baas 1980: 238).

The constitution is constitutive of reality, in that in many societies it provides a necessary requirement for the individual comprehension of political and societal reality (Brodocz 2003: 24). In this, the constitution, in particular in its liberal-legal understanding, forms – even if not always explicitly conceived as such – an intrinsic part of how society is understood and how it understands itself (Brodocz 2003: 25). But the fundamentally symbolic nature of constitutions also means that intense political and societal conflict over how to understand the constitution and its symbolism is a perennial possibility, and may flare up in moments in which the essential nature of a political community is being questioned. In many contemporary societies, this seems to be exactly the case (one may think of the US, the UK, or, as I will discuss below, the case of Poland).

Case study: The 1997 Constitution of Poland

Despite many acclamations of the "end of transition" and "democratic consolidation," the post-1989 liberal-constitutional projects in East-Central Europe did not necessarily result in constitutional stability, and in increasingly consolidated and pacified societies (De Raadt 2009). A case in point is Poland. The adoption of the 1997 Constitution can hardly be understood as a "constitutional moment" in the sense of the creation of a widely shared and uncontested constitutional framework for Polish democracy. As argued by the American constitutional law scholar Bruce Ackerman, the "1997 constitution was enacted during a moment of popular alienation from politics."[1]

A significant dimension of constitutional politics in post-communist societies consists in a meta-conflict over the nature and substance of constitutions. Indeed, one could depict the democratization trajectories as struggles over interpretations of constitutionalism, as does Emilia Kowalewska in her concept of "competing constitutionalisms" (Kowalewska 2020). The meta-conflict regards distinctive procedural, regulatory, and institutional dimensions (not least with

---

1   According to Ackerman, the original constitutional moment of the early 1990s, in which widespread available support could have been channeled into a legitimate "revolutionary constitution," was wasted (Ackerman 2019: 281).

regard to core institutions of liberal democracy, such as the Constitutional Tribunal and the Supreme Court), but equally regards the symbolic and value-based dimensions of definitions of the political community, commonality, and identity. In this regard, contestation is about the constitution as a symbol (which in itself comprises instrumental and value-based dimensions and their specific relations and interactions).

The duality of symbolism in the text of the Polish constitution

The 1997 Constitution has often been portrayed as a product of political compromise (Wyrzykowski understood the Constitution as a "constitutional compromise" between secularized, civic-liberal forces, such as the Freedom Union, and socialist forces, i.e. the post-communist Alliance of the Democratic Left, Wyrzykowski 1999; cf. Herold 2013). The pragmatic approach towards a constitutional compromise followed the "moderate-liberal" spirit of the dissidents who had engaged in the Roundtable Talks. The Talks had put emphasis on a pragmatic form of negotiations with the Communist Party elite as well as on evolutionary change, rather than a revolutionary attempt at radical change (Herold 2013: 488). In the constitutional discourse from the early 1990s onwards, compromise became represented as a core democratic value, without which democracy could not be built and which could provide a legitimating basis for the new Polish democratic system (Herold 2013: 489). In the parliamentary debates, the notions of "compromise" and "synthesis" were often expressed, also to claim a broad societal basis for the constitutional document (Herold 2013: 490). The governmental forces equally asserted that the "Citizens' Draft" of the extra-parliamentary, center-right opposition was taken into account in the drafting of the official constitution (Herold 2013: 490).

From a symbolic perspective, and notwithstanding the compromise, the contents of the Constitution can however be interpreted as involving strong tensions between significantly variegating visions. In this sense, it could be argued that the 1997 Constitution contains a contrasting symbolism, which is particularly evident in the preamble. The "belated" adoption of the Polish Constitution in 1997, the constitution that replaced the provisional, so-called Little Constitution of 1992, provides an extraordinary example of the codification of (at least) two quite clearly defined political cultures or political grammars in a singular constitutional document. In particular the preamble to the Constitution can be seen as expressing two different interpretations of democracy and nationhood, referring to both an "ethic of rights" and an "ethic of identity,"[2] and has as such been a relatively frequent object of interpretation of the symbolic side of the Polish constitution (see Brier 2006; Hałas 2005; Přibáň 2007; Zubrzycki 2001, 2006).

The Polish Constitution of 1997 reflects two distinct and relative coherent visions of democracy and the constitutional order (Zubrzycki 2001: 636).[3] One perception of democracy that has been clearly codified in the Constitution is based on a civic, secular, and Europeanist vision of the Polish constitutional order, while the contrasting vision is relatively more complex in that it is based on an ethno-cultural and nationalist vision, and includes ideas of a historically rooted and culturally homogeneous Polish nation while simultaneously invoking a strongly Catholic definition of the Polish nation.

In particular, the preamble reveals a struggle or "cultural war" between the two main visions of democracy. This becomes clear in the hybrid or dualistic nature of many of the provisions of the preamble. The first sentence seems to unequivocally refer to an identitarian understanding of a Polish cultural community that is connected by its past and future: "Having regard for the existence and future of our Homeland. . ."

The following words seem to confirm an ethic of identity by means of the formulation "We, the Polish Nation." This confirmation is, however, immediately amended, and actually connected by a hyphen, by the statement "all citizens of the Republic." In this, the second part clearly invokes a political, rights-based, rather than a pre-political, culture-based understanding of the individual members of the Polish democratic polity. This compromise, suggested by Tadeusz Mazowiecki, was the result of the aforementioned fierce debate between supporters of a civic and those of an ethno-cultural definition of the nation (the first suggestion by Mazowiecki was "We, Polish Citizens" but this was unacceptable for the center-right and the Catholic Church, Zubrzycki 2006: 88). Such formulations of compromise often reflected concessions made by the constitution-making majority to the extra-parliamentary forces of the center-right.

---

2   In my book *Multiple Democracies in Europe,* I distinguished between political cultures on the basis of different "democratic ethics." An ethic of rights prioritizes the idea of universalistic, individual human rights, whereas the ethic of identity puts emphasis on shared cultural and historical components of a collective identity, see Blokker 2010.

3   The discussion below is a condensed version of a more comprehensive discussion of the Polish Constitution that appeared in Blokker 2010.

The dialectic nature of the preamble consists therefore in its rights-based and value-based nature, or, in other words, in the attempt to define the political community simultaneously in civic, rights-based and universal terms, and in terms of a particular Polish community with strong roots in the past (including references to the struggle for survival of the nation at the times of absence of the Polish state) as well as in Christianity (cf. Zubrzycki 2001). Whereas the first can be detected in the invocation of civic values and a secular understanding of the Polish polity, the second, value-based "spirit" comes to the fore in the articulation of a cultural, historical, and religious understanding. In some instances, the constitution clearly reflects a compromise between secular and cultural-nationalist ideas, as in the following sentence that was suggested by Tadeusz Mazowiecki: "Both those who believe in God as the source of truth, justice, good and beauty, As well as those not sharing such faith but respecting those universal values as arising from other sources." Similar statements of a dual nature can be found throughout the preamble: "for our culture rooted in the Christian heritage of the Nation and in universal human values. . ... Recognizing our responsibility before God or our own consciences."

A number of statements have a clear invocation of a past-oriented and cross-generational attachment to the Polish nation: "Poland, Beholden to our ancestors for their labours, their struggle for independence achieved at great sacrifice. . ... Recalling the best traditions of the First and the Second Republic. . . Obliged to bequeath to future generations all that is valuable from our over one thousand years' heritage."

Other statements are clearly evoking a singular ethic of civic equality and of universal rights:

> Equal in rights and obligations towards the common good. . ... Aware of the need for cooperation with all countries for the good of the Human Family. . ... Mindful of the bitter experiences of the times when fundamental freedoms and human rights were violated in our Homeland. . ... Desiring to guarantee the rights of the citizens for all time, and to ensure diligence and efficiency in the work of public bodies. . ... Hereby establish this Constitution of the Republic of Poland as the basic law for the State, based on respect for freedom and justice, cooperation between the public powers, social dialogue as well as on the principle of subsidiarity in the strengthening the powers of citizens and their communities. We call upon all those who will apply this Constitution for the good of the Third Republic to do so paying respect to the inherent dignity of the person, his or her right to freedom, the obligation of solidarity with others, and respect for these principles as the unshakeable foundation of the Republic of Poland.

The two democratic discourses that emerge from the preamble are in many instances clearly in tension and invoke different ethics of democracy in their propositions of what the finality of the democratic community should be. While an ethno-cultural definition of the nation does not necessarily need to go against a civic, liberal understanding of democracy (as in a "liberal nationalist" perception, see Auer 2004), i.e. when both religious and universal, civic values are acknowledged, the ethno-cultural definition is sometimes formulated in a mutually exclusive sense, thereby obstructing an inclusive reading of the nation: "Bound in community with our compatriots dispersed throughout the world."

The exclusivist reading of a national identity is further reinforced by the abovementioned references to "ancestors," their "great sacrifice," and "future generations" that invoke a closed community with common ethno-cultural characteristics that are stable over time (cf. Zubrzycki 2001).

The dual democratic visions and dual symbolics of the 1997 Constitution seemed to many observers to indicate a remarkable reconciliation between diverging political forces. The reconciliation, however, never really solidified, as becomes clear from the constitutional politics around the adoption of the 1997 Constitution, but even more from the continuous conflict over the Constitution in the two decades after its adoption.

Constitutional politics

The preamble, and more generally the Polish Constitution as such (cf. Blokker 2010), reflects a polarized society. The 1997 Constitution was the outcome of a constitution-making process that was highly protracted (Wyrzykowski 1999) and contested. In the process, competing understandings of the constitution clashed. The process was supposed to be completed with the 1997 referendum on the new constitution, but, as a matter of fact, the constitutional conflict is continuing until this day, marking the lack of closure of "metapolitical" questions. As George Sanford has remarked, the Polish constitution-making process in the 1990s was "incredibly prolonged and torturous" (Sanford 2002: 79). The difficulties existed in the lack of consensus between significant political groups about the constitution's contents (in relation to such matters as religion and human rights) as well as about the overall role and standing of the Constitution (as constituting a deep rupture with the preceding order or as a negotiated compromise). In Robert Brier's terms, the 1990s saw a "constitutional dispute" which needs to be "understood as a symbolic struggle over the cultural hegemony in the [post-1989] Third Republic" (Brier 2006: 112).

As further discussed below, the contested nature became visible, for instance, in the fact that the formal constitution-making procedure, producing a formal parliamentary draft largely promoting a liberal-democratic position, was paralleled by a grassroots, civil society-created "Citizens' Draft" (*Obywatelski Projekt Konstytucji Solidarności*), produced by the conservative forces, later gathered in the Solidarity Electoral Action party (AWS). The latter united a range of conservative forces coming from the right wing of the 1980s Solidarność movement.

The constitutional counter-project was formulated early in the transition. A societal or civic project was initiated by a group of people gathered in the so-called *Kosarzyski Club*, which in the 1980s predominantly debated social and philosophical matters, but in the 1990s started to address matters of a new constitution for Poland. Its efforts led to the formation of the Social Constitutional Commission (*Społeczna Komisja Konstytucyjna*), which started working on a draft parallel to the official parliamentary one (Kowalewska 2020: 916–17; Hałas 2005). A key figure was conservative politician and chairman of Solidarność, Marian Krzaklewski[4] who coordinated the alternative constitutional initiative as president of the Social Constitutional Commission. The Commission devised a separate draft as early as 1993, which was to reflect the "values and ideas of the 35 per cent of the population, which was excluded from the official "constitutional coalition" (Herold and Wandan 2014: 273). Krzaklewski argued that the constitutional text could not be "accidental, it cannot reflect momentary [*bieżących*] political agreements, it has to be the permanent work of the nation. The constitution has to be based on a moral and ethical foundation, on a clear vision of the human person and of society" (cited in: Brier 2006: 114). The draft followed in a way the traditional logic of the Solidarność movement in the 1980s, pitting "us vs. them," or society against the authorities and questioned the legitimacy of the parliamentary coalition in a political-cultural sense. It questioned whether the official project represented national tradition, religion, culture and identity, and the actual will of the people (Herold and Wandan 2014: 279). As claimed by Krzaklewski in a speech in the National Assembly, "Does the National Assembly of the 1997 parliament really want to go down in Polish history as the National Assembly which after one thousand years of the existence of a Christian Poland threw God out of the constitution?" (qtd after Brier 2006: 126).

---

4   Krzaklewski had been member of Solidarity since 1980 and in 1989 became a member of its National Executive Committee.

Significantly, the alternative, bottom-up constitutional draft reflected ideas of Christianity, patriotic and national values, as well as social values (Kowalewska 2020: 917–18). In other words, its symbolism was deeply grounded in a collectivist understanding of society, emphasizing axiological and identitarian dimensions, in which individuals were to be always already part of a common project with historical, religious, and cultural overtones. In Brier's words, the rightwing conservative forces put forward a nationalist and religious "master narrative," which emphasized "Catholicism as an indispensable part of the identity of Polish society," understood the democratic model created by the constitution as a political community grounded in a distinctive culture and prioritized the idea that the "Constitution needs to express national values" (Brier 2006: 144).

Maik Herold and Solongo Wandan have interpreted the successful mobilization around the Citizens' Draft[5] and its influence on the constitution-making process as revealing the existence of an "alternative constitutional subject" (Herold and Wandan 2014: 273). They indicate, in this, separate, conflicting visions on the symbolic nature of the constitution, as either a unifying and pacifying force between a plurality of societal groups or rather as the confirmation of a distinctive, historical, conservative and homogeneous understanding of Polish society.

As mentioned, to promote the latter understanding, the right-wing coalition Electoral Action Solidarity (AWS) mobilized a range of small right-wing parties against the existing left-liberal constitutional coalition and the "prospect that Poland's new constitution would be adopted by a parliament dominated by the SLD [the post-communists]" (Brier 2006: 9). The historian Brier, who has engaged in a comprehensive historical study of post-1989 constitution-making in Poland, has argued that the "framing process was accompanied by an extraordinarily bitter and aggressive dispute. Especially when this process reached its decisive stage between 1993 and 1997, the constitutional issue polarized Poland's political scene in an ever more ferocious debate" (Brier 2006: 7). As Brier recalls, at the time of the finalization of the draft of the formal constitution, a reporter of one of the country's leading daily newspapers [*Rzeczpospolita*] saw the political scene characterized by "a complete bipolarity" and

> one side [the Social-Democrats, SLD] unanimously convinces the citizens that this constitution is the best that could happen to us because otherwise we would be left

---

5   In May 1994, ca. 900.000 signatures had been gathered for the citizens' draft. See Herold and Wandan 2014: 275.

with the Stalinist constitution from 1952. The other [the AWS], however, calls the constitutional compromise national treason [*targowica*] and perceives the constitution as
a threat to our social life and national identity (Brier 2006: 9).

Major dimensions of the conflict about the constitution regarded not so much
electoral matters or the most adequate way of framing rights, but rather "cultural or symbolic issues," such as the role of religion (in particular with regard
to an *Invocatio Dei*) or the content of national traditions to be reflected in the
preamble (Brier 2006: 10; Hałas 2005). Indeed, in Brier's view, the "debate's
two main participants – the SLD and the AWS – used these symbols to cast
the constitutional dispute as a confrontation between two mutually exclusive
value systems and collective identities" (Brier 2006: 10). The debate concerned
much less constitutional particulars, and rather a form of meta-politics about
the nature of the political community (as a pluralist, liberal democratic community or rather a "Catholic nation").

The constitution-making process hence failed to include all relevant political and social actors, in that the parliamentary constitution-making process (1994–1997) was driven by post-communist and center-right forces, but
excluded the sizeable nationalist, religious right, which claimed to continue
the tradition of Solidarnosc. Indeed, Krzaklewski strongly argued against the
draft constitution as violating the convictions of larger part of society (Brier
2009: 65), while others denounced the particularist, interest-based nature of the
document and its reflection of a singular ideological orientation. Center-right
forces regarded the final as the outcome of a political deal between secularized,
civic-liberal forces and socialist forces, constitutional rather than as reflecting
a society-wide, inclusive compromise. This was somehow corroborated by the
confirmatory referendum held in 1997, as the Constitution was only endorsed
by 53.5 per cent of the voters, while the overall voter turnout was just 42.9 per
cent. This meant de facto that 22.58 per cent of Polish eligible voters voted in
favor (cf. Skąpska 2019).

Post-2015 symbolical meta-politics

The cultural war in Poland has intensified since the coming to power of PiS
and continues to be defined by a clash between liberal, Europeanist forces and
conservative forces. The conservative right – in recent years often defined as
rightwing populists – has radicalized since the early 2000s, and in particular
since PiS' first government in 2005–7, which strengthened resentment against
the left-liberals and against specific institutions, such as the Constitutional
Tribunal (Buzogany and Varga 2018; 2020). The conflict between liberal and

conservative forces remains connected to the struggle over constitutional symbolics and has in important ways deepened. During the 2000s, PiS countered the post-1989, liberal-democratic "Third Republic" by the project of a "Fourth Republic" (Brier 2009), which included at least two draft proposals for a conservative constitution (of 2005 and 2010).

In the period of PiS' second government (from 2015 onwards), its explicit constitutional project has however been substituted for by an approach of "executive decisionism" (Bill and Stanley 2020: 7), which in important ways conflates constitutional and ordinary politics. What is crucial in this approach is that the formalistic, liberal, and pragmatic symbolism of the 1997 Constitution, grounded in the rule of law and in liberal legalism (at least as it is understood by left-liberal forces), is swept away by a moralistic approach that denies the symbolic standing of the Third Republic. The foundations of the democratic Republic, based on liberal understandings of the rule of law, human rights, and political pluralism, are portrayed as a threat to the Polish nation and as a rejection of Polish cultural and political history. The political project of PiS, pursued through executive decisionism based on unlimited majority rule (in strategic terms a necessity because PiS' lack of a constitutional majority), effectively undermines the liberalism, formalism and proceduralism of the Third Republic, by violating constitutional norms, packing the Constitutional Tribunal with loyalists, extensively reducing the separation of powers (in particular, by reducing the independence of the judiciary), reducing media plurality, and limiting the freedom of action of left-liberal civil society organizations (Sadurski 2019).

This politics is not merely destructive of the old order, but pursues an alternative, collectivist, religious and nationalist project, the contours of which were already present in the constitutional vision of the conservative right from the 1990s onwards. The earlier constitutional project has now however become largely a majoritarian, populist attack on the 1997 Constitution as higher law by putting its most significant safeguards and principles on hold. The distinctive populist dimension consists in the disregard for higher constitutional norms and the prioritization of majoritarian politics over law, thereby significantly reducing the possibility for oppositional forces and (liberal) civil society to engage in politics. As Bill and Stanley have argued,

> [i]f PiS saw the political-institutional system of the Third Republic as insufficiently pluralistic, its attempts to address this resulted not in more diversity of thought and action, but in the emergence of an arbitrary and monistic political system: a mono-power of PiS's own. The disappearance of PiS's earlier project for a new constitution was symptomatic of the new mode of governance (Bill and Stanley 2020: 8).

In this regard, PiS' conservative project is not so much defined by "arbitrariness," but by the ongoing pursuit of a distinctive, illiberal constitutional project "by other means." PiS has by now (anno 2020) almost entirely dismantled the liberal-democratic order that had been the core aspiration of the 1997 Constitution and is replacing this order with a majoritarian and religious-nationalist one. Grażyna Skąpska, an astute soiological observer of constitutionalism in post-communist societies, identifies the Polish approach as one of "abused constitutionalism," which consists in the "violation of an existing and binding constitution by its very guardians, especially by the president and constitutional court, in order *to bring about fundamental changes to the political system*" (Skąpska 2019: 427; emphasis added). Skąpska further argues that "it reflects a constitutional nihilism which completely ignores the binding constitution, or, at best, refers to it selectively and expediently" (Skąpska 2019: 427). In Skąpska's view, the nihilistic approach towards the 1997 Constitution of the current PiS government is possible in the first place, because the Constitution never really became part of the "habits of the heart" of (part of) Polish society; in other words, a form of "constitutional patriotism" never emerged in any significant sense. As Skąpska observes, "the principles communicated in the text of a constitution do not frame public discourse or provide arguments for social actors; they fall on deaf ears" (Skąpska 2019: 430). She characterizes the situation of Polish society as one of "negative constitutional consensus," that is, a

> considerable part of society's lack of support for liberal constitutionalism and open disregard for its cornerstones, that is, for such constitutional principles as the rule of law, checks and balances, the accountability of government, the independence of the judiciary – the disregard which in Poland takes the form of an abused constitutionalism (Skąpska 2019: 430).

But besides the societal indifference or "mind-numbness," Skąpska importantly also refers to a second dimension that explains the fact that the PiS political program somehow finds significant societal support, in terms of a widespread adherence to "cultural nationalism:"

> Citizens have a different concept of the nation as a politically organized community from the concepts expressed by liberal democratic constitutionalism. They demand a different political culture – one that appeals to traditional values to counter fears about contemporary challenges such as globalization, migration waves, the cumulative strength of mega-corporations, and the new influence and power divides on a worldwide scale (Skąpska 2019: 431).

Skąpska hence points at the emergence of a "new form of constitutionalism: instead of a liberal democratic one, it is a constitutionalism that expresses and protects the ethnic and religious identity of the nation" (Skąpska 2019: 434).

To sum up, Polish populist conservatives claim that liberalism – in its promotion of modernity, Western civilization (allegedly grounded in moral decline, hyper-individualism, and consumerist thinking), and political pluralism and multiculturalism – is undermining Polish culture, religion, and national identity (Wolff-Powęska 2018: 59). As elaborated upon above, this conservative critique of the liberal-democratic system *in statu nascendi* has been part and parcel of the post-communist transition (Bill and Stanley 2020: 4). The main point of contention was – and in important ways remains – the transformation of 1989 and in particular the Roundtable Talks and its resulting compromise. In many ways, the 1997 Constitution is simply seen, by conservative forces, as an institutional confirmation of the compromise approach. In this, it ought to be replaced by a radically different order. As Bill and Stanley argue, "[n]early three decades on, Polish politics is still dominated by these 'metapolitical' questions" (Bill and Stanley 2020: 2), meaning, whose is to rule Poland and what political shape is Poland to take after communism. The so-called "liberal consensus" that was predominant in the 1990s was hence contested from the outset: "[f]rom the beginning of the transition, conservative groups and social movements had chafed at liberalism's assumption of its natural superiority" (Bill and Stanley 2020: 4). This also means that the legacy of the famous Solidarność trade union, and its key role in the 1989 transformation, remains deeply contested to this day (Kim 2020: 190).

Conclusions

The contemporary conservative, populist critique on liberal democracy in Poland can only be understood if carefully analyzed in the context of the post-1989 transformation, which witnessed an alliance between left-liberal forces and post-communist ones, while conservative, rightwing forces remained relatively marginalized until at least the second decade of transformation. A key focus of the conflict between these two prominent political forces has been the Constitution, its symbolism, its distinctive role in Polish society, and the interpretation of its norms.

The left-liberal view of the Constitution, in particular that of the SLD (but with regard to liberal-legal dimensions equally supported by the Freedom Union (*Unia Wolności*[6]), promoted a social-democratic understanding of the

---

6   The Union included all of the intellectuals, members of Solidarity, who had participated in the Roundtable Talks.

Polish state and emphasized societal diversity and pluralism, that is, the importance of protecting individual groups in a diverse society (Brier 2006: 149–50). The governmental proposal was defended by references to a pragmatic approach (which consisted, for instance, in favoring a compromise with various political forces) and the need for modernization (Brier 2006). The pragmatic approach also meant that a reference to the identitarian and symbolic dimension in the left-liberal draft remained largely absent:

> The overall structure of the SLD draft was ostensibly void of any references to values or to history and there was no reference to an overarching "preconstitutional" system of values or ideas which justified the constitution's articles. A central claim of SLD was, as a consequence, the state's strict neutrality in terms of religion or world view (Brier 2006: 149).

The left-liberal approach to the constitution was one of a "structure of power which had to be restricted for the sake of the citizens' freedom to have their private convictions" (Brier 2006: 150). The emphasis was hence on the instrumental-rational and negative dimensions of constitutions. As argued by Brier,

> The role of the state, as defined by this frame, is to protect the individual citizen's right to these diverse ideas and opinions. The concept of freedom of this frame is, therefore, negative: Freedom is primarily freedom *from* the tutelage of the state or from other institutions like the Catholic Church (Brier 2006: 151–52; emphasis in original).

Core dimensions of the left-liberal constitutional proposal were a democratic state, grounded in human rights and the rule of law.

As discussed in the chapter, from the early 1990s, the conservative political forces increasingly positioned themselves in stark contrast to this "liberal consensus." The conservative understanding of the constitution was in stark contrast to the liberal, negative, Europeanist approach, and posited a constitution that reflected the historical Polish nation, with as key forms of identification Polish traditions and Christianity. As discussed, the increasingly potent conservative counter-voice played an important role in the constitution-making process of the 1990s (Blokker 2020). But the conservative forces became politically significantly stronger from the early 2000s onwards with their embodied in PiS. The latter managed to mobilize various conservative political forces, intellectuals, as well as movements of "conservative civil society."

PiS emerged hence as the main political opponent of liberalism and continued the strong critique on the official 1997 Constitution and its nature of a compromise, originally initiated by AWS. The Third Republic, i.e. the Polish post-1989 project for liberal-democracy, was strongly criticized by PiS, in the name of a Catholic Poland, a united and historical nation, and a promotion of traditional values, such as the family (Folvarčný and Kopeček 2020: 171). The emphasis on the negative, instrumental dimensions of the left-liberals, for a good part realized in the 1997 Constitution, where contrasted with a radically different constitutional understanding, one that reflected an already existing, historical Polsih nation with its traditions and religious outlook. In other words, the conservative project strongly prioritized extra-constitutional identity markers, of which the constitution is to be merely a formal expression. The identitarian and axiological dimensions of the constitution become hence of primary importance, whereas the instrumental, regulatory dimensions are largely approached as subjective to the nation and its collective project.

As examined, PiS started outlining a project for a different Poland in the form of a "Fourth Republic," which was to create a deep rupture with both the preceding communist order, but equally with the ill-founded liberal democratic order (Brier 2009). PiS' project for a Fourth Republic indeed criticizes forms of "imitative modernization," liberal pluralism, and Europeanism. In its stead, PiS endorses Christianity, whiteness, and traditional views of society (Bill and Stanley 2020: 4–5). In its 2005 constitutional project, for instance, PiS claimed: "The need for a new constitution today results from the need to overcome the great crisis of confidence, [a] crisis [that] has different dimensions, but its most visible feature seems to be a great confusion, a total lack of clarity as to what rules determine the functioning of our social and public life" (PiS 2005).

The 1997 Constitution was portrayed by the conservative forces as an exclusionary and unholy compromise between left-liberal and post-communist forces, and its institutions as bastions of continuity with communism. PiS, initially an "anti-establishment party" (Folvarčný and Kopeček 2020: 168) but since 2015 firmly rooted in government, strongly criticizes the post-communist transformation as having led to the betrayal of the Polish nation. The changes of 1989 are criticized as heralding in an era in which the state fails to "defend the interests of the individual, the family, society and the nation" (Folvarčný and Kopeček 2020: 173). PiS, as a "stringent critic of the liberal-democratic system" (Folvarčný and Kopeček 2020: 175), strongly condemns independent judicial institutions,[7] liberal civil society, and media pluralism, and argues in favor of a strong political center that promotes the historical values of the nation.

What is striking in the conservative, populist approach to the constitution is that it almost eradicates the modern-constitutional narrative of liberal-legal

---

7   In its 2014 programme, PiS argues that "the people cannot be denied influence over the functioning of this third power," cited in: Folvarčný and Kopeček 2020: 175.

institutions and replaces it with a historical and "societal" understanding of the constitution;[8] not as grounded in universalistic norms and values, but rather as a collective understanding, always already part of Polish society. Despite its emphasis on the past, the traditionalist-conservative approach at the same time consists in a project for the creation of a new society or "Fourth Republic." As András Sajó argues with regard to the illiberal constitutions in East-Central Europe, they enable the "creation of a new social structure," "new social relations of dominance and stratification," and clear forms of "rent seeking" (Sajó 2019: 405). As Sajó further rightly observes, the conservative project stresses unity and pretends societal integration, but in reality, divides society in friend and enemy (that is, those belonging to the traditional order, and those that contest it).

To conclude, the Polish symbolic struggle over the 1997 Constitution shows how different dimensions of constitutions – instrumental-rational and substantive-rational – may strongly clash in competing projects of constitution-making. In current times, it appears evident that in many societies the dominant, liberal-legal understanding of constitutions, with its symbolism of universalism, human rights, and the rule of law, faces strong counter-projects that tend to stress symbolic, identitarian, and value-based dimensions of constitutions, which are allegedly more deeply grounded in enduring societal structures and forms of interaction. This hyper-symbolic approach to the constitution denies the symbolic value and relevance of liberal legalism as a meaningful language for political communities and societal integration and criticizes its lack of capacity in endorsing commonality. The excessive emphasis on identitarian symbolism is itself, however, equally, or arguably even more, problematic as an integrative force. This is not least due to its pretense of being "societal" and close to the people, while in fact strongly denying society's essential diversity and pluralism, which is more effectively symbolized in the liberal language of human rights and limitations on political power.

References

Ackerman, Bruce (2019) *Revolutionary Constitutions: Charismatic Leadership and the Rule of Law.* Harvard: Harvard University Press.

Auer, Stefan (2004) *Liberal Nationalism in Central Europe.* London/ New York: Routledge Curzon.

---

8 Kowalewska interestingly approaches the Citizens' Draft as a "civic" or "societal " constitution.

Baas, Larry R. (1980) "The Constitution as symbol: Patterns of meaning," *American Politics Quarterly*, 8(2), pp. 237–256.

Balkin, Jack M. (2011) *Constitutional Redemption*. Cambridge, Mass.: Harvard University Press.

Bill, Stanley and Ben Stanley (2020) "Whose Poland is it to be? PiS and the struggle between monism and pluralism," *East European Politics*, pp. 1–17.

Blokker, Paul (2010a), Multiple Democracies in Europe. Political Culture in New Member States. London/New York: Routledge.

_____ (2010b), "Democratic Ethics, Constitutional Dimensions, and Constitutionalisms", in: Alberto Febbrajo and Wojciech Sadurski (eds.), Central and Eastern Europe After Transition: Towards a New Socio-legal Semantics, pp. 73-98. Farnham/Burlington: Ashgate.

_____ (2020) "Constitutional Resistance in Populist Times," *Federal Law Review*, Online First.

Brier, Robert (2006) *A Politics of Meaning. Culture and Constitution-Drafting in Poland's Third Republic*, unpublished PhD-thesis, Frankfurt (Oder): European University Viadrina.

_____ (2009) "The Roots of the "Fourth Republic" Solidarity's Cultural Legacy to Polish Politics," *East European Politics and Societies* 23(1): 63–85.

Brodocz, André (2003) *Die symbolische Dimension der Verfassung: Ein Beitrag zur Institutionentheorie*. Wiesbaden: Westdeutscher Verlag.

Buzogány, Aron and Mihai Varga (2018) "The Ideational Foundations of the Illiberal Backlash in Central and Eastern Europe: The Case of Hungary," *Review of International Political Economy* 26(6): 811–828.

_____ (2020) "The Foreign Policy of Populists in Power: Contesting Liberalism in Poland and Hungary," *Geopolitics*, pp 1–22.

De Raadt, Jasper (2009) "Contested constitutions: legitimacy of constitution-making and constitutional conflict in Central Europe," *East European Politics and Societies*, 23(3): 315–338.

Castiglione, Dario (1996) "The Political Theory of the Constitution," in: *Political Studies*, XLIV: 417–35.

Folvarčný, Adam and Lubomír Kopeček (2020) "Which conservatism? The identity of the Polish Law and Justice party," *Politics in Central Europe*, 16(1): 159–188.

Gonenc, Levent (2002) *Prospects for Constitutionalism in Post-Communist Countries*. The Hague/London/New York: Martinus Nijhoff Publishers.

Hałas, Elżbieta (2005) "Constructing the Identity of a Nation-State. Symbolic Conflict over the Preamble to the Constitution of the Third Republic of Poland," *Polish Sociological Review*, 149(1): 49–67.

Herold, Maik (2013) "Ordnungsbegründung als politisch-kultureller Deutungskampf. Der Verfassungsdiskurs im demokratischen Polen nach 1989", in Hans Vorländer (ed.) *Demokratie und Transzendenz. Die Begründung politischer Ordnungen*, pp. 473–508. Bielefeld: Transcript Verlag.

Herold, Maik and Solongo Wandan (2014), "Verfassungsgebung jenseits der Konstituante: Solidarność und die politische Mobilisierung in Polen 1993–1997", in André Brodocz et al. (eds.) *Die Verfassung des Politischen*, pp. 271–285. Wiesbaden: Springer VS.

Kim, Sengcheol (2020) *Discourse, Hegemony, and Populism in the Visegrád Four: A Post-Foundational Discourse Analysis*, PhD-thesis, Humboldt-Universität, Berlin.

Krygier, Martin (1996), "Is there constitutionalism after communism? Institutional optimism, cultural pessimism, and the rule of law," *International Journal of Sociology*, 26(4): 17–47.

Levinson, Sanford (1988) *Constitutional faith*. Princeton: Princeton University Press.

PiS (Prawo i Sprawiedliwość) (2005) *Konstytucja Rzeczypospolitej Polskiej. Projekt Prawa i Sprawiedliwości*, Warsaw.

Pitkin, Hanna (1987) "The Idea of a Constitution," *Journal of Legal Education*, 37: 167–69.

Přibáň, Jiri (2005) "Constitutional Symbolism and Political (Dis) continuity: Legal Rationality and Its Integrative Function in Postcommunist Transformations," Adam Czarnota, Martin Krygier, and Wojciech Sadurski (eds) *Rethinking the Rule of Law after Communism*, pp. 295–322. Budapest: CEU Press.

_____(2007) *Legal Symbolism. On Law, Time and European Identity*. Aldershot, UK/Burlington, USA: Ashgate.

_____ (2009) "Symbolism of the Spirit of the Laws: A Genealogical Excursus to Legal and Political Semiotics," *International Journal for the Semiotics of Law – Revue Internationale de Sémiotique Juridique* 22(2): 179–195.

Sadurski, Wojciech (2019) *Poland's Constitutional Breakdown*. Oxford: Oxford University Press.

Sajó, András (1999) *Limiting government: an introduction to constitutionalism*, Budapest: Central European University Press.

_____ (2019) "The Constitution of Illiberal Democracy as a Theory about Society," *Polish Sociological Review*, 208(4), pp. 396–412.

Sanford, George (2002) *Democratic Government in Poland: Constitutional Politics since 1989*. Basingstoke, Hampshire: Palgrave.

Scholl, Bruno (2006) *Europas symbolische Verfassung. Nationale Verfassungstraditionen und die Konstitutionalisierung der EU*. Wiesbaden: VS Verlag für Sozialwissenschaften.

Skąpska, Grażyna (2019) "Abuse of the Constitution as a Means of Political Change: Sociological Reflections on the Crisis of Constitutionalism in Poland," *Polish Sociological Review*, 208(4): 421–438.

Śpiewak, Paweł (1997) "The Battle for a Constitution," *East European Constitutional Review*, 6(2/3), available at: http://www1.law.nyu.edu/eecr/vol6num2/feature/battle.html.

Thornhill, Chris (2011) *A Sociology of Constitutions. Constitutions and State Legitimacy in Historical-Sociological Perspective*. Cambridge: Cambridge University Press.

____ (2019) "Constitution making and constitutionalism in Europe," in David Landau & Hanna Lerner (eds.), *Comparative Constitution Making*, pp. 427–446. Cheltenham, UK: Edward Elgar Publishing.

Vorländer, Hans (2002) "Integration durch Verfassung?" in Hans Vorländer (ed.) *Integration durch Verfassung*, pp. 9–40. VS Verlag für Sozialwissenschaften.

Weiler, Joseph H.H. (2003) *Un'Europa cristiana. Un saggio esplorativo*, Milano: BUR Saggi.

Wigura, Karolina (2020) "Introduction: Diagnosing the End of the Liberal Mind," in Karolina Wigura and Jarosław Kuisz (eds.) *The End of the Liberal Mind: Poland's New Politics* pp. 7–17. Warsaw: Kultura Liberalna.

Winczorek, Piotr (1999), "Axiological Foundations of the Polish Constitution," in Mirosław Wyrzykowski *Constitutional Essays*, pp. 59–71. Warsaw: Institute of Public Affairs.

Wolff-Powęska, Anna (2018) "Trommler der Revolution Jungkonservative und Polens Rechte," *Osteuropa* 3–5: 57–76.

Wyrzykowski, Mirosław (1999) "Introductory Note to the 1997 Constitution of the Republic of Poland," in: Mirosław Wyrzykowski (ed.) *Constitutional Essays*, pp. 7–13. Warsaw: Institute of Pulblic Affairs.

Zubrzycki, Geneviève (2006) *The crosses of Auschwitz: nationalism and religion in post-communist Poland*. Chicago: The University of Chicago Press.

____ (2001) "We, the Polish Nation:" Ethnic and civic visions of nationhood in Post-Communist constitutional debates," *Theory and Society*, 30: 629–68.

TIME AND SEMIOSIS OF HISTORY: SYMBOLIC CONFLICTS OVER REMEMBERING AND FORGETTING

Luba Jurgenson

In the Shadow of the Memory Tree:
a Green Remembrance of the Bloody Past

Abstract: This chapter considers, from a critical point of view, the instrumentalization of symbol of the tree by memory politics in Central and Eastern Europe. The aim is to show how the tree becomes a living monument symbolizing the fighter, the victim, the witness or the righteous and how it is used to create a consensual memory. This "vegetal" memory is meant to be universal while serving national discourses or the discourse of European integration. Although based on ancient traditions, this symbolism of the tree deals with new concerns, including ecology.

Keywords: memory, memory politics, symbol, tree, violence

"The impossible is the Real, quite simply the pure Real," Jacques Lacan said in his seminar (Castanet 2006: p. 5). Without wishing in any way to place this reflection under a Lacanian sign, I can only agree with the formula according to which "the definition of the possible [requires] always a first symbolization" (*Ibid*). For Lacan, the "possible" is therefore not anterior to the real but results of a retrospective elaboration of it. Is possible, that is to say, what can be grasped by thought, what can be structured, what has been the object of symbolic mediation.

Extreme violence is one of those realities that are perceived as "impossible" even by those who testify to them: the survivors. This is why it is sometimes perceived as a fantastic or absurd episode (Borowski 1977: 127; Shalamov 2013: 283, 286, 290). In order to become "possible" at the level of the societies, catastrophic episodes must be integrated into the symbolic space. It is this symbolization – with its plural and complex schemes – that makes it possible to memorialize and narrate these events and underpins the notions of collective, communicative, cultural memory, post-memory, etc. In this perspective, metaphors such as "silence" or "unutterable," which have become commonplace in the field of memory, are already cultural items and, in a sense, symbols, bearers of their own universal and vernacular, intellectual and aesthetic history. No work of memory, whether individual or collective, is therefore possible without symbolization. Our object of study lies where these complex fabrics of symbolization are rethought and organized by institutions, in the form of both practices and discourses, according to patterns dictated and sometimes even imposed by memory politics in order to be shared by a large number and to produce common content intended to build, legitimize or perpetuate communities. The policies of memorialization thus involve wide issues like heritage policies, education, toponymy, the distribution of sacred and secular spaces, art, legal sphere, and concern the creation of societal and aesthetic norms as much as the controlling of collective imaginations.

Central and Eastern Europe has the peculiarity of having been, during the twentieth century, the scene of particularly murderous violence perpetrated by actors from all sides, and especially by the two main totalitarian regimes in Europe, Nazism and Communism (Snyder 2010) (and, to a lesser extent, Italian fascism). The two memories are intertwined, inseparable although often separated either because of the specialization of the researchers, or because these memories have been instrumentalized in new homogenizing societal projects. Due to this specificity, until the 2000s, Central and Eastern Europe presented a constellation of memories often carried by local actors, drawing from an arsenal of eclectic symbols, without an official discourse unifying them. This relative freedom of the local was due to the fact that there was no real national consensus on the interpretation of some events to be commemorated or musealized. In the years that followed, marked by the emergence of regressive and closed community memories, some of these symbols were essentialized and 'nationalized,' while others were used for negotiations between local associative memories and national ones.

The focus will be on memorial policies (memorial, place of memory). The aim is to show how certain key symbols, which seem universal, occasionally serve as a source of identities and memories that reinforce a positive and traditional image of the societies to which they are addressed. How shared symbols produce discourses that separate. These symbols are multiple and their uses are various. Among them are the wall of faces and the wall of names, the stele, the wagon, the suitcase, etc. They circulate across countries and even continents and constitute an alphabet of universal memory but, depending on the materials used and the scenography, they compose messages that form strong identities. As we cannot, in the context of this article, analyze all these symbols, we will focus on one: the tree, solicited in various ways in memorial scenographies (Chevalier 2015; Jurgenson 2018; Schama 1996, especially pp. 5–7). In recent years, this figure has gained importance in the sphere of public as well as private memory. Its polysemic radiance is undoubtedly one of the reasons for this. Indeed, it expresses the twofold concern to commemorate the dead and to work for the safeguarding of the planet.

Planting and caring

In European culture, the symbol refers to the Tree of Life of the book of Genesis in the Bible (which has multiple variants in other symbolic systems). Since antiquity, the tree has been seen as a mediator between heaven and earth, symbol of the elevation and regeneration of the living, and participates in the mythologies of all peoples. (Brosse 1999). With the emergence of the question of Anthropocene, we have seen in recent years an increase in publications on trees which include both scholarly and general public issues, such as the essay by the forest engineer Peter Wohlleben (Wohlleben 2015), bestseller translated into several languages. As a metaphor of the soul (heritage of belief in metempsychosis), it invites one to meditation: a secular alternative to prayer in modern places of memory. The tree marks a boundary between the real space (a land, a region, a landscape, with its climatic conditions, its social fabric, its forestry practices) and the symbolic one. It thus delimits heterotopic islands dedicated to memory while at the same time being integrated into everyday life. The tree, finally – and this is probably what explains its success in recent memory policies and initiatives – is an organism that can and must be cared for. In return, it will take care of us, symbolically and truly (it is our 'green lung'). Its presence in places of remembrance means that life goes on despite past disasters, and it is up to us to perpetuate it. But, at the same time, the tree is dependent on man in these places of acculturated nature, it requires human intervention and personalized follow-up: it is an object of exchange (we take care of it, it purifies our air) and concern (we give it symbolic value, it keeps our memory); in other words, it is an object of human responsibility and of an ethics of care. This ethics based on practice consists of a set of gestures and words that aim to preserve not only the health but also the dignity of the person. The tree, which seems to exist outside of discourse and to be a symbol requiring no mediation device, because it is internalized by vernacular cultures, produces the illusion of a natural memory.

The discourse on the recognition of otherness, the principle of assistance (especially to vulnerable people), the concern for the other that the ethics of care has put forward, is implicitly nourishing the pedagogy of memory. The future peace promised by the commemoration of the victims of violence or heroes who died in battle is not simply the absence of war but an art of living together: strengthened by the lessons of the past (the abandonment of victims), each person will look out for others. Not only for his neighbor, but also for the environment. The other, nowadays, is not necessarily human, it can be animal, vegetal or even mineral (the soil). Sustainable peace is no longer conceivable without sustainable development, and the tree is naturally involved into this new memorial and ecological configuration, which is also commercial if we think of the immense and new service sector designated under the name of 'person's care.'

Thus, the archaic symbol meets new concerns. The question of care for others has emerged in connection, among other things, with the ageing of European societies. But it is also linked to the interest that historians and memory specialists have taken in the fate of civilians in wars and the role of women, especially nurses, both in the rear and in the front line (Shukan 2018). This new openness to others was first brought about by feminist thought (Gilligan 1982), within philosophy and psychology in conjunction with the action theory (Frankfurt 2004). Others disciplines are examining the question today: sociology, anthropology, political science. The discourse of care has quickly come under criticism (Tronto 1993). Yet it must be noted that the rhetoric of care is not unrelated to the general trend within European states where the values of freedom are increasingly taking second place to those of security.

The tree thus appears not only as a 'soul' – a form of reincarnation of the deceased – but also as a potentially vulnerable body in need of services such as fertilization, watering, pruning. Planting a tree in memory of a deceased person is both an ecological gesture for the health of the planet and a posthumous "restorative care" for the victims who were once abandoned to their fate.

Of course, urban initiatives that involve planting memory trees do not claim an ethic of care. One must not confuse the memory, ecological and caring discourses, although they are co-present in the public space and sometimes mobilize the same audiences, because they reflect the major concerns of our time. It is the discourse of memory that interests us here first and it is through this discourse that we approach the other two. Historical memory, whether institutionalized or associative, has the property of being protean and nourished by the societal issues that are contemporary to it. Memory is constructed in the present, as shown by certain museums that incorporate events as they are assimilated by societies, such as the Museum of the Great Patriotic War in Kiev, for example, where a room is dedicated to the soldiers who died in Afghanistan.[1] In Western Europe, some museums devoted to the Second World War integrate the more recent issues of human rights, migrants and even the question of discrimination in the broadest sense for educational purposes (the Kazerne Dossin, a memorial, museum and documentation center on the Holocaust and human rights, inaugurated in 2012). Safeguarding memory and the defense of

---

1   Fighters of the Soviet-Afghan war (1979–1989).

human rights also go together for the International Memorial Association, the main actor in the memory of the Gulag in Russia. This openness to the present makes memory porous to contemporary discourse and debate, for better or for worse.

The history of the ancient practice of planting a tree in memory of the deceased is not recounted here. This transhistorical and transnational symbol speaks "directly" to its recipient, regardless of his or her community and religious affiliation, that is, via the symbolic arsenal of one's own culture. It is the bearer of an emotional "pedagogy" accessible to all, irrespective of the visitor's level of education and knowledge of the event which is commemorated. The tree does not need translation, as it is based on tradition. As a living monument in the open air, it creates a commemorative landscape for individuals and groups, an inscription of the past in the very body of nature. The unifying message of hope in a peaceful living-together that the tree transmits is founded on its ability to develop, to grow, and to last: the tree is in the process of becoming. If its roots are stretched towards the past, its branches are stretched towards the future (Chevalier, 2015, 2018). It thus participates in a process of "development."

The tree is therefore part of a common project for humanity. But by this very fact, it lends itself to appropriation by memory policies which, under the cover of its a priori apolitical universality, spread community messages marked by withdrawal into national memories.

The fighter as a tree

On 1 August 2014, a "memory tree" was planted in the Polish capital, in the Saxon Garden, near the Tomb of the Unknown Soldier. This young oak tree commemorated the 70th anniversary of the outbreak of the Warsaw Uprising.[2] The mayor of Warsaw, Hanna Gronkiewicz-Waltz, could be seen in the pictures of the ceremony with a shovel in her hand. Next to her was General Zbigniew Ścibor-Rylski, President of the Warsaw Insurgent Union (died in 2018). As a symbol of strength, endurance and longevity, the oak tree is a vector of transmission, the general emphasized this signification: "Our generation had to be

---

2   The Warsaw Uprising against the German occupiers (1 August – 2 October 1944), organized by the Polish resistance (Armia Krajowa), aimed to liberate the city from German forces but also to preserve Polish sovereignty in the face of the advance of the Red Army and the threat of sovietization. The Red Army, having arrived on the other bank of the Vistula, did not come to the aid of the insurgents, leaving the Germans to complete the destruction of the city. (Davies 2004; Białoszewski 1970).

as strong as an oak tree. . ... Let the younger generations also be strong like this tree, which will still be there in a hundred, two hundred years' time." The tree, as has already been said, is a symbol of peace in memory devices. It is not surprising, then, that we are reminded of this by the veteran's message: "May there never be war, may peace always reign, so that these younger generations will never know what we have known." Another formula, used by the General, may however come as a surprise: "We have won thanks to our perseverance and to our great, great love for our country." In view of the tragic outcome of the uprising, one might think that it was a purely moral victory, but that is not what he seems to be saying. The mayor then goes on in the same vein: "Seventy years ago, the Warsaw Uprising broke out, a heroic explosion, which was the culmination of a five-year underground struggle of the Polish underground state. The final battle for an independent and autonomous Poland." She continued: "We wish to keep the memory of all those who died at that time. We want to save their stories from oblivion, so that future generations will know to whom they owe the opportunity to live in peace in an independent homeland, in a beautiful, free and developing Warsaw."

A startling shortcut – when one considers that the insurrection was crushed in blood, causing 200,000 victims (including 180,000 civilians), and leading to the destruction of the city; that this carnage was made possible by the non-intervention of the Red Army, which was contemplating it from the other bank of the Vistula; which Red Army was thus paving the way of almost fifty years of communist oppression, which the insurgents had just tried to avoid. In short, the commemorative discourse erased those decades, mixing up 1944, when the USSR was, in fact, taking power in Poland, with 1980, the other revolt that formed the basis of Polish identity after 1989. The younger generations, who were supposed to be as strong as the oak tree, were thus given a summary of history in which the misfortunes of the past were absorbed in a uniform rhetoric of success. The strength of the oak tree and the observation of development clearly had the capacity to transform a defeat into a victory. The message inscribed on the act deposited at the root of the tree was more neutral: "in memory of the 63 days that were the culmination of the five-year underground struggle of the Polish underground state for freedom and independence of the fatherland" (https://dzieje.pl/aktualnosci/drzewo-pamieci-w-70-rocznice-wybuchu-powstania-warszawskiego).

It seemed to be forgotten that the Polish underground state, represented by the government-in-exile, would be left out of the Allied decisions for the new division of the world at the Yalta conference; that Anders' army, a survivor of

Soviet captivity, then fighting in Italy, would be banned from the victory parade in London and its soldiers scattered around the world.

Victory is more likely to be commemorated than defeat. Similar examples can be found in every country. It is therefore easy to understand why the Warsaw Uprising Museum, which celebrated its tenth anniversary in 2014, wanted to be "a place of homage and not of martyrdom" (Kurz 2016: 272; Kurz 2007). However, the triumphalist speeches delivered on 1 August 2014 are not insignificant and are not content to comfort and heal the wounds of the past. By ignoring the failure to create an independent Poland after the war, the *coup de force* of Soviet diplomacy and the eagerness of the allies to sacrifice Poland to Stalin, the speech also seems to want to make us forget the debate that has been stirring Polish society since 1989 about the meaning to be given to the Uprising (Napiórkowski 2016).

> Freedom of speech meant, for some, that one could finally glorify the uprising and definitively inscribe it as a constituent element of national identity [something which had been impossible under Communism, L.J.] and, for others, that one could henceforth speak, without being accused of collaboration with the authorities, of the crime of outbreaking a desperate struggle in the middle of a city with a population of one million (Kurz 2016: 271).

By presenting the uprising as a victory, this kind of questioning was avoided.

In Russia, where the crimes committed against the Polish citizens following the German-Soviet pact have long been denied and are mostly ignored by institutional memory, the symbolism of the tree also serves "the patriotic education of youth and transmission between generations." This was the stated aim of the national action "Tree – Memory," carried out from 22 April to 15 May 2016 by KEDR (acronym of Konstruktivno-ekologicheskoe dvizhenie Rossii, Constructive Ecological Movement of Russia). The action, which was addressed to all educational institutions, consisted of planting "memorial trees" in the company of veterans of the "Great Patriotic War" (fewer and fewer in number, such as those of the Warsaw Uprising), in order to celebrate the 71st anniversary of the victory. The tree was to be marked with a plaque in the name of the veteran and it was understood that the institution responsible for the tree would promise to take care of it. The action has been expanded across the country in the following years, with the memorial tree being transformed into memorial gardens in many areas, planted in memory of the soldiers who fell in the "Great Patriotic War," in the presence of veterans or, increasingly, on their behalf. Many new associations have joined KEDR, such as the Victory Volunteers, under the patronage of the Moscow Victory Memorial Museum.

The young people who plant the trees become *de facto* heirs to the veterans, the transmission taking the form of legacy within an extended family: the nation. Some initiatives combine national memory (presented as the sum of regional memories) with family memory. For example, the "Garden of Memory" initiative, led by the Victory Volunteers, which plans to plant 27 million trees in memory of the 27 million victims of the "Great Patriotic War," proposes that participants "keep the memory and traditions of [their] family as well as the memory of the entire country." The garden is conceived as a place where "one can transmit the history of one's family to one's children and grandchildren, where one can come to commemorate the members of one's family who fell for the fatherland." Family traditions are thought to be the soil for an emerging national tradition: "It is not simply an action, it is the foundation of a new tradition that will preserve the achievements of the ancestors in the centuries to come" (https://садпамяти2020.рф/.)

In a country marked by strong centrifugal tendencies, the tree hero, the tree fighter, is called upon to federate family and local memories into a national imagination, to homogenize and bring together while allowing for regional variations. In this sense, the 'fighter' celebrated in Russia is very different from the one who took part in the Warsaw Uprising. But, as in Poland, the use of the symbolism of the tree closes the discussion that had emerged at the end of the 1980s, particularly around the German-Soviet pact that the "Great Patriotic War," which began in June 1941 and not in September 1939, purely and simply excluded from its scope. The official commemorations of the "Great Patriotic War" make it increasingly possible to evoke the "positive" role of Stalin or at least to display his effigy. Memory gardens are not necessarily in line with this trend, but they accredit it through the accompanying rhetoric. From red Stalin became green.

Certainly, the heroic deeds commemorated by these trees do not have the same significance in the long history of national memory. If in Poland the memory and myths of the Uprising had waited for the collapse of Communism to become institutionalized, in Russia the founding myth of the Great Patriotic War is part of an official tradition that was already very strong in Soviet times. The dismantling of Red Army monuments in the countries of the former USSR and Central Europe 'liberated' by the Soviets exasperated the need to give new symbolic forms to the figure of the combatant. It is therefore not a matter of comparing events, but of comparing practices. In both cases the tree, once planted, is unifying: under its benevolent gaze, the complexity of problematic memories melts into the landscape.

The victim/martyr tree

These national, commemorative and ecological actions are inspired by associative practices which, upstream, used the symbolism of the tree in order to maintain and make visible memories (the victimized and not heroic ones) that had remained clandestine during the communist period. The tree symbolized all the more "naturally" the violence of the past as the forests were the scene of mass crimes, both communist and Nazi. Thus, the Polish Catholic association PARAFIADA carried out, between 2008 and 2010, the project to have 22,000 trees planted by secondary school students to commemorate the victims of the Katyń crime[3] in their region. In Russia, on the site of Boutovo, near Moscow, no new plantations are planned, but this former polygon, one of the important mass graves of the Great Terror,[4] has been given the status of a "garden of memory." Long before its inauguration in 2017, some actors of memory, including the Memorial association and the Church, worked for the recognition of the site and the families helped to convert the trees into living monuments. In Levachovo near St. Petersburg, in Kommunarka near Moscow, in Sandarmokh in Karelia, in Kouropaty in Belarus, in Bykovnia in Ukraine and in many other places, trees were associated with the commemoration long before these places were officially recognized as heritage sites. Descendants had created the tradition of covering them with "memorial signs:" embroidered napkins, traditional in Ukraine, or, more often, photographs of the deceased protected from the weather by plastic bags, stuck to the trees with strips of tape.

---

3 Massacre by the NKVD (Lavrenti Beria's decree of 5 March 1940) of nearly 22 thousand Poles taken prisoner by the Red Army during the invasion of Poland in September 1939. Detained in the camps of Starobielsk, Ostashkov and Kozielsk, they were murdered in at least five locations, the most famous of which, the forest of Katyń near Smolensk, became emblematic of the martyrdom of Poles in the USSR. The massacre was long denied by the Soviets, who were blaming the Germans for this crime, and was finally acknowledged by the Russian Duma on 26 November 2010. This recognition was preceded by the broadcast of Andrzej Wajda's film *Katyń* on Russian television. In the vast literature devoted to Katyń, we should especially mention *Na nieludzkiej ziemi (Inhuman Land)* by Józef Czapski.

4 Peak of Stalinist terror (1937–1938) which struck all strata of the population and resulted in about two million victims, of whom nearly 700 thousand were shot, the others sent to the Gulag camps and deportation sites. This period is also referred to as *ejovchtchina*, after Ejov, who was then the head of the NKVD (People's Commissariat for Internal Affairs).

Photo 1.

Photo 2.

Many of these pictures come from the prison files that the descendants were able to consult in the archives: faces from the front and in profile fixed on film a few days or even hours before the execution. In these mug shots the deceased appear in their absolute vulnerability. Violence is implicitly displayed through the capture, on the threshold of death, of this ultimate face. The emotional choc caused by these images seems to come precisely from the contrast between the bureaucratic "neutrality" that went with their production and the meaning they take on in retrospect. Sometimes the portrait is only seen from the front, as the family probably could not access the file or preferred to leave a less dramatic archive here. This spontaneous and popular commemorative gesture is destined to continue alongside official devices such as steles and plaques. It expresses how an important segment of the society deals with the past on the fringes of memorial policies, in parallel with the memory that is built by the State and the Church, but in connection with popular beliefs that the latter, indirectly, reactivates, raising the victims to the rank of new martyrs. On some sites, such as Boutovo, families can pray to their own ancestor who has become a saint (Rousselet 2016), or even, in a more archaic register, the tree itself becomes the reincarnated ancestor. These images, which therefore sometimes have the status of icons, also attest to the way in which this "wild" memory manages to resolve one of the thorniest dilemmas confronting any attempt to commemorate the victims of the Great Terror: many of the people buried in Kommounarka or Boutovo were themselves, before their arrest, among the actors of the repression who participated, directly or indirectly, in setting the death machine in motion. Thus, among those shot in Kommunarka are the former owner of the premises, Iagoda, and his family, the "darling of the party" Nikolai Bukharin, the People's Commissioner for Justice Nikolaï Krylenko,[5] etc. The graves contain the bodies of criminals and their victims, criminals who in turn became victims. The condemned, exhibited on the photographs in the immediate proximity of death, stripped of the paraphernalia of power, are now equal: all of them were given the status of enemies of the state by the "gaze" of the camera lens, according to the same rules of serial violence. We simply must recognize that there is a "grey zone" which, according to Primo Levi, "contains within

---

5   Genrikh Iagoda (1891–1938), Ejov's predecessor at the head of the NKVD (1934–1936), was arrested on 3 April 1937 and shot on 15 March 1938. Nikolai Bukharin (1888–1938), the party intellectual, was among those who brought Stalin to power. Victim of the Great Terror, shot on March 15, 1938. Nikolai Krylenko (1885–1938), People's Commissar for Justice and Prosecutor General of the Russian Soviet Federated Socialist Republic. Arrested in October 1937, shot on February 10, 1938.

itself enough to confuse our need to judge" (Levi 1988: 27). If the common commemoration of the executioners and victims is a source of debate, the tree participates in spite of itself in the project of societal reconciliation between the descendants of criminals and the descendants of victims, advocated by the official authorities.

However, these forest memories are vulnerable, as we have recently seen in Russia: they are likely to be dismantled and/or reconverted. This is the case of Sandarmokh. The two main actors of the memory of the place, Yuri Dmitriev and Sergey Koltyrin were arrested respectively in 2016 and 2018 (the latter died in prison on 2 April 2020). Sandarmokh is the subject of a rewriting of history reminiscent of that of Katyń: since 2016, the state has been supporting the hypothesis that the bodies buried at Sandarmokh are those of Soviet prisoners from Finnish concentration camps (Higgins, 2020; Werth, Flige, 2020).

So there is a friendly tree, patriotic and educational, and an enemy tree, which needs to be converted. In addition, there are witness trees, which stand at the scene of massacres and ensure their sanctity. As well as heir trees, such as this mirabelle plum tree that was planted in Tekla Square Bądarzewska-Baranowska in Warsaw, from the seeds of a mirabelle tree that grew in the ghetto and was cut down in 2016.

Polish sculptor Lukasz Surowiec has also turned to trees in a different vein. In 2012, he created a living work of art for the Berlin Biennale: he brought 320 birches from the area around Auschwitz-Birkenau to Berlin, "to work against forgetting." The trees were spread over the whole city. Commemorating Berlin's Jews deported to the death camps consisted, in his approach, in giving back to Berlin a part of its "heritage:" these trees, nourished from the land of the dead, returned to the country that orchestrated the assassination of those whose remains symbolically inhabit them. At the Grunewald memorial in Berlin, some of them, ghosts or living archives, grow on the terrace in the middle of the station square, sheltered behind grey steles.

At the Biennale, young shoots of these *Birken* of Birkenau were distributed to city dwellers who pledged to take care of them.

The stele facing them, at the bottom of the ramp that led the victims to the trains, carries the inscription: "In memory of more than 50,000 Berlin Jews who, between October 1941 and February 1945, were deported by the National Socialist State, mainly from Grunewald station, to extermination camps and murdered. A reminder to all of us: we must oppose without hesitation and with courage any act of contempt for human life." Commemorating the victims of genocide is an opportunity to recall that we must help the vulnerable and the oppressed "with courage," i.e. by risking our lives, but in a world where

Photo 3.

everyone would be willing to do so, such a situation could not happen again. The plaque is clearly not addressed to those who could identify themselves with the victims, but to those who, as impassive bystanders of violence, would have left the victims to their fate. The unifying "we" is called upon to compensate this neglect of the duty to help others. By caring for a tree, the bystander repairs this indifference in retrospect, at the same time perpetuating peace in a reunified Europe: the plaque in front of the bunch of birch trees shows Germany and Poland joined together to form a tree leaf, crossed by lines that suggest a round trip.

The tree of the righteous

But what about those who have actually risked their lives to oppose acts of contempt for the lives of others? The various symbolism of the tree referred to was inspired, among other things, by the initiative of Yad Vachem who, in 1963, planted an "Avenue of the Righteous" to commemorate not the combatants or the

Photo 4.

victims, but the saviors. Several former Soviet countries – Ukraine, Belarus, the Baltic States – have seen such avenues appear since their independence. In some of them, one cannot see the dark wood of the past for the trees of Righteous. The past in question, particularly in Ukraine and the Baltic countries, is that of collaboration with the Nazi occupiers. Celebrating the saviors is only justice, but the promotion of the figure of the righteous is sometimes part of a strategy of making people forget what was not done to save Jewish lives or what was done to lose them. These national memories tend towards simplification. They point to a victimized past, to the very real sufferings under communism (sometimes ignoring collaboration with the Soviet regime, a question which we are unable to deal with in this chapter), leaving the complexity of attitudes during the period of German occupation in the shadows. In Ukraine and the Baltic countries, the double genocide thesis emerged (Bechtel 2019, Katz 2019), which equates the persecutions suffered under communism and the Shoah. The imbalance, in the international public arena, between the centrality of the Shoah on the one hand, and the peripheral place left to Stalinist repression (particularly the Holodomor

Photo 5

and mass deportations[6]) on the other, only exasperates these national and ethnic memories in Eastern and Central Europe.

Let us stop on one of the alleys of the Righteous, that of Baby Yar in Kyiv, a place as symbolic of the genocide in the East as Auschwitz is for the West. It was here that the largest massacre perpetrated by the Einsatzgruppen in the USSR took place on September 29 and 30, 1941 (33,771 Jews were shot in this ravine, according to German sources). It was also the first mass execution organized by the occupying forces of the Wehrmacht: a crucial stage in the realization of the "final solution." Having become a place for Sunday walks for the Kyiv inhabitants, the park that lies on the site of the former ravine has been enriched in recent years with numerous monuments (about thirty), through which different groups commemorate their victims. This multiplication of monuments attests to the plurality and complementarity of the memories but also to the memory wars that are played out there. Indeed, Jews were not the only victims to be murdered in this place. All in all, more than 100,000 people were executed at Babi Yar: Roma, clergymen, prisoners of war and, in a macabre twist of irony, Ukrainian nationalists, also persecuted by the Nazis. In this polyphony, the Alley of the Righteous, created in 2011, enjoys a disproportionate visibility. More than 600 Kyiv inhabitants are commemorated as saviors of Jews, of whom only 150 have been recognized by Yad Vashem. The difference can be explained by the fact that the foundation "Memory of Babi Yar" created its own status of "Babi Yar's Righteous" in 1988, which tends to widen this category, sometimes arbitrarily, to the entourage of people who have really saved Jews.

The proliferation of the Righteous at Babi Yar is intended to mask the presence of local auxiliaries during the massacre and, more generally, the question of Ukrainian collaboration. Here again, the tree serves a consensual and restorative memory on the surface, but it is divided and conflictual in depth. Questions of memory divide Ukraine, especially in a situation of conflict with Russia: the anti-Russian view of the events prevails in the west and the pro-Russian view in the east (Ostriitchouk 2013). Russia tends to minimize the criminal aspects of the Stalinist regime and so does Ukraine towards the

---

6   The Holodomor (from Ukrainian *moryty holodom*, 'to kill by starvation') was a man-made famine in Soviet Ukraine (1932–1933) that killed millions of people (mostly Ukrainian). It was part of the wider Soviet famine which affected the major grain-producing areas of the country. Mass deportations: in this case, the repressions that hit the territories annexed by the USSR following the pact Molotov-Ribbentrop in the years 1939–1941 and from the end of the war.

anti-Jewish dimension of its engagement with the occupier during the Nazi occupation. Babi Yar's memory is caught in this complexity.

The project to create a garden of the Polish Righteous in Muranów, on the site of the former ghetto and close to the Polin Museum, has also been the subject of much controversy. In the rush to celebrate the Poles who helped the Jews, it is forgotten that there was no consent in Polish society for this help, that those who gave it were doing so against the general feeling, that the righteous feared their neighbors, sometimes even their own family members, more than the Germans. The multiplication of monuments, plaques and other celebrations will certainly not encourage a deep reflection on the attitude of Poles during the Occupation. On the other hand, it will relieve thousands of Poles from the duty to ask themselves some fundamental, though disturbing, questions about their past. (Grabowski 2012, Grabowski 2013, Molisak 2020). Too much visibility given to the figure of the righteous, in a place of Jewish suffering, has been perceived by many intellectuals and actors of memory as a marginalization of the disturbing memory, which is replaced by the comforting memory of a common Polish-Jewish suffering and of a Poland in solidarity with its Jews. Since Poland has carried out a great deal of research on Polish-Jewish relations (an inappropriate term, since the Jews in question were Poles) under occupation, the redundant exploitation of the figure of the Just appears to be a regression and a denial. Finally, wherever the Righteous takes on too much importance, tree hides the truth about the abandonment of the Jews during the war or participation in the extermination. On these places of memory dedicated to Righteous one finds, highlighted in the gesture of planting, the concern for the other is proposed as a model of living-together. The figure of the savior is intended to reassure the visitor that this concern has never been lacking in her or his community, even in the most apocalyptic moments.

These few considerations on the symbolism of the tree and its political use in the public space are not a condemnation of planting projects per se. This is not to deny that trees do good to the planet. Moreover, the symbolism of trees, as we have tried to show, is far from being unequivocal. While it serves memories based on national identities, it can also serve multidirectional memories (Rothberg 2009). For example, memory trees planted on the occasion of the centenary of Polish Independence in 2018, in the spirit of "patriotism," have been used in parallel to commemorate Jewish history in several cities.

Nor does this article seek to minimize the importance of the ecological question in its relation to memory. On the contrary, it is a promising field of research that is bound to develop. Remarkable works have been produced in recent years highlighting the ecological dimension of mass violence (Domanska,

Leociak: 2017; Praczyk: 2018). The critical approach adopted here simply aims at tracing out a few avenues for a study of the politics of symbolization in their complexity.

References

Bechtel, Delphine (2019) "Légiférer l'histoire en Ukraine," *Memories at Stake* 9: 94–98.

Białoszewski Miron (1970) *Pamiętnik z powstania warszawskiego*. Warsaw: Państwowy Instytut Wydawniczy.

Borowski, Tadeusz (1977) *Wspomnienia. Wiersze. Opowiadania*. Warszawa: Państwowy Instytut Wydawniczy.

Brosse, Jacques (1999) *Mythologie des arbres*. Paris: Plon.

Castanet, Didier (2006) "L'impossible, c'est le réel, tout simplement:" Jacques Lacan," *L'En-Je lacanien* 7: 5–7.

Chevalier, Dominique (2015) "Retour réflexif sur la construction d'un objet géographique mémoriel," *Géographie et cultures à Cerisy* 93–94: 347–366.

_____ (2018) "Un fossé moral est-il visible dans le paysage?" *Memories at Stake* 7: 48–52.

Czapski, Józef (1949) *Na nieludzkiej ziemi*. Paris: Instytut Literacki.

Davies, Norman (2004) *Rising '44: The Battle for Warsaw*. New York: Viking Books.

Domańska, Ewa, Leociak, Jacek (eds.) (2017) *Środowiskowa historia Zagłady. Teksty Drugie* 2.

Frankfurt, Harry G. (2004) *The Reasons of Love*. Princeton: Princeton University Press.

Gilligan, Carol (1982) *In A Different Voice: Psychological Theory and Women's Development*. Harvard: Harvard University Press.

Higgins, Andrew (2020) "He Found One of Stalin's Mass Graves. Now He's in Jail," *The New York Times*. Available at https://www.nytimes.com/2020/04/27/world/europe/russia-historian-stalin-mass-graves.html?smid=em-share (accessed 17 May 2020)

Grabowski, Jan (2012) "La "chasse aux Juifs" dans la société rurale en Pologne: 1942–1945," *Le Genre humain* 52: 285–301.

_____ (2013) "La dénonciation des Juifs en Pologne pendant la Deuxième Guerre mondiale," *Archives juives* 46: 77–90.

Jurgenson, Luba (ed.) (2018) *Does Memory Blend into the Landscape? Memories at Stake* 7: 41–121.

Katz, Dovid (2019) "On the Abuse on Law (Baltics)," *Memories at Stake* 9: 88–93.

Kurz, Iwona (2007) "Przepisywanie pamięci: przypadek Muzeum Powstania Warszawskiego," *Kultura Współczesna* 53: 150–162.

_____ (2016) "Le musée de l'Insurrection de Varsovie: muséographie, muséophotie, muséosensorium" in Delphine Bechtel, Luba Jurgenson (eds.), *Muséographie des violences en Europe centrale et ex-URSS*, pp. 269–284. Paris: Kimé.

Levi, Primo (1988) *The Drowned and the Saved* (trans. Raymond Rosenthal). London: Michael Joseph.

Molisak, Alina (2020) "Commémorations des Justes en Pologne d'aujourd'hui – mémoire ou oubli?" in Kinga Callebat, Agnieszka Grudzinska (eds.), *Représenter la Shoah après 1989. Entre la France et la Pologne*, Paris: Petra (forthcoming)

Ostriitchouk, Olha (2013) *Les Ukrainiens face à leur passé. Vers une meilleure compréhension du clivage Est-Ouest.* Bruxelles: Peter Lang.

Napiórkowski, Marcin (2016) *Powstanie umarłych: historia pamięci 1944–2014.* Warszawa: Wydawnictwo Krytyki Politycznej.

Praczyk, Małgorzata (2018) *Pamięć środowiskowa we wspomnieniach osadników.* Poznań: Wydawnictwo Instytutu Historii UAM.

Rothberg, Michael (2009) *Multidirectional Memory: Remembering Holocaust in the Age of Decolonization.* Stanford: Stanford University Press.

Rousselet, Kathy (2016) "L'Église orthodoxe russe et les dispositifs mémoriels à Boutovo: de la mort du proche à l'histoire nationale" in Delphine Bechtel, Luba Jurgenson (eds), *Muséographie des violences en Europe centrale et ex-URSS*, pp. 57–73. Paris: Kimé.

Schama, Simon (1996) *Landscape and Memory.* New York: Vintage books.

Shalamov, Varlam T. (2013) *Works in Seven Volumes* (Vol. 2). Moscow: Terra-Terra.

Shukan, Ioulia (2018) "Émotions, liens affectifs et pratiques de soin en contexte de conflit armé. Les ressorts de l'engagement des femmes bénévoles dans l'assistance aux blessés militaires du Donbass," *Revue d'Études comparatives Est-Ouest* 2: 131–170.

Snyder, Timothy (2010) *Bloodlands: Europe Between Hitler and Stalin.* New York: Basic Books.

Tronto, Juan (1993) *Un monde vulnérable. Pour une politique du care.* Paris: La Découverte.

Werth, Nicolas, Flige, Irina (2020) "Sandarmokh, un charnier de la Grande Terreur," *Histoire* 470: 68–75.

Wohlleben, Peter (2015) *Das geheime Leben der Bäume: Was sie fühlen, wie sie kommunizieren – die Entdeckung einer verborgenen Welt.* München: Ludwig Verlag.

Joanna Nowicki

Controversies over Symbolism of Reconciliation and Forgiveness

Abstract: The issue we discuss here is the symbolic policy adopted in Poland after the fall of the Communist regime and the controversies it may have generated. We analyze it on the basis of two concrete examples: the doctrine of reconciliation and forgiveness introduced with success by Tadeusz Mazowiecki, and the result of another vision of so-called *historical politics* which allowed the PIS government to dispute and sanction the narrative of the recently created Museum of the Second World War in Gdansk, dismissing its director.

Keywords: memory, museums, reconciliation, symbolic politics/historical politics

Introduction

Myths and political symbols in Central Europe have been a subject of interest to us for a long time. In the preparation of our collective work on this subject (Delsol, Maslowski, & Nowicki 2002), we have benefited from the particularly interesting expertise of Jean Jacques Wunenburger (2002). In his written introduction, he asked, "whether political life, both national and international, can – and must – be entirely determined by political and legal rationality alone, as it has imposed itself since the Age of Enlightenment, and postulated that "the imaginary appears . . . to obey a diversity of rhetorical, symbolic and hermeneutical functions that participate in the construction of political life," suggesting that "the culture of symbolic representation should not be reduced to mere passions hostile to rationality" (Wunenburger 2002: 1–10).[1]

The issue we wish to discuss here is the symbolic policy adopted in Poland after the fall of the Communist regime and the controversies it may have generated. We will analyze it on the basis of two concrete examples: on the one hand, the doctrine of reconciliation and forgiveness introduced by Tadeusz

---

1   All translations mine unless otherwise noted.

Mazowiecki, who became the first Prime Minister from the opposition in the Eastern bloc, and on the other hand, the narrative of the Museum of the Second World War in Gdansk, which is disputed and sanctioned by the Law and Justice Party (PIS) government, which dismissed the museum's director.

In our view, these two examples illustrate two important aspects of *symbolic politics*: its ability to forge common values and motivate attitudes that transcend collective traumas (*Kochajcie nieprzyjacioly wasze!* [Love your enemies!]) and the temptation on the part of the rulers to use it for partisan ends, transforming it into ideology.

Symbolic politics

Since we are dealing here with *symbolic politics,* it is first of all necessary to define it. Controversies are already beginning at this stage, showing that the concept is polymorphous and far from reaching consensus. For Pascal Ory (2000), symbolic politics is one of the three instruments that a political power has at its disposal, in addition to public power and rhetoric. The researcher reserves for symbolic politics a different place from that occupied by speech and insists on its unifying role, recalling the etymology of the symbol: The symbolon is never defined as well as in the form of a sign of recognition, in which, as we know, it opposes the dia-bolic of division" (Ory 2000: 525–536). J. J. Wunenburger (2002), for his part, includes it in the more general reflection on the role of the imaginary in the construction of the City:

> Isn't the imaginary also a ground, a base, a terrain on which the image of the city is built? Its symbolic forms will contribute to the emergence of models, norms and the value of being together. In other words, a society can only take its destiny into its own hands, with an overall vision of its history, by giving itself an interpretation of what has happened, is happening to it, can happen to it. This construction of itself as a community in progress inevitably calls for founding images, unifying narratives, federating symbols (p. 8).

To this more anthropological conception of symbolic politics (Ory explicitly acknowledges the use of an interpretative grille borrowing its vocabulary from ethnology – the *emblem* is associated with the *amulet*, the *monument* to the *totem*, *rituals* compared to the founding rite or *rite of passage*, etc.). Used by different actors with the aim of consolidating a sense of belonging to a political community, one can contrast a vision that is more focused on the use made of it in political action. The shift can then take place between *symbolic politics*, seen as a means of strengthening the cohesion of a community, and historical politics seen as "a narrative about the past, different from that of historians," a sort of pedagogy of the State that serves to shape attitudes considered desirable (*Historia est magistra vitae*), defended for example by Klub Jagiellonski (Barszcz and Pilawa 2019).

The definition that this milieu tries to promote refers first to the words of Tomasz Merta, Counsellor of the Law and Justice Party (PIS), and later viceminister of culture and national heritage, supervisor for the establishment of historical politics in Poland:

> The choice of a tradition does not mean forgetting, nor the right to arbitrary manipulation, but the possibility of emphasizing certain aspects more in line with the contemporary state of consciousness. Such a historical policy leads to a constant renewal of the narrative about the past, a narrative that we wish to tell ourselves and our children. This does not necessarily contradict the aims and fruits of the work of historians, but it does not always correspond to them (Barszcz and Pilawa 2019).

The authors then propose their own definition: "We define historical politics as a way of imposing a narrative in the international context by proposing an unequivocal representation of the past using concepts involving value judgements, such as guilt, responsibility, sacrifice and pride" (Barszcz and Pilawa 2019).

Historical politics (for external use) are distinguished here from pedagogy (practiced within the State) and their success is measured by the presence or absence of the proposed narrative in international relations. The authors of this theory point to what they call "the paradox of historical politics, which should be conducted in such a way that no one is aware of its presence" (Barszcz and Pilawa 2019).

This rapid confrontation of viewpoints on the different conceptions of the role of the imaginary and the symbolic in political life also shows the complexity of their analysis. Indeed, one can think with Ory and Wunenburger that symbolic politics is not only normal but indispensable for understanding what escapes a purely rational analysis of political phenomena. It is only when it manifests itself in an extreme way that this excess brings it closer to propaganda, and in any case, as Ory (2000) points out: "As a creator of forms, symbolic politics is, by the same token, shaped by conjuncture" (p. 531).

"Kochajcie nieprzyjacioly wasze" – Love your enemies

Our first example shows how symbolic politics based on a Christian-inspired utopia has been able to produce a political doctrine in force and to change the attitudes, convictions and behavior of a large part of the Polish population, which has moved from massive anti-Germanism to a peaceful neighborliness and intense economic cooperation with former German enemies.

Poland's democratic opposition, which was composed of lay people and Catholic intellectuals (Michnik, 1979), seized upon symbolic politics as a program of reconciliation and forgiveness. Its doctrine was conceptualized long before the fall of communism and was taken up by the social movement Solidarność, whose moral foundations were described by the Catholic priest and professor of philosophy, Józef Tischner (1983). When the situation allowed it, i.e. after the election of the first non-communist Prime Minister in the former Eastern bloc, Tadeusz Mazowiecki, his government set it up by drawing on all available sources both inside the country and in political exile.

A volume published in 1983 in Paris in the Polish language and titled, "Love your enemies" (Salij), traces the history of this realistic utopia, which became a political ideal throughout the centuries in the history of this country, where the matrix of the Catholic religion influences political discourse and nourishes national sentiment.[2] In the introduction to this important work, Father Jacek Salij, who made the choice of the texts that constitute it, shows indeed the existence of a long tradition of respect for the enemy in Polish religious, political and national thought, which in his opinion remains insufficiently recalled. What are the reasons for recalling this tradition? First of all, for Salij, a society that obtains the source of esteem for others, from elsewhere than positivist sources alone, will not shed blood lightly. A society which is convinced of the greatness of the human being considers that even the enemy should not be the object of hatred, and will value civic courage and martyrdom more than a revolt undertaken in a movement of despair.

It was in this spirit that the Polish bishops, aware of the gulf that separated the Poles after the atrocities of the Second World War, decided to address an appeal to the German bishops, titled: "Appeal of the Polish bishops to the German bishops" (1965):

> Dear German Brothers, do not hold it against us for listing all the evil that happened here in the last millennium. It should not be so much a warning, but rather a justification ... In spite of all this, in spite of this hopelessly charged situation in the past, in this situation, Dear Brothers, we implore you, let us try to forget. No polemics, no Cold War, but the beginning of a dialogue, initiated today by the Council and Pope Paul VI.... In this Christian, but also very human spirit, we extend our hands to you,

---

2   My presentation at the 35th Congress of International Society for the Sociology of Religion, June 2019, Barcelona was an analysis of this realistic utopia (*Analyse de cette utopie réaliste dans le cas polonais*).

you who are sitting in the Council that is ending, and we give you our forgiveness and ask for forgiveness (p. 146).

This letter was met with violent attacks by the press of the regime of the People's Poland, which cultivated anti-Germanism and did not spare its attacks against religion and the Catholic Church. The response of the bishops came a few months later:

> We understand the emotion that this formulation could provoke, when we said, 'we forgive.' The most difficult element in Christian love, the principle that does not exist in any other religion, the principle that seems from the human point of view very difficult to respect, the principle of love of one's enemies, 'love your enemies, do good to those who hate you' (Mt 5:44). For many, this seems contrary to the human order.... But this principle is the condition of hope, is the upsurge of all efforts towards social progress to resolve apparently inextricable contradictions (Polish Bishops 1975: 436).

These words, which may seem far from the political reality of the time, resonated with the philosophers who became dissidents and helped the democratic opposition conceptualize its action. Among these philosophers was Leszek Kolakowski. In his speech in Frankfurt on the Meine on 16 October 1977, which he titled, "Education for Hate, Education for Dignity," he asked why all totalitarian systems need hate and incite hate. Kolakowski's hypotheses were that hatred internally destroys those who hate and renders them helpless in relation to the State, which means spiritual suicide, self-mutilation, and the breaking up of solidarity among even those who hate. The philosopher then shows the asymmetry between love and hate: to live in hate is to live in death. Yet totalitarian systems need hatred even against their own societies. Education in hatred is education in self-satisfaction, which makes those who receive it morally and intellectually helpless, making them feel that they possess absolute values and truths. When we truly hate, we lose the sense of criticism of ourselves and of what we hate. In totalitarian systems, it is important to poison the spiritual fabric of man with hatred, thus depriving him of dignity. Education for democracy, on the contrary, is education for dignity: it means instilling the ability to fight while remaining free from hatred (Kolakowski 1977: 184–188).

This is indeed the choice of Tadeusz Mazowiecki. The foundation of his thought is *Christian personalism* (with the inspirations of Mounier, Maritain, Tischner, Wojtyła). He expresses his convictions in number 1 of the Wiez Review, which can be considered as a manifesto of his generation. Mazowiecki (1958) maintains that one does not have the right to capitulate, that one cannot free oneself from the necessity to make choices, one cannot remain indifferent, "to wash one's hands of it." Christians are condemned to bear witness with their lives, not by participating in movements that call themselves Christian (hence his doubt about neo-Thomism which, in his opinion, did not know how to respond to the challenge of Nazism). Personalism does not consist in searching for a minimum of common values, but in accepting collaboration with people with the most diverse ideas, with different visions of the world. He advocates looking for positive or interesting aspects in opponents and, if these cannot be found, he prefers silence rather than hate. While affirming himself as a Catholic, he stood against the idea of a confessional state, and of denominational exclusiveness at the individual level. Mazowiecki believed in the virtues of dialogue: "Dialogue is a way to discover new aspects of reality, an exchange of values . . . a method of enriching social life, one of the forms of its development" (As quoted in Hall 2017: 125).

While asserting that a particular person is more important than a nation, social class, race or any other category, he respected the history of each nation by speaking out against any standardization, saying that even if it did not touch political sovereignty it touched *spiritual and cultural sovereignty* and provoked reverse reactions by distorting the development of a nation. He discussed the meaning of compromise in the field of values— in politics this did not mean capitulation or submission. A society must be able to show its capacity for self-defense in protest, while retaining the capacity to remain, itself, its own subject. For Mazowiecki, the most evocative example of this utopia of reconciliation that became reality was what he calls, "The Revolution of the Round Table," which took place in January and February 1989 before the fall of the Berlin Wall. His desire: to sew the national community back together, without the spirit of revenge. In a text written later, he defended the idea of a peaceful revolution, looking to the future and not to the past:

> I said that this passage would be difficult, but it does not necessarily have to cause an explosion. On the contrary, it will be a return to normal. **The principle of combat, which leads more or less quickly to the elimination of the enemy, must be replaced by the principle of partnership.** Otherwise, we will not succeed in moving from a totalitarian system to democracy (Mazowiecki 2013, emphasis added).

The strong symbol of this German-Polish reconciliation policy is of course the image of the sign of peace between Mazowiecki and Kohl at a solemn mass held on 12 November 1989 in Krzyzowa (in memory of Baron Helmuth James von Moltke and the Kreisau Circle, a group of anti-Nazi German resistance fighters) — the echo of a similar gesture between Adenauer and de Gaulle in the cathedral of Reims in 1963 which cemented the Franco-German reconciliation.

There then remained the problem of internal enemies: collaborators of the rejected regime, agents, informants. The debates and polemics around what has been called *lustration* reflect this. Mazowiecki's (2013) attitude is again nourished by these personalist convictions:

> I would have been naive and unwise if I thought that by drawing this line, we could separate ourselves from this past and simply cross it out. The mortgage of which we became the inheritors was also the weight of injustice and suffering. Judging them in court could not be the priority. The principle of collective responsibility did not come into play. Playing with the Security files in a political game was a poison in public life until now and a wound to the national community. / Our bloodless victory did not have the verve of military victories to which Poles are accustomed. The transition from submission to independence from a one-party authoritarian system to democracy, from economic decline to development required a look to the future . . . A way to connect people rather than separate them (Mazowiecki 2013).

The culmination of this reconciliation work at that time was the work on the preamble of the 1997 Constitution – between believers and non-believers – which is now considered by the former President of the European Council, Donald Tusk (2019), as "a model of its kind for Europe in crisis," a Europe which is plagued by a "sclerosis of conciliation:"

> we, the Polish nation — all citizens of the Republic,
> as much as those who believe in God,
> source of truth, justice, goodness and beauty,
> as those who do not share this faith
> and who draw these universal values from other sources,
> . . . conscious of the responsibility before God or before our own conscience,
> establish the Constitution of the Republic of Poland
> as a fundamental right of the State (Constitution 1997).

All these examples show that a pacifist, humanist, spiritual utopia has been able to nourish political action among a people subjected to a totalitarian regime. The symbolic force of texts about the painful past, of images that modify this past without forgetting it, and of declarations for the future (as the Constitution), is undeniable.

Museum of the Second World War in Gdansk

Our second example, that of the controversies provoked by the removal from office of the director of the Museum of the Second World War in Gdansk, shows how a meticulously elaborated narrative by a collective of specialists from several countries, and an impressive number of representatives of civil society, could have been blocked by this alternative vision of symbolic politics, which has become *an institutionalized historical policy*.

Once in power, the PIS decided to adopt its own vision, effectively abandoning, without admitting it, the moral injunction of forgiveness that had animated Tadeusz Mazowiecki and the following governments, while choosing what has been formalized under the name of *historical politics*, based, officially, on the emphasis on four guiding concepts: guilt, responsibility, sacrifice and pride (Barszcz and Pilawa 2019), but many believe that the Law and Justice government has established revenge and vengeance as the rule of political combat and has gone so far as to promise the *stigmatization* of elites who do not think like the government (the word "stigmatization," used by the leader of the PIS, Jarosław Kaczyński, in the 2019 election campaign, has caused controversy).

Pascal Ory (2000), in his analysis of symbolic politics, underlines the importance of *the monumental*: "In more than one respect, the monumental appears as the keystone of the emblematic system. It is, in a way, an emblem hypertrophied in space and time, endowed with a quality of stability and durability, which has added the demonstration of erecting power to the exhibition of values" (4).

Let us give voice to the dismissed director, Pawel Machcewicz (2017), who commented on the museum project, a project which had been debated at length, including in the press, but above all, which had been the subject of numerous consultations with a large number of historians, both Polish and foreign, specialists in the Second World War:

> We wanted to show that the end of the Second World War had a completely different meaning for Western Europeans, to whom it brought freedom, while it brought the Poles — certainly liberation from Nazism — but it was also the beginning of a new occupation: it opened the period of Moscow's dependence and very quickly meant the establishment of the communist dictatorship (see Milosz's *The Seizure of Power* or Sandor Marai's *Remembrance of Hungary*). This period ended only in 1989, which meant the effective end of the war for the nations that found themselves in the Soviet bloc (24).

Prof. Tomasz Szarota, consulted on the Museum project, adds:[3]

> We wanted to show the world the fate of Poles in World War II, but also to show Poles the suffering and martyrdom of other nations, the existence of an international resistance movement. In this sense, the Museum could be an antidote to our national

---

3   These opinions from Szarota, Semka, Gmyz, Gawin and Żaryn can all be found in Paweł Machcewicz's, 2017 book, *Muzeum*.

weaknesses, which are the simultaneous existence of a certain megalomania with an inferiority complex.

The project was available on the Museum's website and rather quickly sparked protests. For example, Semka and Gmyz protested against the "universalization" and "Europeanization" of the exhibition. Dariusz Gawin, who has become the designer of so-called "historical politics," compared the museum project with The Museum of Europe in Brussels, which he considers to be the "result of European political correctness that has nothing to do with national memories." He also criticized what he felt was "crypto-pacifism," which resists the glorification of wars and military virtues.

Another historian, Jan Żaryn, director of the Institute of National Remembrance's Public Education Office, saw in the museum project the desire to create "European consciousness at the detriment of national memory," which for him was a matter of social engineering, by also being "a reflection of Brussels' imperialism with regard to the members of the Union."

Apart from this controversy between a national or European or even international vision of the world conflict, what is interesting for our purposes are the arguments of the head of the PIS, Jarosław Kaczyński, who criticized in the project the attitude towards Germany, which he described as a posture of "an ugly girl" (in French, one would say of a poor cousin), who symbolized Poland's submission to its powerful western neighbor. This is best understood after learning about the basis of the historical policy defended by PIS: pride regained.

Donald Tusk responded publicly to these criticisms by referring to the action of Wladyslaw Bartoszewski and his efforts to normalize relations with the Germans. The title of the historian's book "Warto być przyzwoitym" [It's Worth Being an Honest Man] entered the Polish language as a fixed expression of a certain moral attitude that he defended. It was mentioned on the day of his funeral with gratitude.

Another dimension of these discussions concerned the way in which history was interpreted, but also the attitude to be taken toward neighbors, Poland's place in Europe, and international relations. The debate allowed the Euroskeptics to respond to the pro-European enthusiasm of the Polish people by insisting on the need to defend Poland's specificity. For the pro-Europeans, it was an opportunity to insist on the need for a better understanding of Polish history within European history. The controversy was also about the meaning to be given to sovereignty and the place of national States in today's world.

On a purely museographic level, the designers of the museum wanted to highlight the experiences of ordinary people, their lives. Public opinion surveys showed that it is precisely this aspect that seemed to be the most important in the memory of the Second World War in Poland, much more than geopolitics, battles, or historical facts.

This short summary of the arguments in this debate shows that it was a multi-level issue: it cannot be analyzed from a single intellectual point of view. From a discussion between specialists (historians, political scientists) it quickly became political and then societal, which supports J. J. Wunenburger's thesis on the role of the collective imagination in the constitution of living together in a community. Museums have become one of the important places where this imaginary is expressed, which is why they are the subject of political controversy all over the world. Several international examples are summoned by Paweł Machcewicz (2017) in his book and lead him to say that museums have become a matter for politicians and not a matter reserved for specialists in history or historical mediation.[4]

---

4   The designers of this Museum affirm that they considered other museums that were created in a particular political context or with a political backdrop. They were interested in the Holocaust Memorial Museum in Washington, D.C., the first of its kind initiated by Carter in 1977, which one might think he also did to reinforce ties with Israel (Linenthal 2001). The political backdrop did not prevent it from playing an important role in creating a model of a *narrative history museum* (i.e. telling a story according to a specific scenario). It has been visited by more than 40 million people since its opening in 1993.
This museum inspired the Museum of Terror in Budapest and the Warsaw Uprising Museum in the Polish capital. The political context of the creation of the Berlin History Museum or the House of the History of the Federal Republic of Germany in Bonn (an expression of the historical politics initiated by Kohl and criticized by liberals and the Left. The argument of criticism was to use the museum to create a new national identity removing permanent self-criticism) (Machcewicz 2017: 45). The term *Geschchtspolitic* would be copied in Poland 20 years later.
The House of Terror in Budapest (Terror Haza) was for Machcewicz an example of the instrumentalization of museums for political ends. This Museum, opened in 2002, is located in a building that was formerly the seat of Hungarian fascists, and beginning in 1945 was the seat of the Communist Security Services. The thesis of the museum is to demonstrate the resemblance between the two types of totalitarianism and a certain continuity in the attitudes of their leaders. Twenty percent of the exhibits are dedicated to the war; the rest concerns the post-war period. The real historical record is different: the repression of Hungarian Jews largely went beyond Hungarian Stalinism. A second important point: the fascists and the communists are presented as foreign forces— German or Soviet. They do not show the collaboration of the Hungarians with the Nazis. The Hungarians are shown as victims of

The history of the Museum of the Second World War in Gdansk is reported in detail in the book by its dismissed director (Machcewicz 2017). It all began in 2008 when he was appointed adviser to the Prime Minister to carry out the institution's project. He began by visiting foreign countries, notably France, to examine the Great War Museum in Péronne, where he was struck by the simultaneous presence of three narratives: those of France, Great Britain and Germany. He also visited the Museum of the Great Patriotic War in Kiev, created at the time of the Soviet Union, "Ukrainianized" after 1991, which gave a kind of hybrid. This museum made him understand how the exhibition changes according to the political situation of the country.

Another museum he visited was the one in Moscow, which focused on great victory over Nazism. Russian officials made no secret of their skepticism about his planned design of the Museum of the Second World War in Gdansk, which he had planned. They suggested sending a Russian specialist to help the Polish colleagues, an invitation declined by Machcewicz and his team. Another visit, to The National Word War II Museum in New Orleans, was made solely from the American point of view, a counterexample for the Polish team.

The team surrounded itself with many advisors, the main one being Krzysztof Pomian. The authors of the winning project were the Belgian firm Tempora in Brussels, Christophe Gaeta and Dodier Geinaert, and the French museology specialist Isabelle Benoit. Among the foreign personalities involved were Elie Barnavi, a professor in Tel Aviv and former Israeli ambassador to Poland. Several personalities from the intellectual world were involved in writing the narrative for this exhibition: Wladyslaw Bartszewski, Krzysztof Pomian, Norman Davies, Timothy Snyder, Ulrich Herbert, Henry Rousso, and Pavel Polian.

Very soon, everyone understood that a *European narrative* of the Second World War was not possible. All that could be done was to try to detach oneself

---

two totalitarianisms. Viktor Orbán wanted to show the horrors of the communists and his own contribution to the elimination of the communist system. Today, this museum is an important tool in the hands of Orbán (Machcewicz 2017: 48).

We can show other examples of this type of appropriation, such as Putin in his attitude toward memorials, for which leaders defended the Goulag Perm 36 Museum, transformed and disfigured since its creation. The Warsaw Uprising Museum was seen as a huge success for Lech Kaczyński. He also used it against those who did not make the effort to commemorate this national tragedy. The true debate concerning the uprising that took place in Poland — heroism or suicidal decisions— was not presented there.

from national visions by international comparisons within each theme. This reflection shows the importance of the debate on European heritage, seen as a response to the postmodern visions that announced the end of the great narratives (Kowalski 2013), or even as a moral duty— such as Arjacovsky's (2016) work on European consciousness, influenced by Ricoeur and his reflections on memory and history, forgiveness and the need for translation.

The narration suggested for the exhibition was intended to resemble the writing of a film script or a play with a major role given to the scenography (Machcewicz 2017: 123). The exhibition occupies 6,000 square meters, making it one of the largest museums in its category. The objects themselves have also been given major roles. When Machcewicz left the museum in 2017, the team managed to find 40 thousand objects, which shows a great commitment of the civil society that has appropriated this narrative. When the conflict around the Museum broke out, many people wanted to remove their donations of personal memorabilia from their families, which shows that the controversy was not purely institutional or political but also societal Some objects have a strong symbolic significance, such as the souvenirs of the officers massacred in Katyń, or the objects found during the exhumation of the victims of the pogrom in Jedwabne, or the T-34 tank which symbolized the victory of the Red Army over the Third Reich but also the Sovietization of Central and Eastern Europe.

The designers of the exhibition also insisted on the role of sound (for example, listening to funeral music of the Orthodox church while watching the hecatomb of Soviet prisoners, three million of whom starved to death in German camps.) They report on several debates, for example the linguistic debate on the word *bystander* or *witness* (which does not suggest passivity) or on the term *total war* or *war of annihilation*. The designers' point of view was to focus on historical truth and not on the Polish *raison d'état* or historical politics.

The less visible aspect of this dispute was purely political. PIS made historical politics one of the key elements of its electoral program, wanting to show its difference from the so-called liberal and left-wing circles. The fact that Donald Tusk initiated the Museum project took a major electoral argument away from PIS, hence the desire to block this project, to discredit it in the public eye. At the time of the creation of this comparative narrative, the atmosphere in Poland was optimistic about the country's place in Europe. It changed afterwards (nationalism, xenophobia, fear of the Other, etc.). The international composition of the Scientific Council of the museum raised a first controversy, revealing this atmosphere where the Polish right-wing expressed its fears over the loss of the museum's Polish character.

The opening of the Museum in 2017 took place in a completely different atmosphere. The last room wanted to show the victory of freedom and democracy, Poland's entry into the E.U., but also the war in Donbass and the refugees from Aleppo. This fragment of the exhibition was removed in October 2017 when PIS took back control of the building, which was felt as a censorship by the exhibit designers. A few hundred people were nevertheless able to view this film.

Conclusion

The two examples discussed in this text illustrate, in our view, a mechanism that many scholars of symbolic politics warn against (as does, for example, Grégory Aupiais in his 2005 text "Les politiques symboliques"). This mechanism consists in transforming a symbolic policy into a compulsory doctrine, imposing it using the tools available to the public authority as the only legitimate doctrine, while suppressing any other interpretation. In this concrete case, the case of the Second World War Museum in Gdansk can be analyzed as an illustration of the passage of the doctrine of reconciliation and forgiveness, chosen in Poland during the democratic transition, drawing on the era of dissent, and successfully applied by Tadeusz Mazowiecki, toward *historical politics* which, under the guise of defending the honor of victims and national heroes, leads to divisions within Polish society— the exact opposite of the aims of a good symbolic policy. In order to achieve this, it does not hesitate to control public discourse through laws, including the amendment of the law on the Institute of National Memory (IPN) of February 2018, which has aroused very strong reactions in Poland and abroad, particularly in Israel, the U.S.A., Ukraine and Germany. It is another related problem widely discussed in France, for example, in connection with memory laws.

This statement from the Polish Pen Club (2018), which followed this case, expresses it very well:

> The so-called 'politics of shame' gives way to a 'shameless' policy that looks like a provocation. . . . The choice of the date of the International Day of Remembrance of the Victims of the Holocaust for the adoption by Parliament of the decree on the Institute of National Remembrance and the anti-Semitic atmosphere that it provoked. . . . The aim is to introduce thematic censorship. . . . This 'narrative security machine' creates a mythologized image of war, showing in particular its aspect related to the battles and martyrology of this nation. Anti-Germanism, anti-Ukrainian sentiment and anti-Semitism serve anti-European sentiment. . . . All this causes conflicts within the country which may be irreversible.[5]

---

5   In. Gazeta Wyborcza, 8/02/2018 – https://wyborcza.pl/7,95891,22998454,oby-niepodlegla-polska-przetrwala-ten-samobojczy-paroksyzm.html

Let us hope that the serious tone of this declaration will not prejudge the future and that our collective reflection on symbolic politics in Central Europe will make it possible to propose some intellectual tools to be better armed against such excesses. Controversies surround *historical politics* which has poured into nationalism, when it was initially cosmopolitan, open and forward-looking instead of being primarily conservative. People with strong European convictions deplore this turning point, which can be seen as a step backwards, in reaction to changes that were too rapid for some, and desired for others.

References

Arjacovsky, Antoine (2016) *Histoire de la conscience européenne*. Paris: Salvator.

Aupiais, Grégory (2005) 'Les politiques symboliques,'' *Hypothèses* 8 (1): 17–22, available at https://www.cairn.info/revue-hypotheses-2005-1-page-17.htm (accessed May 25, 2020).

Barszcz, Agnieszka & Pilawa, Konstanty (2019) "Polityka historyczna, Próba programu pozytywnego," *Klub Jagielloński*. Available at https://klubjagiellonski.pl/2019/01/28/polityka-historyczna-proba-programu-pozytywnego/# (accessed May 25, 2020).

Constitution of the Republic of Poland (1997) available at: https://www.refworld.org/cgi-bin/texis/vtx/rwmain/opendocpdf.pdf?reldoc=y&docid=5d4943894 (accessed May 26, 2020).

Hall, Aleksander (2017) (ed.) *Architekt wolnej Polski*. Kraków: Znak.

Kolakowski, Leszek (1983), Speech in Frankfurt on the Meine on 16 October 1977, which he titled, "Wychowanie do nienawiści – wychowanie do godności" [Education for Hate, Education for Dignity], in Salij, Jacek (1983) *Miłujcie nieprzyjacioły Wasze, miłość nieprzyjaciół w Polsce. [Love your enemies, the love of enemies in Poland]*, pp. 184–188. Paris: Éditions du Dialogue.

Kowalski, Krzysztof (2013) "Debate about European Heritage," *O istocie dziedzictwa europejskiego – rozważania [Reflections on the essence of European heritage]*. Kraków: Międzynarodowe Centrum Kultury.

Linenthal, Edward T. (2001) *Preserving Memory. The struggle to create American's Holocaust Museum*. New York: Columbia University Press.

Machcewicz, Paweł (2017) *Muzeum*. Kraków: Znak.

Mazowiecki, Tadeusz (1958) *Rozdroża i wartości* [Intersections and values], Warszawa: Biblioteka "Więzi."

_____ (2013) "Dlaczego nie skreśliłem zdania o "grubej linii?" [Why did I not remove the phrase 'thick line?'], *Gazeta Wyborcza*. October 28, 2013 ed.

https://wyborcza.pl/1,75398,14854434,Dlaczego_nie_skreslilem_zdania_o_
_grubej_linii____TEKST.html (accessed May 30, 2020).

Michnik, Adam (1975) *L'Église, la gauche-le dialogue polonais*, Paris: Du Seuil.

Ory, Pascal (2000) "L'histoire des politiques symboliques modernes: un questionnement," *Revue d'Histoire Moderne & Contemporaine* 47-3: 525-536.

Polish Bishops (1965) "La lettre des évêques polonais aux évêques allemands," *Miłujcie nieprzyjacioły wasze*. November 18, 1965 ed. p. 146.

_____ (1975) "Parole des évêques polonais sur la lettre aux évêques allemands," *Listy pasterskie Episkopatu Polski, 1945-1974*, p. 436, Paris: Éditions du Dialogue.

Salij, Jacek (1983) *Miłujcie nieprzyjacioły Wasze, miłość nieprzyjaciół w Polsce. [Love your enemies, the love of enemies in Poland]*. Paris: Éditions du Dialogue.

Tischner, Józef (1983), *Éthique de Solidarité*, Limoges: Librairie Adolphe Ardant et Critérion,

Tusk, Donald (2019) *Speech given May 3, 2019 on the subject of European challenges of the 21st century*. University of Warsaw.

Wunenburger, Jean-Jacques (2000) *Utopie de la raison, essai sur la politique moderne*, Paris: La Table Ronde.

_____ (2002) "Introduction" in Chantal Delsol, Michel Maslowski & Joanna Nowicki (eds.), *Mythes et symboles politiques en Europe centrale*, pp. 1-10. Paris: Presses Universitaires de France.

Elżbieta Hałas

Polymorphous Time of Transformation in Poland and Semiosis of History

Abstract: After three decades, "systemic transformation" is visibly a conflictful place of memory. The passage of time facilitates such symbolic struggles, since to the divisions between memories of participants and witnesses presenting their different claims to "living history" (narratives of the first order embedded in life-worlds) it adds the breaches between narratives of the second order, which constitute the objectified texts of culture, including historical narratives providing distanced forms of explanation.

All this proves the importance of continuing research on the process of systemic transformation in Poland. The politics of symbolization was a constitutive dimension of this transformation. It comprised various strategies of making and managing the meanings of ongoing changes. In particular, the historical discontinuities and continuities were to be represented. In the semiosis of history, orientation towards the past was as important as the emergence of significant events, punctuating the time of transformation.

Assuming that time conceived qualitatively (i.e. meaningful in social and cultural terms) is a correlate of human actions, systemic transformation will be analyzed from the angle of producing a multitude of times, depending on several fields of action. Together they form a polymorphous time of transformation. The differentiated rhythm and pace of these times will be analyzed, with a particular focus on symbolic practices related to the past.

Keywords: post-communism, semiosis of history, systemic transformation, time

The time of transformation and the transformations of time

The time of systemic transformation is an emergent time. It is the combined effect of all changes that manifest themselves in the historical process viewed from the angle of agency. It involves disrupting the expected continuity of this process and identifying new significant markers in the semiosis of history. In this sense, time encompasses the events that mark its significance, as in the case of war time, postwar time, the time of revolution or the time of transformation. Importantly, in all of these examples time flows forward, towards the future where new events await along the vector of time. In effect, this spatializes time: those new events are akin to a series of points in space. Within this time, where something is "taking place," we are positioned somewhere "in time;" in the analyzed case, in the time of transformation.

Time can also manifest itself in a different sense as "someone's" time or a time "of something," e.g. "the time of Solidarity:" as the time of acting subjects, either individual or collective. This is "some" time: time that is experienced or lived through. When we refer to time in this second sense, we are in fact dealing with a multitude of times, and when we place this multitude of times "in time" in the first sense, we can consider the multitude of times an attribute of being in time. This polymorphous nature of the time of transformation deserves analysis and reflection. Thus, we will discuss several varieties of time. Namely, the time of post-communist transformation in Poland, even when analyzed in historians' narratives, will be a reconstructed present time: the time of the ongoing transformation. Depending on the field of action (Fligstein, McAdam 2012: 9) where new significant events appear, the following varieties of time can be distinguished: time of institutions, time of practices relating to the past, time of symbolic politics of dead bodies, political time, civil society time, economic time and time of international relations.

Time embedded in institutions and its irregularities

Let us begin our analysis with a look at the time of institutions as a variety of "someone's" time, in the sense of time of persons or individual subjects and time of a collective subject. Every acting subject simultaneously constitutes its own time. In particular, time is a constitutive element of institutions. George H. Mead drew attention to this phenomenon (Maines 2001: 43–47; Mead 1964), as did Fernand Braudel (1971) from the perspective of their long duration. Here, when referring to the time of institutions, I mean the time of functioning that is constitutive for them and subject to conventionalized rules.

When dealing with the time of transformation, it is particularly important to characterize the time of political institutions, taking into account both their constitutive time and their irregularity. This irregularity manifests itself in departures from the normativity of institutional time, such as shorter terms of office.

The analysis performed here, rooted in the structure of meanings carried by political history, deals with semiosis of history and politics of symbolization in Poland between 1989 and 1999. This period spans the first decade of trans-formational changes and the beginning of the second decade. A decade is an external reference system for analyzing phenomena, a measure of time used by historians (Braudel 1971: 46 f). Political institutions (the Parliament, where the length of terms of office established by law may differ from their actual duration; the government, an institution where the expected and actual duration of a cabinet's functioning may also differ; and the presidency) all provide their own significations regarding time. They shape the temporal perception of ongoing processes of collective life. Namely, we say "it happened during the rule of Prime Minister X," "during the presidency of Y," "during the Sejm's term of office." Political institutions with an inherent duration of functioning, i.e. with their inherent institutional time, manifest their symbolic power in social space in a principled manner, by imposing temporal categorizations in advance. Through their existence and action, political institutions structuralize the meaning of history by performing their unique function of sociosemiosis. Unless a social historian or anthropologist decides to approach time from a different angle, showing other dimensions of cultural time (Hałas 2010), political history focused on political institutions will dominate both in popular temporal perception and in professional, historical analysis of collective time.

I deal here with socio-political processes only on the plane of meanings and semiosis, i.e. with so-called collective performances, as opposed to the psychologically oriented concept of collective mentality. My starting point for the analysis of the polymorphous time of transformation is the time of political institutions. These are the dominant, symbolic representations of political history, and here we will begin our analysis of the time of transformation in the symbolic dimension.

In the period that interests us, the time of political institutions (viewed as a variety of the time of transformation) was structuralized in a way that gave it a unique rhythm and pace. The Parliament, i.e. the Sejm and Senate, functioned over four terms of office (Table 1)[1]

The prime ministers' cabinets changed nine times over this period. The subsequent prime ministers and their terms of office are shown in Table 2.

The analyzed time of institutions spans three presidential terms of office (the first, brief one ended with Jaruzelski's resignation and an early election). The presidential terms are presented in Table 3.

---

1   *Analiza aktów prawnych. Opracowania tematyczne OT-608*, Kancelaria Senatu. Biuro Analiz i Dokumentacji [*Beginning and end dates of Sejm and Senate terms of office since 1989. Analysis of legal acts. Thematic studies OT-608*, Chancellery of the Senate. Analysis and Documentation Office] 2012: 3.

Tab. 1. Beginning and end dates for Sejm and Senate terms of office (1989–2001)

Sejm term	Senate term	Duration	Regular / Irregular
10th	1st	from June 18, 1989 until November 24, 1991	Irregular by contract
1st	2nd	from November 25, 1991 until May 31, 1993	Irregular (dissolved before the end of term)
2nd	3rd	from September 19, 1993 until October 19, 1997	Regular
3rd	4th	from October 20, 1997 until October 18, 2001	Regular

Tab. 2. The prime ministers' cabinets from August 24, 1989 until October 19, 2001

Prime minister	Term of office	No. of full months
Tadeusz Mazowiecki	August 24, 1989 – January 4, 1991	16
Jan Krzysztof Bielecki	January 4, 1991 – December 6, 1991	10
Jan Olszewski	December 6, 1991 – June 5, 1992	5
Waldemar Pawlak	June 5, 1992 – July 10, 1992	(1)
Hanna Suchocka	July 10, 1992 – October 26, 1993	15
Waldemar Pawlak	October 26, 1993 – March 7, 1995	4
Józef Oleksy	March 7, 1995 – February 7, 1996	11
Włodzimierz Cimoszewicz	February 7, 1996 – October 31, 1997	22
Jerzy Buzek	October 31 1997 – October 19, 2001	47

Tab. 3. Presidential terms of office from August 24, 1989 to October 19, 2001

President	Term of office	No. of full months
Wojciech Jaruzelski	December 31, 1989 – December 22, 1990	12
Lech Wałęsa	December 22, 1990 – December 22, 1995	60
Aleksander Kwaśniewski	December 23, 1995 – December 23, 2000	60

Aleksander Kwaśniewski was subsequently elected for another term (December 23, 2000 – December 23, 2005), opening the first decade of the 21st century. Importantly, the first and third presidents during the initial decade of transformation came from communist party structures. The first president, General Wojciech Jaruzelski, had introduced martial law in Poland on December 13, 1981, attempting to suppress the Solidarity movement. Thus, Jaruzelski's and Kwaśniewski's presidential terms of office mean that the first decade of transformation can be termed "post-communist," but as shown above, five out of eight successive prime ministers in this period came from post-Solidarity formations, despite the persuasive rhetoric of an emerging post-communist enigma (Staniszkis 1999).

The time of political institutions, both as the time normatively embedded in them and as the time produced by their functioning, provides a temporal framework of meaning for other processes of social life, forming an interpretative and discursive frame. The irregularity of the time of political institutions results from deviation from the conventions of that time. A normalized rhythm of institutional time in the form of anticipated cycles of change is typical. Remarkably, the first decade of transformation begins with institutional ruptures in the form of deliberately short terms of all political institutions, contractually marking the new beginning. After that, the time of the presidency acquires a regular rhythm. The time of parliamentary institutions exhibited arrythmia only once. The time of governance is fraught with irregularity due to unstable political coalitions, but the pace of this institutional time also calms down in the last years of that crucial decade of transformation.

The time of transformation in historians' narratives

This analysis does not deal directly with the process of moving away from communism or with the democratization process. It focuses on the symbolic dimension of transformation and on politics of symbolization as a tool for controlling this process.

Historians, especially those dealing with political history (the one whose classic model was defined by Leopold von Ranke) focus primarily on event history, elevating some occurrences over others to the status of historical events. Moreover, as the main temporal reference for their narratives they use the semantic frames of time that are constitutive for and produced by political institutions. However, in these narratives they introduce their own categories of periodization, carrying out semantic structuralizing, which, unlike the institutional significations described above, is interpretive. Thus, there are two levels of the symbolic constitution of time. The first level consists of the structure of the meanings of time embedded in the social reality of institutions, while the second one is built on interpretations given to the institutional texture of this reality. Without denying the moderating impact of the scientific historical method aiming at scientific objectivity, historians' narratives undeniably more or less openly co-create the ideological image of historical processes. Historians themselves have often addressed this issue (Topolski 1995). The narrative constructed retrospectively by a historian also carries evaluations in its rhetoric.

The basic construct used by historians to forge a framework of meanings for events in the process of ongoing changes is the "systemic transformation" (Roszkowski 1995; Dudek 1997). This abstract category has become part of common discourse and entered the collective imaginary (Hałas 2000). Historians' narratives dealing with the time of transformation and dating from the first decade of this period frequently use the metaphor of a "fall," referring to the "fall of communism" or the "fall of the communist regime" (Roszkowski 1995; Dudek 1997). This metaphor contrasts with the concept of transformation. It carries an image contrasting with the idea of purposeful change, which implies that certain invariables are retained (Hałas 2000).

During the first decade of systemic transformation, historians reached for imagery that served as rhetorical measures. The aim was to root memory in a special event to further construct the narrative of event history and agency of its protagonists and antagonists. The symbol of the Round Table (negotiations in February 1989 between the communist party and opposition representatives) was introduced in historians' narratives, as expressed in titles such as "The Way to the Round Table," "Around the Round Table". The symbolism of the Round Table and its evoked power are built in these narratives using rhetorical means such as "one of the most amazing and momentous events of this century" or "the Round Table agreement had historic consequences, initiating peaceful transformations towards democracy and free market economy throughout the Soviet Bloc" (Kowalski 1996).

In such narratives of event history, the "June election" (June 1989) gained an elevated symbolic status. Although it was not yet a free election, the turnout on June 4 (voting for non-communist party candidates) was relatively high (62 %). In the second round on June 18, which decided who would fill the seats reserved for candidates put forward by the communist authorities, the turnout was only just over 20 %. The event narrative and its rhetoric build a current symbolic representation of the ongoing historical process. However, explanation of the historical process and interpretation of its meaning are necessary to create an orderly vision of the social world, to control the ongoing process of transformation. Symbolic power over the semiosis of history is at stake in political struggles in which historians inevitably participate as sense producers with their narratives.

The term "Mazowiecki's government" marks a new beginning in historians' narratives about the time of transformation. "Mazowiecki's government" was meant to be "the first non-communist one" after 40 years of communist rule, despite the fact that this government included communists (e.g. General Czesław Kiszczak, minister of the interior). Such narratives formed the political myth necessary in the process of molding a new collective imaginary (White 2000).

Such a symbolic status in historians' narratives in the historiography of the first decade of transformation was also given to the first non-communist president, the most famous Solidarity leader, Lech Wałęsa. Likewise, a slogan from the June 4, 1989 election campaign became established in the rhetoric of historians' narratives: "Wałęsa's team" in regard to non-communist candidates in the contract election. The phrases "acquiring power" to describe the outcome of the contract election or "Solidarity's victory" in this election have a similarly mythologizing function.

The core metaphor signifying the time of transformation, taken from the political discourse and included in historians' narratives, is the "thick stroke" (Polish: *gruba kreska*) metaphor, a paraphrase of the "thick line" (*gruba linia*) metaphor used by Prime Minister Mazowiecki in his exposé:

> "The government I will create is not responsible for the mortgage it inherits. However, that mortgage has an impact on the circumstances in which we have to act. We cross off the past with *a thick stroke*. We will be responsible only for what we have done to bring Poland out of its current state of collapse."[2] The paraphrased expression used in historians' narratives has a connotation close to crossing out.

This "thick line" metaphor signifies the beginning of a new historical time, which required a clear demarcation. In the historical process, however, historical narratives cannot be cut off from the past. In the analysis of symbolic transformation processes, a deeper study of the rhetoric of transformation is still waiting for an analytic scrutiny that will more accurately show the use of language as an instrument of symbolic power to manage and control the ongoing process. The rhetoric of transformation and its metaphors shaped the common understanding of ongoing changes and built the meaning of the time of transformation in the collective imaginary.

Significantly, the language and rhetoric of historical narratives in the first decade of transformation contain contradictory ideas, which is not an uncommon phenomenon in socio-cultural processes (Archer 1996: 143–184).

---

2   Prime Minister Tadeusz Mazowiecki's exposé, August 24, 1989.

Having announced the fall of communism, historians must then declare its viability when talking about the victory of post-communists (Dudek 1997).

After the rise to power of the coalition of the post-communist party and its satellites, the Democratic Left Alliance (*Sojusz Lewicy Demokratycznej*, SLD) and the Polish People's Party (*Polskie Stronnictwo Ludowe*, PSL), and then after Aleksander Kwaśniewski's victory in the presidential election, new metaphors appear in regard to the time of transformation: "splitting Poland in half" (Kwaśniewski's slight advantage in the presidential election), "the specter of the PRL," "renewal of historical disputes."

On the one hand, free parliamentary elections are viewed as the final transition from the Polish People's Republic (*Polska Rzeczpospolita Ludowa*, PRL) to the Republic of Poland (*Rzeczpospolita Polska*); on the other hand, the activity of Jan Olszewski's government is considered the first true attempt to break with the legacy of the PRL by undertaking the so-called lustration, which involved disclosure of ties with the communist secret service (Staniszkis 1999).

Although the Solidarity social movement was suppressed during the martial law period, historians' narratives commonly use the term "Solidarity camp" when referring to non-communist formations on the political stage of the transformation period. Thus, historians also use such expressions as "the collapse of the Solidarity camp" or "crisis and collapse of the Solidarity camp" (Roszkowski 1995, Dudek 1997). Historical narration is fraught with contradictory meanings of the time of transformation, since it first speaks about the fall of the communist regime, then about post-communism and the collapse of the Solidarity camp. However, this does not apply to all historical narratives, as exemplified by an author who presents the election on June 4, 1989 and Mazowiecki's government as a continuation of events related to the threat of Soviet intervention and the martial law introduced on December 13, 1981. He eschews the term "fall of communism," focusing instead on Poland's regained sovereignty, and emphasizes the importance of three processes: the collapse of the great Solidarity movement as a driving force for Poland's extrication from the Soviet system, revival of the political ideology of National Democrats and Christian Democrats (or, more broadly, of national ideology), and the significance of the Catholic Church's search for a place in the new political situation (Topolski 1995).

Attempting to describe the time of transformation, historians disagree on how to date the breakthrough that marked the beginning of the Third Republic. They indicate the commencement of the Round Table talks (February 6, 1989), the parliamentary election on June 4, 1989, or December 29, 1989, when the name "Polish People's Republic" was abolished and replaced by "Republic of

Poland" (Hałas 2016: 129–146; Majcherek 1999). This shows the work on historical time performed by historians as the producers of semiosis of history, as well
as the arbitrary character of the conventions of enumerating significant events.
Historical narratives which are correlates of current processes remain inevitably fraught with a bias that stems from a particular nearsightedness of the
performed observations and interpretations. Participants in the Thirty Years'
War could not name the events they were observing as the Thirty Years' War.
However, "systemic transformation" in historians' narratives is not a retrospective explanation, but rather a prospective interpretation with performative
consequences.

The multitude of transformation times

The starting point of this part of the analysis is the timeline of events from
February 6, 1989 to March 12, 1999. They are analyzed depending on what field
of activity they occurred in: the field of political activity, the field of economic
activity, the field of strictly social activity, i.e. the civil society field, the international field, in which Poland defines its place in Europe and in the world,
or the field of symbolic actions related to the past: the dissolution of organizations that operated in the PRL, most notably the Polish United Workers'
Party (*Polska Zjednoczona Partia Robotnicza*, PZPR), new rituals of commemoration, etc. This enables us to analyze the time of transformation and its symbolic dimension more deeply and in a more multilateral manner than if we
were referring solely to the time of political institutions and to the semantic
framework created by historians' narratives. The analyzed time of processes
and events in the above-mentioned categories covers 11 years between the symbolic date of the Round Table talks and Poland's accession to North Atlantic
Treaty Organization (NATO) structures on March 12, 1999 (Table 4).

Not surprisingly, among the 275 events noted as important in the public
sphere, recorded in the analyzed timeline between February 1989 and March
1999, events in the political and social fields predominate.

Symbolic actions involving reference to the past are also very visible in public
practices registered in the timeline of events. An intriguing aspect is the relatively small number of events considered important in the economic field, and
therefore associated with the transformation of the Polish economy during the
period of rapid change metaphorically termed "shock therapy." Events determining Poland's place in Europe and in the world also represent only 10 % of
the total number of events in the timeline, i.e. those that give meaning to the
time of transformation (Figure 1). Importantly, the analysis is based on the

Tab. 4. The multitude of transformation times
(from February 6, 1989 to March 12, 1999)

Variety of time	1989	1990	1991	1992	1993	1994	1995	1996	1997	1998	1999	Total	%
Political time	13	15	7	6	6	6	4	6	8	11	5	87	32 %
Economic time	2	2	5	1	3	1	-	1	1	2	-	18	7 %
Civil society time	11	8	5	14	12	13	3	2	3	11	1	83	30 %
Time of Poland in Europe and in the world	3	5	10	3	-	3	-	1	1	1	1	28	10 %
Time of operations performed on the past	10	8	3	4	6	7	4	3	1	11	2	59	21 %
Total	39	38	30	28	27	30	11	13	14	36	9	275	100 %
%	14 %	14 %	11 %	10 %	10 %	11 %	4 %	5 %	5 %	13 %	3 %	100 %	

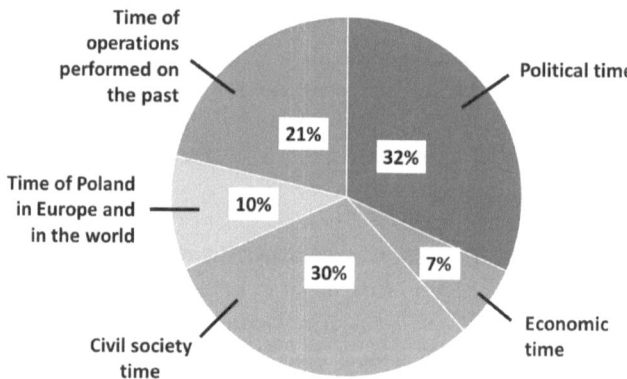

Fig. 1. Multiple times generated by events during the first decade of transformation

PT – political time; ET – economic time; CST – civil society time;
TP – time of Poland in Europe and in the world; TOP – time of operations performed on the past

Fig. 2. Polymorphous time of transformation

calendar of events presented during the first decade of transformation and not retrospectively.

For political time, 1989 is clearly the most important year (more precisely, the political time of transformation begins with the Round Table talks in February 1989), along with 1990, when the number of events increased (Figure 2). The density of political time did not increase again until 1997, when the so-called post-Solidarity formations came into power. In contrast, towards the end of the rule of the cabinets of Waldemar Pawlak and Józef Oleksy (politicians belonging to post-communist formations), political time becomes "diluted:" few events are recorded in the timeline. Furthermore, the period when the above-mentioned governments were in power, i.e. the end of the 1990s, brought no notable events in the economic field, nor events capable of changing Poland's place in Europe and in the world. A similar stagnation regarding events in the international field can be seen in 1993, when the governments of Hanna Suchocka and Waldemar Pawlak were in power.

In the field of economy, the greatest number of important events was recorded in 1991, when the government was led by Jan Krzysztof Bielecki. The smallest number of these events was recorded in 1995 (the rule of prime ministers Waldemar Pawlak and Józef Oleksy). The beginning of 1999 also brought no significant new events in this field.

The time of events in the social field is characterized by a swift rhythm in 1989, the year which initiated the transformation, then in the years 1992–1994 and again in 1998. This time includes various civic initiatives, but above all it is marked by social unrest. It should be noted that in the years 1995–1997, i.e. in the middle of the studied period, the rhythm of social time slows down significantly: few events are recorded in the timeline.

In the international field, i.e. in the field of events defining Poland's place in Europe and in the world, the number of milestone events in the timeline was greatest in 1991, during the rule of Jan Krzysztof Bielecki.

Of particular interest to us is the field of symbolic actions and references to the past. Events belonging to this field are recorded in the timeline mostly in 1989 and 1990, at the beginning of the transformation; hence the proposed term "symbolic transformation" (Hałas 2016).

Interestingly, the rhythm of symbolic actions slows down significantly in the following years. Its weakening is particularly evident in 1991 and 1992, while in 1997 these events disappear almost entirely. Subsequently during the rule of Jerzy Buzek, a prime minister from a post-Solidarity formation, this rhythm abruptly intensifies once again in a literal eruption of symbolic actions.

Interestingly, when we take into account events from all fields recorded in the timeline as important in the public sphere, one sees that their number decreases in the years 1992–1993 and decreases to just one third in 1995, 1996 and 1997, during the rule of Waldemar Pawlak, Józef Oleksy and Włodzimierz Cimoszewicz: prime ministers from post-communist formations.

The time of operations performed upon the past

Events in the timeline involving operations performed on the past in the first months from the start of the Round Table talks signified the rejection of communism. On February 11, 1989, a commission was established to commemorate the victims of the Stalinist repression, and on February 15 the Sejm established the hitherto forbidden anniversary of Poland's return to independence on November 11, 1918: Independence Day.

The rehabilitation of persons convicted by communist courts began with the Supreme Court's acquittal of activists of the Polish Socialist Party (*Polska Partia Socjalistyczna*) convicted in 1948. Proceedings were initiated in the matter of posthumously restoring the Polish citizenship of General Władysław

Anders (commander-in-chief of the Polish armed forces during World War II outside the country), of which he was deprived by the PRL government.

Some organizations symbolizing the repressive communist system's actions against the Solidarity movement, such as the Patriotic Movement for National Rebirth (*Patriotyczny Ruch Odrodzenia Narodowego*, PRON) and the Volunteer Reserve of the Citizens' Militia (*Ochotnicza Rezerwa Milicji Obywatelskiej*, ORMO) became dissolved. However, others, including such fundamental ones as the communist party and its satellite peasant party, dissolved themselves only to continue operating under new names. This occurred in accordance with a more broadly prevalent model of transformation of communist European parties (Kertzer 1996).

Operations on the past recorded in the timeline do not reach deep into the past. They cover a relatively recent past, the living history present in the memory of living generations: above all, the PRL period. These actions are related to the installation of communist rule and the beginnings of this system in Poland, but not to the most recent past, i.e. events that immediately preceded the transformation, such as the suppression of the Solidarity movement and the imposition of martial law. Just like during the "thaw" of 1956, these operations on the past concern the Stalinist period, 1944–1956, already condemned during the so-called thaw; the past still remembered by the victims, perpetrators and witnesses.

The time of operations on the past emerges as a result of various initiatives involving a response to the communist past. These initiatives most often aim to bring about certain qualitative changes in the symbolic sphere. These include: rehabilitation of former sites of memory, i.e. sites associated with persons and events from Polish history that had been excluded from the collective memory in the PRL period, and creating new organs for this purpose, such as the Commission for Commemorating Victims of the Stalinist Repression (*Komisja do Spraw Upamiętniania Ofiar Represji Okresu Stalinowskiego*).

New sites of memory related to events from the PRL period are created. Of primary importance among them is commemoration: celebrating the anniversary of the signing of the August Agreements between the Solidarity movement and the communist authorities on August 31, 1980. Therefore, these symbolic operations on the past have a selective character in the symbolism of the transformation period. Affirmation of the symbolism of the August Agreements goes hand in hand with symbolic denial. The time of these operations on the past can therefore be called the time of negating the past.

These operations fall under various types of decommunization initiatives: abolishment, transformations, lustration, vetting. Their goal is to "settle accounts" with the communist past and condemn it. This time of operations on the past has a variable rhythm. Three periods can be clearly distinguished: 1989–1992, 1993–1997 and 1998–1999.

The years 1989–1992 bring a "thickening" of initiatives, such as "restoring" places of memory in the public sphere (restoration of national holidays on November 11 and May 3); rehabilitation of persons convicted by PRL courts for political reasons; dismantling PRL government structures and institutions. The time of operations on the past is very fast-paced in this initial period.

As regards measures undertaken to settle accounts with the past, including its condemnation, such initiatives are not frequent in this initial period of transformation, in accordance with the policy of the so-called "thick stroke." There are no events which would indicate a determination to undertake such measures, especially attempts to draw consequences against former functionaries of the communist system. The lustration initiative undertaken during the rule of Jan Olszewski's government was a failure. The country's highest authorities also avoid any direct condemnation of the PRL period; certain elements are considered illegal, but they are not openly condemned.

Between 1993 and 1997, the time of operations on the past slows down and remains steady. Its rhythm is mainly determined by initiatives aiming to directly draw consequences against PRL officers: specific persons, rather than structures. Trials of persons responsible for crimes committed during the PRL period begin. The Sejm decides that these crimes shall not be subject to the statute of limitations. Indirect measures are undertaken to settle accounts with the past, introducing statutory changes such as the Act on veterans and the Act on uniformed pensions. During this period, the Sejm also adopts the Lustration Act on April 11, 1997, during the rule of the SLD-PSL coalition.

Between 1997 and 1999, the time of operations on the past accelerates again. Lustration-related initiatives are undertaken faster: the amendment to the Lustration Act and the Act on vetting of judges. Lustration enters the implementation phase after the second list of persons covered by the Lustration Act, who admitted to cooperating with the PRL secret service, is published on March 2, 1999.

There are also attempts to condemn the PRL's communist system, as shown by decommunization initiatives: the parliamentary debate on the bill of April 3, 1998, followed by the Act of June 18, 1998, or the resolution condemning the actions of PRL authorities during the revolt in March 1968. A novel initiative was the Act on the Institute of National Remembrance, which enabled citizens to access "files," i.e. materials concerning them collected by the PRL secret service.

The symbolic politics of dead bodies

In Poland, as in all other post-communist countries, the 1990s were a time when history "returned" and became present in the form of remains and ashes formally reinterred in new burial ceremonies (Verdery 1997). In contrast to the field of action defined as operations on the past, I distinguish a subfield of symbolic actions in which the past is embedded in the present. Here, the temporal direction is opposite. In operations on the past, present actions are oriented towards the past (significant elements from the communist era are removed from the present), whereas in the case of symbolism of dead bodies, what was removed from the semiosphere during the communist period is restored. In this way, a time of commemoration is created (Connerton 1999).

From an anthropological point of view, the symbolism of dead bodies is very rich and provokes interpretations from the perspective of cultural anthropology, regarding universality and particularity of rituals (Cohen 1998). Public rituals of ceremonial reburial would have gained no symbolic value, were it not for the deep semantic and axiological content associated with revering the dead body in Western culture. The cult of relics, which gave rise to reverence surrounding the remains of rulers, and in Poland also of national martyrs, is an example of this. All Saints' Day and the Day of the Dead, celebrated in Poland at the beginning of November each year, show that cemeteries are important sites of memory that help create a moral bond between generations.

The ceremonial reburial (including symbolic ceremonies where no actual remains are being reinterred) of members of the Second Polish Republic's ruling elite: high-ranking military officers and politicians, representatives of the Polish Government in Exile, soldiers of the Home Army (*Armia Krajowa*, AK), including those executed under Stalinist rule, played an important role in validating the transformational changes for those social strata that identified with anti-communist opposition and cultivated independence traditions. Honors publicly given to representatives of ideologies and values that had been anathema until recently (especially personages from the Second Polish Republic's elites) were a clear message that the framework of interpretation of the social world is undergoing radical changes (Table 5).

Between 1990 and 1999, the new daily "Gazeta Wyborcza" alone published 55 reports from the funeral ceremonies of politicians, military personnel and other representatives of the elite, hitherto discredited as political opponents or

Tab. 5. List of symbolic funerals between 1990 and 2000

Year	Name and surname	Function	Date of birth	Date of death	Date of reinterment
1990	Bolesław Wieniawa-Długoszowski	General	22 VII 1881	1 VII 1942	1 VII 1990
1991	Kazimierz A. Tumidajski	General	28 II 1897	4 VII 1947	14 IX 1991
1991	Leopold Okulicki	General	12 XI 1898	24 XII 1946	
1992	Kazimierz Sosnkowski	General	19 XI 1885	11 X 1969	12 XI 1992
1992	Józef Ignacy Paderewski	Prime Minister of the Second Republic of Poland	18 XI 1860	29 VI 1941	29 VI 1992
1992	Aleksandra Piłsudska	Wife of Marshal Piłsudski	12 XII 1882	31 III 1963	28 X 1992
1992	Michał Tokarzewski-Karaszewicz	General	5 I 1893	22 V 1964	IX 1992
1993	Józef Haller	General	13 VIII 1873	4 VI 1960	23 IV 1993
1993	Ignacy Mościcki	President	1 XII 1867	2 X 1946	1993
1993	Ludomił Rayski	General	29 XII 1892	11 IV 1977	May 1993
1993	Sikorski	General, Prime Minister of the Polish Government in Exile	20 V 1881	4 VII 1943	17 IX 1993
1994	Tadeusz Bór-Komorowski	General, Prime Minister of the Polish Government in Exile	1 VI 1895	24 VIII 1966	30 VII 1994
1995	Stanisław August Poniatowski	King of Poland	17 I 1732	12 II 1798	14 II 1995
1995	Tadeusz Pełczyński	General	14 II 1892	3 I 1985	1995
1996	Ignacy Prądzyński	General	20 VII 1792	4 VIII 1850	1997
1997	Mariusz Zaruski	General	I 1867	8 IV 1941	
1997	Zygmunt Szyszko-Bohusz	General	18 I 1893	20 VI 1982	

(*continued on next page*)

Tab. 5. Continued

Year	Name and surname	Function	Date of birth	Date of death	Date of reinterment
1997	Paweł E. Strzelecki	Geographer, explorer	20 VII 1797	6 X 1873	29 XI 1997
1999	Hieronim K. Dekutowski, *nom de guerre* Zapora	Home Army commander	24 IX 1918	7 III 1949	
1999	Zaporczycy	Home Army soldiers			
2000	Stanisław Mikołajczyk	Prime Minister of the Polish Government in Exile	18 VII 1901	13 XII 1966	2000

criminals. The largest number of these accounts (25) was published in 1993, which can be called the year of symbolic politics of dead bodies. In that year, the most important funeral ceremonies took place: of President Ignacy Mościcki (1867–1946) and General Władysław Sikorski (1881–1943), General Józef Haller (1873–1960) and General Ludomił Rayski (1892–1977).

Also important for this type of symbolic politics was the preceding year, 1992, which saw the funerals of statesman and co-creator of Polish independence Ignacy Paderewski (1860–1941), General Kazimierz Sosnkowski (1885–1969), General Michał Tokarzewski-Karaszewicz (1893–1964) and Aleksandra Piłsudska (1882–1963), the wife of Marshal Józef Piłsudski (1867–1935).

The symbolism of these burials and its political functions during the transformation become even more significant if one takes into account the public discourse surrounding the exhumation of collective graves of Poles (soldiers of the Home Army – *Armia Krajowa*), Germans, Ukrainians and Soviet soldiers at that time. During this period, about 90 reports on these exhumations appeared in the press. The time of symbolism of dead bodies remains dense throughout the first decade of transformation, but its event density decreases after 1998.

The symbolism of the exhumation of victims of the Katyń massacre committed by the NKVD requires a separate analysis. Only in "Gazeta Wyborcza" this exhumation was reported over 300 times between 1989 and 1999, and the frequency of these reports reached its apogee in 1994 and 1995: 43 and 79 accounts respectively. Thus, these two years should be regarded as years of symbolic politics of dead bodies of the victims of the Katyń massacre. In public discourse, this symbolism clearly fades out towards the end of the first decade of transformation.

Notably, public visibility and the symbolism of the Katyń massacre became apparent and intensified over time after the last Russian troops withdrew from Poland on the symbolic day of September 17, 1993 (the date of the Soviet invasion of Poland in 1939). It was on this day that the body of General Władysław Sikorski was reinterred in Wawel in St. Leonard's Crypt, next to the royal tombs. These symbolic actions broke the taboo of silence which had surrounded the NKVD's crime against Polish officers in Katyń, Ostashkov, Kozielsk, Miednoje and Kharkov until the end of communist rule in Poland.

Political time

The events analyzed above are a function of the field of political action. They reflect the dynamics of processes occurring in the field of practices that constitute the politics of symbolization. This is demonstrated by the analysis of political time, generated by the actions of political institutions that determine its rhythm, pace and meaning. The actions that generate political time co-determine the whole transformation process. This rhythm is marked by three phases.

The most significant milestones of political time occurred in the first years of transformation, up until the adoption of the "small Constitution" in October 1992. During this period, political events set swift changes into motion, resulting in a denser transformation time: a large number of events occurred during this period. The significance of this time lies in changes taking place in the future-oriented present.

The present time represents the end of a certain stage: the end of the Polish People's Republic, and the beginning of a new one: transformation towards a democratic system. Significant points in the political time of transformation mark the beginning of this new stage. They cluster densely precisely in this first period: the Round Table talks, legislative initiatives introducing political changes as a consequence of the Round Table, the first government with a non-communist prime minister, the first free presidential and parliamentary elections.

Focusing on the present as transformation gives this political time a uniquely short temporality. This means that reference to the future is limited, although this time is oriented towards change. However, this future is close to "now." No events represent visions reaching far into the future. A short perspective of future time dominates.

Similarly, the past is also a near past. It selectively reaches only as far as the PRL period, which represents a mostly negative reference. During this period, the time of transformation becomes politicized, and thus the domination of politics can be observed in many areas of life, as well as in visions of the past and future.

Initiatives undertaken during this period transform the social space. A new framework for the functioning of the state and society emerges. Systemic changes introduce a new institutional order in Poland and new rules for moving in the social space (principles of the rule of law, principles of democracy, the principle of sovereignty of society and its participation in power, and the principle of pluralism). The breakup of the so-called Solidarity camp paves the way for practical functioning of the principles of parliamentary democracy. New actors appear on the political scene and gain a say.

The transformation of social space involves dismantling the structures of the Polish People's Republic, as well as removing some elements of the old institutional order and its principles of institutional functioning. The old political space becomes dismantled; changes include abolition of censorship, dissolution of the Security Service (*Służba Bezpieczeństwa*) and the Volunteer Reserve of the Citizens' Militia, transformation of the Citizens' Militia (*Milicja Obywatelska*) into the Police (*Policja*).

After 1993, the political field of systemic transformation changes much less rapidly. The most important changes, those initiating the democratic system, have already been introduced. The nascent democratic state is slowly beginning to function at its own pace. Further elections and referendums are held; political parties are active. However, the state's fragility is revealed by the subsequent failures of governments. Mechanisms of the democratic system's functioning also exhibit their side effects: power struggles, party disputes, conflicts in relations between the president and the parliament. The views of particular parties and their programs become more and more divergent in comparison to the previous consensus regarding the introduced fundamental changes.

Legal regulations and legislative initiatives concern more detailed areas of life; the aim is to adapt those areas to the initiated democratic system. These regulations and initiatives are a consequence and concretization of the changes from the first period. They are much less spectacular, and appear much more slowly. The timeline shows "empty" periods in political time, a lack of significant events in the calendar. As regards the introduction of further political changes, political time now "stands still."

The temporal orientation during this period is primarily towards the present. The focus is on the here-and-now events of the political scene. The past as a reference point is the recent past, the past of the PRL. As for the future, a short temporal perspective remains typical.

After 1997, time accelerates again to some degree. Changeability is visible once more and interpreted as bold reforms (administrative reform, social security reform, health care reform, education reform). The guarantor of stability is to be the Constitution of the Third Polish Republic, adopted on April 2, 1997.

When the coalition of two post-Solidarity formations, the Solidarity Electoral Action (*Akcja Wyborcza Solidarność*, AWS) and the Freedom Union (*Unia Wolności*, UW), came into power, the communist past became an obviously negative frame of reference. This period, as shown above, brought the largest number of legislative initiatives related to settling accounts with the PRL (repeated lustration and decommunization initiatives, the Act on the Institute of National Remembrance) in the entire analyzed decade. During this period, a new territorial division of the country was also introduced. This was the most conspicuous manifestation of spatial transformation and had the additional symbolic value of breaking with the past and with the identity of the PRL.

Civil society time

The basic principle for expanding the space of society's activity within the state is the principle of society's sovereignty and its participation in power. Society acquires subjectivity, confirmed by such institutions as free elections, referendums, forming political parties, the right to freely organize into associations, the ability to protest and organize strikes. Thus, the field for all social initiatives broadened as a result of systemic transformation. New fields and levels of participation emerged. However, society's readiness for actual involvement in this enlarged space is an entirely different matter.

As in the case of the above-presented political time, civil society time also passes through three phases. Between 1989 and 1992, the timeline of events shows the introduction of a number of legal regulations regarding society's "mobility" in the new political space: the Act introducing the Republic of Poland, the Act on freedom of association, the Act on political parties, the Act on electoral law. This period can be read as a kind of "initiation" into public participation in state life. The first free presidential and parliamentary elections took place and the first legal political parties were formed (and many new ones subsequently sprang up in rapid succession). These events intensified and occurred in large numbers over a short period. Along with the new legislation, the state discursively presents a wide field of possible civic activities.

The turnout in subsequent elections during this period is indicative of the society's involvement, or lack thereof, despite emerging opportunities: in elections to the Contract Sejm – 62 %, in local elections – 42 %; in the first free presidential election: first round – 60.6 %, second round – 53 %; in the first fully free parliamentary elections – 43.2 %.

An avalanche of strikes, protests, pickets and demonstrations grew in intensity from 1992 onwards. The speed with which they spread remained very fast until 1996. Apart from dissatisfaction, mainly with the country's economic situation, this also shows the consolidation of the fundamental principle of a democratic state, i.e. the society's belief in its own subjectivity and the associated possibilities. By 1997, approximately 290 political parties had formed. The turnout in elections, however, showed no significant change in political culture and remained more or less at the same level.

In 1996 and 1997, the number of protests decreased and two referendums were held, enabling the public to participate directly in the decision-making processes of the state. The turnout in both of them was low (enfranchisement referendum: 34.4 %; constitutional referendum: 46.8 %).

From the end of 1997 onwards, strikes intensified once again. The Sejm adopted a new law on political parties, which set higher requirements for registration. During this period, the public expressed dissatisfaction with the country's future territorial division. These actions intensified from January to July 1998. In the first elections to the three levels of local government on October 11, 1998, the turnout was not very high, only 40%. Thus, civil society time distinguishes itself as a time of symbolic protests, especially in its first and third phase during the decade.

Economic time

Actions undertaken in the economic field generate another variety of transformation time: economic time. The timeline of transformation includes events that mark the transition from a statist economy, a planned economy, a scarcity economy to a free market economy. The principles of the economy's functioning underwent a fundamental change. The state's monopoly on undertaking economic activities was removed. New actors and new market economy institutions emerged.

Interestingly, not many important events on the timeline are landmarks of economic time. This is in stark contrast to other varieties of time, the meanings of which are various dimensions of the semiosis of history. Moreover, economic time signified by meaningful events that were important for the economy is not synchronized with the other times, which went through the three phases described above. In the case of economic time, only two phases are visible. The period from 1989 to 1993 generated a dense time of events in the economic field, whereas later years generated a much slower time. In some years no important events were noted in the field of economy.

Fundamental changes began with the adoption of a package of economic laws known as the Balcerowicz Plan. These laws came into force on January 1, 1990. The Balcerowicz Plan is the most significant symbol of systemic transformation regarding economic changes. Changes occurred swiftly in this period.

After 1992, activities in the economic field were focused on gaining membership in various economic organizations of Western Europe and the world. This goal was reached in 1996, when Poland became a full member of the Organization for Economic Co-operation and Development (OECD).

Between 1989 and 1999, the timeline of events contains only 18 occurrences associated with the field of economy. Two thirds of these events occurred during the first period of transformation, before 1993. This does not mean a complete lack of significant events in the economic field. The fact that economic transformation has scarcely any markers on the timeline in this period, despite being a very significant dimension of systemic transformation, raises a question regarding the politics of symbolization in this dimension. This reveals a hiatus in the semiosis of history between the plane of activities and the plane of expression (Hałas 2017). Metaphorically speaking, economic time is silent; it does not speak for itself.

The time of international relations

Activities in the field of international relations generate their own variety of time. The space of international relations expands over time. The qualitative change is that Poland, within confirmed and inviolable borders, gains the ability to act internationally as a sovereign entity with a new identity. The Yalta system collapses, the structures of the former Soviet Bloc fall apart: the Council for Mutual Economic Assistance and the Warsaw Pact cease to exist. Russian troops, a symbol of the alliance with the former USSR, withdraw on September 17, 1993. The space for cooperation with other countries (primarily those with which Poland did not maintain relations during the PRL period, such as Israel) broadens; relations with other countries gain a new quality and extend to new areas of cooperation. Many countries lift the visa requirement for Poles. Polish borders open up, enabling Poles to travel freely and emigrate.

The political space in the immediate vicinity of Poland also changes. As an independent actor on the international scene, Poland gains the ability to participate in shaping it. Relations with neighboring countries, who also recently became new actors in the international space, determine Poland's credibility.

This variety of time also passes through three phases. The first period between 1989 and 1992 is characterized by intense international relations and growing activities in this field. During these years, Poland confirms its Western borders, reestablishes diplomatic relations with countries with which those relations had been broken off during the communist period, and expands its cooperation with other countries. During this phase, the Third Republic also normalizes its relations with neighboring countries. These changes occur very swiftly. All the most important shifts in the quality of Poland's international relations take place in this period.

After 1993, Poland's position in international space stabilizes. Various types of activities are undertaken as part of international cooperation and marked on the timeline. The timeline shows bilateral visits and the participation of representatives of the Republic of Poland in international conferences. During this period, relations with the Vatican become settled by signing a concordat which had been the subject of political disputes in earlier years.

After 1994, the time of international relations remains oriented mostly towards the future, as the rhythm of this time was partly determined by efforts to obtain Polish membership in various structures of Western Europe, primarily in the European Union and NATO. The timeline of recorded events reveals the growing dynamics of this variety of transformation time, culminating in the official start of negotiations with the European Union and in Poland's accession to NATO on March 12, 1999. NATO membership and the future EU membership, due to historical events, changed the geopolitical position of the Republic of Poland.

The field of actions associated with international relations generates a specific variety of transformation time consisting of events that changed the place of Poland in Europe and in the world, relevant for the future. Here, the temporal orientation of time contrasts remarkably with the field of actions oriented towards the past and with the temporal perspectives of other times discussed above.

The presented analysis shows that the semiosis of history is more multidimensional and more complex as regards temporal orientations than the model where an orientation towards the past occupies a privileged place to guide the future. The analyzed time of transformation is not uniform but polymorphous.

References

Analiza aktów prawnych. Opracowania tematyczne OT-608, Kancelaria Senatu. Biuro Analiz i Dokumentacji [*Beginning and end dates of Sejm and Senate terms of office since 1989. Analysis of legal acts. Thematic studies OT-608, Chancellery of the Senate. Analysis and Documentation Office*] 2012: 3).

Archer, Margaret (1996) *Culture and Agency. The Place of Culture in Social Theory*, Cambridge: Cambridge University Press.

Braudel, Fernand (1971) *Historia i trwanie*. Translated by Bronisław Geremek. Warszawa: Czytelnik.

Connerton, Paul (1999) *How Societies Remember*. Cambridge: Cambridge University Press.

Cohen, Anthony P. (1998) *The Symbolic Construction of Community*. London: Routledge.

Dudek, Antoni (1997) *Pierwsze lata III Rzeczpospolitej 1989–1995. Zarys historii politycznej Polski [The First Years of the Third Republic 1989–1995. An Outline of the Political History of Poland]*. Warszawa: Wydawnictwo GEO.

Fligstein, Neil and Doug, McAdam (2012) *A Theory of Fields*, Oxford: Oxford University Press.

Hałas, Elżbieta (2000) "Transformation in Collective Imagination," *Polish Sociological Review* 3: 309–322.

_____ (2010) "Time and Memory. A Cultural Perspective," *Trames. Journal of the Humanities and Social Sciences* 14 (4): 307–322.

_____ (2016) "Symbolic Transformations: State Symbolism and the Fall of Communism in Poland" in Elżbieta Hałas (ed.), *Life-World, Intersubjectivity and Culture. Contemporary Dilemmas*, pp. 129–146, Frankfurt am Main: Peter Lang.

_____ (2017) "The Orientation of Culture and the Memory of the Past in the Making of History," *Sign System Studies*. Special issue: Semiotics and History: Boris Uspenskij 80. 45 (3/4): 361–379.

Kertzer, David I. (1996) *Politics & Symbols. The Italian Communist Party and the Fall of Communism*. New Haven: Yale University Press.

Kowalski, Sergiusz (1996) *Narodziny III Rzeczpospolitej [The Birth of the Third Republic]*, chapter I. Warszawa: WSiP.

Maines, David R. (2001) *The Faultline of Consciousness: A View of Interactionism in Sociology*. New York: Aldine de Gruyter.

Majcherek, Janusz (1999) *Pierwsza dekada III RP 1989–1999 [The First Decade of the Third Republic: 1989–1999]*. Warszawa: Wydawnictwo Rzeczpospolita.

Mead, George H. (1964) "The Nature of the Past" in George Herbert Mead, *Selected Writings*. Andrew J. Reck (ed.), pp. 345–354. Chicago: The University of Chicago Press.

Roszkowski, Wojciech (1995) *Historia Polski 1914–1995 [The History of Poland from 1914 to 1995]*. Warszawa: Wydawnictwo Naukowe PWN.

Staniszkis, Jadwiga (1999) *Postcommunism. The Emerging Enigma*. Warsaw: Institute of Political Studies. Polish Academy of Sciences.

Topolski, Jan (1995) *Polska XX wieku 1914–1995 [20th-century Poland 1914–1995]*. Poznań: Wydawnictwo Poznańskie.

Verdery, Katherine (1999) *The Political Lives of Dead Bodies. Reburial and Postsocialist Change*. New York: Columbia University Press.

White, Hayden (2000) "Catastrophe, Communal Memory and Mythic Discourse: The Uses of Myth in the Reconstruction of Society" in Bo Stråth (ed.) *Myth and Memory in the Construction of Community. Historical Patterns in Europe and Beyond*, pp. 49–74. Brussels: Peter Lang.

SYMBOLIC CONSTRUCTION OF COMMUNITIES: NEW BEGINNINGS AND NEW DIVIDES

Ulf Hedetoft

The Crowned Eagle and the Mythical Turul: Populism and the Symbolization of National Identity in Poland and Hungary. History, Politics, Religion

Abstract: The article focuses on the symbolism connected with the populism vibrant in both Hungary and Poland. It shows how both countries moralize history, politics and religiosity in each their own way. At the same time, the two versions of political symbolism are not identical, but are interestingly different – Hungary's pivoting around images of victimization, Poland's around defiant resistance. On the other hand, though the two countries have travelled different routes, they have arrived at much the same political conclusions. The article attempts to explain how and why this has happened.

Keywords: national identity, populism, religion, Hungary, Poland

Introductory

The phenomenon that we regularly talk about as populism is no easy analytical object. It presupposes that concepts like nationalism, people, popular reactions, elites and borders are determined, that the interconnectedness between them stands out clearly, and that historical processes and contemporary consequences are linked in a convincing manner. This is not mainly because the materiality or the economic contexts of these issues are at stake, but because populism is centrally dependent on symbols, abstractions and identity perceptions, ie on less (or more?) than apparently rational and logical explanatory models of reality. Populism depends on images of martyrdom, historical vindication and righteous revenge, on moralities divorced from selfish gain, and on the belief in the superiority of the national identity allegedly given to its people – a people which can consequently be construed as divinely sanctified. Mainstream nationalism (see e.g. Anderson 1983; Gellner 1983; Billig 1995) may be an abstraction, but it nevertheless rests on an economic basis that has been twisted and turned by means of the necessary dependency of state and people – and of sections within the people (Hedetoft 1995; 2020). Populism takes this nationalism further into the realm of symbolic abstraction, where the links between symbols and their references, between *signifiant* and *signifié,* are less easy to establish and the room for affective reactions hence are more expansive. In semiotic terms, populism matches the Peircean definition of non-motivated symbols more perfectly than mainstream nationalism, where metaphors and metonyms (so-called indexes) have a place as well (Atkin 2010; Peirce 1977; Sebeok 1994, 28–37; Short 2007).[1] Mainstream nationalism makes a comprehensible distinction between, say, elites and the people, where the former (at least its political segment) *represents* the people following elections. Populism, on the other hand, refuses to recognize the close connection between the two and constructs the relationship as a contradictory duality, where elites only represent their own personal, egoistic interests *at the expense of* the people; elites are thus morally condemned and seen to be (often foreign) agents of interests that must necessarily oppose those of the people (Hedetoft 2020, Chapter 5; Müller 2016, 25–40).

Populists elected to serve in governments, on the other hand, are morally exempt from being part of the elites. They are presented and imagined as an integral part of the people and are symbolized as such. They make sacrifices and lead lives of ascetic constraint, but they do it in a good cause. The people are also regularly asked to make sacrifices (like in ordinary national contexts), but they do it for themselves, their national identity and their cultural sovereignty, not because they have been forced to do so in an alien cause. Those citizens who do not agree with this version of national moralism are not seen to be part of the real, moral people – and become vilified as persons who have lost their way. Thus, populism is able to turn the effect-affect relationship around, denying the commonplace division of nation and state (Hedetoft 1995, 27–34). It conquers the moral high ground over what it sees as political and economic opportunism, taking symbolic revenge over internal as well as external enemies, in the process waving goodbye to any notion of the benevolent Other. The Other is always presented as a threat, a hostile presence, an enemy of the

---

1   Indexes imply that there is some intrinsic connection between the form and the content of signs, whereas symbols postulate a connection, often on the basis of conventions, e.g. the rose as a symbol of love, the colour of a flag as a symbol of a particular nation-state, or the 'non-descriptive' logo of a specific company (eg Mitsubishi or Citroën). This 'non-motivated' association between *signifié* and *significant,* between referent and object, opens up for the intervention of affect, emotionality and misrepresentations of reality to a much larger extent than in the cases of direct iconic representations (eg photographs) or metaphorical connections, and is hence well suited to the pure moralism of populist imaginings.

populist project. All this requires an extraordinary feat of mythical, moral and quasi-religious imagination, in which symbolization plays a key role.

In the following, the symbolism of the political and cultural populism vibrant in both Hungary and Poland will be the object of examination. I will try to show how they both live up to the context, features and requirements described above, in the sense that they moralize history, politics and religiosity in each their own way, while bringing back national symbolism and national identity formations in versions that run counter to the globalizing and liberal tendencies of the last 50 years (Dittmar 2019). At the same time, they are not identical, but are interestingly different and specific. This applies to the form they assume on the background of the histories of the two countries; to the concrete interactions of history, politics and religion; and to the symbolism applied to arouse and thicken the popular imagination whilst tying it to the idea of national existentialism and the cataclysm that would result in case it were to be neglected. In this sense, populism is far from the 'thin' ideology is has been made out to be. It is rather a 'thick' representation of the national phantasmagoria (Kotwas and Kubik 2019).

Let me begin by looking at the symbolic cornerstone of national symbolism in both countries: their *national anthems* and what they tell us about the imaginaries that constitute the national (political and civic) cultures of the two countries.

Setting the stage. The anthems: lament vs. belligerence

Despite what one might expect – that the two anthems are similar and express comparable attitudes to life, history and nation – they are in fact diametrical opposites. The Hungarian "Himnusz" – "God bless the Hungarians – From the rough centuries of the Hungarian people" – is a protracted lament, almost a prayer to God to protect the Hungarian people from the vicissitudes and martyrdom of history. In contrast, the Polish anthem, "Mazurek Dąbrowskiego" (known in English as "Poland Is Not Yet Lost") is a belligerently stubborn and relatively short march – almost a war song – inspiring the Polish people to retrieve all that history has taken away from it, "with a sabre," and thus follow the example of Napoleon Bonaparte.[2] Where the Hungarian implores God to "bless the nation of Hungary" and "extend over it your guarding arm,' the Polish

---

2 The words of the Hungarian anthem were written by Ferenc Kölcsey in 1823; the music by Ferenc Erkel in 1844. It was de facto used as hymn of the Kingdom of Hungary from its composition in 1844 and was officially adopted as national anthem

incites citizens 'to be Polish' and 'save our homeland.' Where the Hungarian wallows in the pain and misery, even slavery, which the Hungarian people have been subjected to throughout history, ending with a plea for divine intervention so that Hungarians – endless "tossed by waves of danger" – can finally enjoy "a time of relief/ They who have suffered for all sins/ Of the past and of the future;" there the Polish extols the recalcitrant spirit of the Polish nation and is certain it will prevail. Similar histories, one might argue, but very different symbolic representations – in spite of the fact that godliness and divinity today could be argued to play a greater role in Poland than in Hungary and that pious subjection is nothing alien to the Polish *habitus*. We need to be able to explain this apparent contradiction. Why are Hungarians portrayed as victims, Poles as victors? Why do Hungarians implore God to intervene on their behalf, while Poles take destiny into their own hands? Why are Hungarians symbolized as submissive and Poles as vengeful?

As so often, I would argue, the answer can be found in history. Not in material history, economic history or even the history of wars, but in the interpreted and thus symbolic history of significant turning points. In one sense, it is not difficult to present a case for the history of Poland being just as tragic as that of Hungary, possibly even worse. Yet, the anthem tells a different story: we are a proud people, we have survived, we will conquer and prevail. Why? I submit that the solution can be found if we look back a century, to the end of WWI and the Versailles Treaty. Prior to that, Poland and the Polish territories had been divided between Russia, Prussia and the Habsburgs – in fact, it is not possible to speak of a Polish nation-state between 1795 and 1918, though the idea of Poland and Polish culture persisted. WWI changed all that, through a combination of external events (the defeat of Germany, the demise of the Habsburg Empire,

---

of the Third Hungarian Republic in 1989.The lyrics are a prayer beginning with the words "Isten, áldd meg a magyart" (God bless the Hungarians).

"Mazurek Dąbrowskiego (Dąbrowski's Mazurka), in English officially known as "Poland Is Not Yet Lost," is the national anthem of Poland. The lyrics were written in 1797 by Józef Wybicki, in Northern Italy, two years after the Third Partition of Poland erased the Polish–Lithuanian Commonwealth from the map. It was originally meant to boost the morale of Polish soldiers serving under General Jan Henryk Dąbrowski's Polish Legions that served with Napoleon's French Revolutionary Army in the Italian campaigns of the French Revolutionary Wars. The music is an unattributed mazurka. When Poland re-emerged as an independent state in 1918, "Dąbrowski's Mazurka" became its de facto national anthem. It was officially adopted as the formal national anthem of Poland in 1926.

and the Bolshevik revolution) and the determined efforts of the Polish independence movement led by Marshal Józef Piłsudski.[3] Poland regained its integrity and sovereignty and was re-instated to its long-lost standing among independent nation-states. The outcome of WWI was a triumph for the Poles in that respect, although they were to play a role as an international bone of contention and a territory up for imperial grabs once more in WWII. More on that later.

The Hungarian situation following WWI was almost the exact opposite (Hedetoft 2020, chapter 9). Having sided in the War with the German losers, Hungary was left in a humiliating position in the Versailles Treaty negotiations and eventually lost about 70 % of its territory and about a third of its ethnic population (about 2 million) at the Treaty of Trianon, which it was compelled to sign on June 4, 1920. From having been a junior part – but nevertheless one part – of the Austro-Hungarian dual monarchy before the War and Budapest an admired cultural center for decades, the country was severely reduced, chopped to pieces after WWI. It was clearly a national tragedy at the time (which Woodrow Wilson, the American President responsible for the founding texts of the Versailles Treaty, disagreed with, but in vain), a historical turning

---

3 Józef Piłsudski has given rise to one oft-mentioned variant of Polishness, ie the friendly and international patriotism of Poland, frequently contrasted with the inward-looking and bellicose ideology of Roman Dmowski, an independence politician of the 1920s and 30s, said to be far more nationalistic than Piłsudski, and right now very popular among populists and other right-wing Polish nationalists. He was the co-founder of Narodowa Demokracja (National Democracy), also known as Endecja, and he has been frequently referred to as the father of Polish nationalism. In his 1927 book *Kościół, Naród I Państwo* (*Church, Nation and State*), Dmowski wrote: "Catholicism is not a supplement to Polishness; it is somehow rooted in its very existence and to an important extent it even forms its existence. The attempt to separate Catholicism from Polishness in Poland, cutting off the nation from religion and Church, would mean destroying the very existence of the nation. The Polish State is a Catholic State. This is not because the vast majority of its inhabitants are Catholics or because of the percentage of Catholics. From our point of view, Poland is Catholic in the full sense of the word, because we are a national state, and our people is a Catholic people." Throughout most of his life, he was the chief ideological opponent of Piłsudski and of the latter's vision of Poland as a multinational federation against German and Russian imperialism (see Kossert 2011). In my view, the contrast between the two positions may well be exaggerated (Piłsudski was quite aggressive, and Dmowski more peaceful than often believed), but it is beyond doubt that the division has serious consequences for contemporary Polish debates on national identity, religiosity, and Polish sovereignty. For further clarification, see Dabrowski 2011 and Wandycz 1990.

point, one which today's Orbánism exploits politically to the full, by casting Hungary as the innocent victim of evil powers. This political cleansing process continues with the no less revisionist interpretation of WWII and Hungary's role therein, symbolized by the monument erected in 2014 in Budapest's Liberty Square (*Szabadság tér*), dedicated to the victims of the German occupation and portraying Hungary as the Archangel Gabriel about to be ravished by the German Eagle. The extent of historical revision was so striking that ordinary citizens have felt it necessary to put in place a 'counter monument' in front of the official one, a 'living memorial' to the victims of WWII killings and its perpetrators. These perpetrators comprise the Hungarian government in two versions: first, as the Horthy regime collaborating with the Nazis; and after 1944 the Arrow Cross party, the Hungarian Nazi movement instated by the Hitler regime in Germany after Horthy was removed from power in Operation Panzerfaust. Both were undoubtedly in varying ways complicit in killing and exporting Hungarian Jews and making Hungary comport itself in accordance with Nazi politics (Eröss 2016), and Hungary had clearly compromised itself through its long-term collaboration with Germany throughout the 1930s as well, pursuing its own revanchist aims while attempting to regain lost territories and lost standing. The failure of this endeavor entailed, not an acknowledgement of historical guilt, but rather an additional layer to the Hungarian symbolization of itself as the archetypally innocent victim of historical injustice and evil foreign design.

Poland's WWII experience was qualitatively different from the Hungarian. The country became one of the central battlegrounds in the showdown between the Nazis, the Allies and the Soviet Union, and had to suffer ravages, death and destruction on a gigantic scale. Its reaction to all this horror was significantly different from the Hungarian attempts at revanchism and its concomitant self-pity on a national scale. Poland never surrendered or bowed to the Nazis. Poland set up its own underground government vying with direct Nazi rule; it formed its own military brigades, which actively and successfully aided and abetted Allied fighting against the Germans; and Polish forces fought under Allied command, e.g. the Polish II Corps, nucleus of the Polish Armed Forces in the West, which was active in the Italian campaign. There were no doubt individual Poles taking a less reputable part in the German concentration camps on Polish soil, but there was no collective and official Polish collaboration with the Nazis, but a lot of determined resistance.[4]

---

4   This is the rational substance to PiS's (*Prawo i Sprawiedliwość – Law and Justice,*

Nevertheless, the outcome of the war was much the same for Poland and Hungary; they both ended up on the Soviet side and became puppet states within the Warsaw pact. Their national mentalities, on the other hand, were configured in very different ways, in harmony with their national anthems. And the symbols put in place to express their respective historical hurt (their symbolic politics of memorization and forgetfulness – Maryniak 2019– and their utilization of religiosity) were hence qualitatively different too.

Sovietism, its breakdown, and the reinvention of national identities

What I refer to as Sovietism in the two countries is meant to indicate the largely indirect but still powerful and unquestionable dominance by the Soviet Union and its ideological worldview in Hungary and Poland between 1945 and 1989, as well as the occasional shift to direct oppression in times of revolt and 'disobedience.' Both countries were forced to act as advanced puppet states, go-betweens and potential territories of war in the struggle between NATO and the Warsaw Pact. Their regimes of suppression reacted to the changing political modalities of the Moscow Center, moving from aggressive Stalinism and its celebration of collectivization and the New Soviet Individual (*Homo Sovieticus*); over Khrushchev's more lenient form of hegemony; the Brezhnev Doctrine, the direct confrontation with the Americans and the various SALT treaties; Andropov and the Second Cold War during the first part of the 1980s; only to finalize in the regime of Gorbachev and the eventual emasculation and breakdown of the Soviet interpretation of communism in 1989. Both countries adapted to these changes as best they could, sometimes quietly, at others more vociferously and rebelliously. There were even direct parallels of timing and revolt, most clearly in 1956, when major protests and riots occurred in both countries, in Poznan (June) and Budapest (October-November), respectively, both trying to take advantage of the 'thaw' that had followed the death of Stalin and the liberalization attendant upon the 20th Communist Congress (see Applebaum 2012, Chapter 18: "Revolutions"). Both rebellions were crushed, in Poland by the Polish army, in Hungary, and with graver consequences, through the direct military intervention of Soviet forces, which led to the death

---

Poland's governing party) recent attempt to criminalize any reference to the Holocaust taking place on Polish soil as being due to the action and participation of Poles. This has since been downgraded to a civil offence, largely because of the pressure exerted by the European and international community.

of some 2500 Hungarians and the enforced exile of about 200000 more.[5] At
the same time, Poland experienced 'the Polish October,' the reformation of its
internal life and the regime of Gomulka, which managed to liberalize the Polish
economy and slacken ties to the Soviet Union. For Hungary, the result was
disastrous, leading two years after to the hanging of Imre Nagy, Prime Minister
at the time of revolution in 1956.[6] While in Poland, the resistance of the Poznan
workers actually involved some positive results. Hungarian martyrdom had
been strengthened, Polish resistance rewarded. The fact that the ensuing Kádár
regime in Hungary had much the same mollifying consequences for Hungary's
relations with the Soviet Union as Gomulka's in Poland matters less in terms of
national identities and the symbolization thereof. Thus, in Poland we find the
proud and defiant Poznan Monument (Pomnik Poznańskiego Czerwca 1956;
Monument of the Poznań June 1956), erected in 1981 in memory of the 1956
uprising (and listing the years of subsequent revolts as well). While in Hungary
monuments commemorating the 1956 uprising are couched in a more pitiful
modality, like the image of Péter Mansfeld, a teenager executed in 1959 immediately after his eighteenth birthday for taking an active part in the fighting and
now represented as a martyr.[7]

  In addition, there has recently been a heated discussion about the new
location for a statue of Imre Nagy, since 1989 placed on a bridge close to and
overlooking the Parliament building, but now moved by the Government to
Jaszai Mari Square, much further away from the central part of Budapest –
possibly in deference to building positive relations with Russia. This would be
unthinkable in Poland. Imagining the Polish government making gestures to
keep Moscow happy would be pure fantasy and would run counter to everything

---

5   Interestingly, the Hungarian revolution started at the Budapest statue of Josef Bem,
    a national hero of both Hungary and Poland, whose contributions to Poland's
    insurrections against Russia (1812–1830) and Hungary's War of Independence (1848–
    49) are commemorated in both countries.

6   Though only just – instated for tactical reasons by Khrushchev on October 23, and
    accepted by the rebels because, though loyal to Sovietism, he was more in line with
    their interests than Mátyás Rákosi, a staunch Stalinist in every sense of that word.
    For a detailed account of the Soviet atrocities in Hungary between 1948 and 1958,
    see Sebestyen 2006, which, though somewhat colored by its revulsion at the Soviet
    leaders and their Hungarian henchmen, nevertheless paints a vivid, authentic and
    empirically documented picture of the state of hypocrisy, terror and personalized
    back-stabbing in this decade.

7   It was not unusual for kids and teenagers to take part in the 1956 revolution, at least
    in Budapest, and many were killed. See Sebestyen 2006, 151.

Image 1: Péter Mansfeld

that Poland represents. In Poland, incidentally, the words 'O Boga' (For God) were added in 2006 to the Poznan Monument, reflecting the increasing sacralization of national identity during the age of populism. The relations of the two populist regimes to the past of their countries are thus in significant ways polar opposites, in spite of the fact that they react in similar manner to membership of the EU, record temporally identical turning point (eg 1918, 1945, 1956, 1990, 2006/7, 2010, 2015), and largely pursue the same nationalizing strategies (see Conclusion). The difference is apparent in their use of national days of remembrance and their religious representations of nationhood. As an example, let us contrast June 4 (Hungary) and November 11 (Poland).

"Áldozatak vagyunk" (We are victims)[8] vs. 'My chcemy Boga' (We want God!): victimization and defiance

The two days are not formally comparable, the Polish being the official Independence Day and the Hungarian a relatively new public celebration, introduced by Viktor Orbán and the incoming Fidesz Goverment on assuming power in 2010.9 Other dates might have been chosen, all mentioned in the Hungarian Constitution: March 15, in memory of the 1848–1849 Revolution; August 20, the day celebrating the founding of the state and its founder, Szent István (Saint Stephen); or October 23, memorizing the 1956 revolt. These – and other dates – all have a longer record than June 4 and tell important symbolic stories about the Hungarian experience. However, June 4 encapsulates the essence of modern Hungary, both for being so recent and for pointing us back to the national tragedy which Orbán wants to hold up to the people – in order to overcome it, certainly, but also in order to keep the same people in a state of permanent emergency, victimization and historical bitterness: Trianon 1920.

June 4 was the day of the signing of the Trianon Treaty 100 years ago; thus, it is not a date for jubilant celebration but for mourning and pessimism. This was the day Greater Hungary broke down, only to be replaced by a much smaller and more insignificant national entity. The Polish November 11 dates back to

---

8   My abbreviation of the last two lines of the national anthem: 'Megbűnhődte már e nép/A múltat s jövendőt!' –'They who have suffered for all sins/Of the past and of the future!'.

9   The full name of the governing party is Fidesz – Magyar Polgári Szövetség (Hungarian Civic Alliance).

almost the same post-WWI period: it is the day Marshal Józéf Piłsudski took control of the reborn Polish state and is hence a day of triumph and real celebration. It was formally abolished as the official Independence Day by the post-WWII Communist regime, but continued as a public day of protest and was restored to its official status after the breakdown of Sovietism in 1989. The day is marked by all the pomp and circumstance imaginable and follows a rigid ceremonial pattern, where the main actors are the President, the Prime Minister and the Minister for National Defense, the Armed Forces and the Honor Guard, Service Commanders, diplomats, army veterans, and the Tomb of the Unknown Soldier. The ceremony comprises the unfurling of the Polish flag, the reading of semi-sacral national texts, the singing of the National Anthem, the playing of the Armed Forces Memorial Fanfare, and wreath-laying at the Tomb. It is all very ritualistic, highly symbolic, pitched to infuse national emotions and popular pride in the joyous event: the recuperation of national/state sovereignty and independence.

Since 2006, however, November 11 has taken on a different character. Nationalist, aggressive and sometimes extremist groups have organized marches of independence, which have increasingly led to violence, rioting and vandalism. As well expressed by Marta Kotwas and Jan Kubik:

> Along the way, however, the manner of celebrating changed as far-right rallies and marches were gaining popularity, attracting publicity, and growing in numbers. This process accelerated after the unveiling of a statue of Dmowski on Warsaw's Rozdroże Square on 10 November 2006. The symbolic space of Warsaw acquired a powerful marker whose presence created a new opportunity to invigorate the Dmowskiite tradition, narrowly nationalistic in tone by contrast to Piłsudskiite open patriotism. As other observers have also noted, 2006 constitutes a critical juncture after which the game of symbolic politics in Poland changed, with far-right narratives and performances acquiring new visibility. At their core were ceremonial invocations of extreme nationalism increasingly intertwined with the nationalized version of Polish Catholicism (Kotwas and Kubik 2019).

Concurrently, since 2012 the President has organized a parallel march, which is presented as a continuation of the official rituals. However, neither that nor counterdemonstrations by liberalists, anti-fascists or 'rainbow' propagandists (Lewis and Waligorska 2019 calls it 'the war of symbols') have been able to outmanoeuver the march organized by extreme nationalists, in terms of numbers or media attention and thus visibility. This became obvious in 2017, when the unofficial march was able to attract more than 60000 participants under the slogan "We Want God" ("My Chcemy Boga"), which also indicates the addition of a strong religious/Catholic element to the celebration of Polish nationalism on November 11.[10] Some of the participants chanted slogans like "Catholic Poland, not secular," others "Death to enemies of the fatherland," while yet others vilified the LGBT movement, calling it anti-Polish and anti-religious. The PiS Government, meanwhile, officially condemned the radicalism, but clandestinely condoned it, and obviously must also take responsibility for the rise and popularity of the phenomenon, since it falls perfectly in line with its own nationalist preferences. The rioting and violence has since abated, but numbers have soared, a total of 250000 people having participated in the 2018 centenary celebrations (which was a combination of the presidential and the public marches) and probably similar numbers in 2019, though here the authorities tried to dissociate themselves from the right-wing extremists. Interestingly, Robert Bakiewicz, the head of one of the organizing groups, in 2017 said that "[w]e are recalling the fighting church, which for centuries was the keystone and fundament of Europe. We want to show Catholicism not as a faith of weakness, but as a faith of strong people." "We have to return to our roots. Our world has abandoned God and Christianity." It is not surprising that one of the slogans chanted by some was "No to the European Union."[11]

There is hardly any resemblance between all this Polish symbolism and the commemoration of June 4 in Hungary. The Fourth of June is a day of mourning and lament, not one of festivity and celebrations. It is commemorated quietly and mainly through speeches, monuments and statues around the country, not in boisterous events or public demonstrations. It is infused with humility and a spirit of tragedy. There are no marches, no joyousness, but a spirit of victimization, bitterness and (occasionally) revanchism. Viktor Orbán's speech to a gathering of youthful participants of the Rákóczi Group[12] and public officials on June 4, 2019, is symptomatic. It took place, not in Budapest, but in the

---

10 The slogan alludes to a religious song with the same name, which is a prayer for the blessing mediated by the 'Saint Lady' (Mary) for all social strata. Originally a French song ('Nous voulons Dieu'), written in 1882, and translated into Polish. In connection with the 2017 demonstration, the slogan became adopted by right-wing militants and harnessed to political and nationalist ends.

11 See Pikulicka-Wilczewska 2017; Koper and Pempel 2019.

12 Francis II 9.Rákóczi (March 27, 1676 – April 8, 1735) was a Hungarian nobleman and leader of the Hungarian uprising against the Habsburgs in 1703–11 as the prince of the Estates Confederated for Liberty of the Kingdom of Hungary. He was also Prince of Transylvania, an Imperial Prince, and a member of the Order of the Golden Fleece. Youth organizing under his name symbolically send an aggressively nationalist message about their intentions and objectives.

remote town of Sátoraljaújhely on the Hungarian-Slovak border, once divided
by the Treaty of Trianon between Slovakia and Hungary. Thus, the location was
deliberately and symbolically chosen to address audiences on both sides of the
border, and, in the spirit of irredentism, also Hungarians living in Slovakia.
Orbán opens in a mood characterized by both sadness and defiance:

> It is now nine years since we decided that the most gloomy day of our national history
> should not just be depressing, but should also give us energy, bring us closer together.
> Since 2010, the anniversary of Trianon has been elevated from a day of sorrow due to
> the division of Hungarian-ness into pieces to a celebration of national togetherness.
> 99 years ago the bells tolled for us. They tolled for us, for our survival. Their mes-
> sage was that we wanted to live in spite of the brutal peace dictate, that we wanted to
> live as Hungary, and we are going to strive to create the legal, cultural and economic
> conditions for our national togetherness. What was once unjust remains so to the end
> of time. Time may heal wounds, but not the amputation."

Trianon was an act of injustice! We were victimized! However, we need to sap
power and energy from the tragedy for unity and resurrection. There is hope
for Hungary and Hungarians, within and outside Hungary, as he subsequently
makes clear in evocative, affective language:

> You probably will have difficulties imagining it, but when I was your age, this kind
> of camp was impossible. At that time, schools would keep quiet about the fact that
> no matter in what direction you might happen to cross the Hungarian border, you
> would nonetheless meet Hungarian people. And today we have reached the point
> that it is once again natural that Hungarian youth from Oberland, Siebenbürgen, the
> Carpathian Ukraine, from Banat and Batschka[13] as well as from the diaspora reflect
> on their common future together. Previously this was the foolhardy dream of cou-
> rageous patriots. Thirty years ago, these courageous patriots founded the Rákóczi
> Group, and this started a completely new chapter in Hungarian politics. The founders
> desired that the time of division and dissipation should be replaced by a time of unifi-
> cation and nation-building in the life of Hungarian-ness."

And he continues to address the young patriots directly:

> Dear Youth, – The earth we stand on was the property of Ferenc Rákóczi II, one of the
> greatest Hungarians, who took the Hungarian side against foreign powers, the side
> of a Hungary which was being pushed back on its own home soil. He subordinated
> everything to this goal: his total fortune, all his landed property, his rank, his honor,

---

13 Regions once belonging variously to Serbia, Austria, Romania and Hungary, now
    mainly contained within Vojvodina in Serbia. It is interesting that Orbán chooses to
    refer to localities that were once Hungarian (in whole or in part) and thus to manifest
    political irredentism as central to his program of Hungarian-ness.

and even his own life. And he proclaimed this goal on his pennant: 'Cum Deo pro patria et libertate! With God for fatherland and freedom!' Fighting and working for a free and Hungarian home, trusting in the help of God. This is a pledge that commits the rest of us to this very day. This work awaits you. Travel the world, collect a multitude of experiences, and never forget that your home is waiting for your return. Contribute your talent and your work to the great collective effort of Hungary. You should not harbour any doubts: together we will again achieve great, strong and successful victories. – Long live Hungary!"[14]

Orbán thus does his utmost to functionalize the day of memory as the day of the future regeneration of a Hungary of strength, greatness and success, while appealing to the young generation to carry the torch. In other words, he appeals to these youthful Hungarians to stop thinking of themselves as pitiful victims and martyrs of a woeful history of defeats and rise to another kind of challenge. However, he does this by reference to exactly that, by keeping the memory of Trianon and everything it stands for alive in the popular imagination. The symbolic dialectic between humiliation and victory, past and future, is conspicuous. June 4 is in one sense an empty, void, zero signifier, and in another replete with symbolic promise of a coming future regeneration: with God for the nation and for freedom! Religiosity plays a role in Hungary too, but more marginally than in Poland. Where "We Want God!" symbolically encapsulates the entire Polish dream of independence, victory and identity, in Hungary God is imagined as a helper, protector and guardian angel, but not as the determining symbol and unifying force that it is in Poland. Even where Hungary is closest to ridding itself of its victimization shackles, it nevertheless is unable fully to make the transition away from its position of inferiority. *Áldozatak vagyunk* is still the underlying trope. The strength conjured up by Orbán is still not a present reality but a project for the future. In the meantime, he appeals to the vanguard to gather experiences, travel the world, and return to rebuild their nation-state. This also throws the alleged inward-lookingness of Hungarian populism into relief: it is de facto not blind to the outside world but wants to take advantage of it for the benefit of Hungary. Thus, Orbán eagerly enters into cooperative arrangements with the USA, Russia, China, Turkey and the Visegrád countries – and other EU countries to boot, where Polish populism comes across as more choosey, proud and self-centered. Russia is out, the EU looked at with suspicion, and only the USA (for reasons of security) and the

---

14 My translation. The entire text (in German) is here: https://www.kormany.hu/en/the-prime-minister/the-prime-minister-s-speeches/viktor-orbans-rede-am-tag-der-nationalen-zusammengehorigkeit. Accessed December 15, 2019.

four Visegrád countries (for reasons of culture and economics) curry favor with the Polish regime.

Nevertheless, although the two countries may have pursued different pathways from the past into the present and the future, we should not overlook that they have reached similar conclusions as regards their position on European cooperation and generally their view of themselves, their identity and the outside world. Polish and Hungarian populism is not identical, their histories and national imaginaries over the past century are different, but they are converging around much the same political and cultural conclusions to their historical dilemmas. This convergence is also visible in the landscape of symbolism. Let us cast a look at the imagery of the national birds of prey: the White Crowned Eagle of Poland and the Mythical Turul of Hungary.

The Eagle and the Turul

The symbolism of the two birds is evocative. They are both undoubtedly national symbols. They are both predatory birds – one real (the Eagle, seemingly iconic) and the other more mystical and symbolic (the Turul). They are also both images of statehood and sovereignty. The Polish Eagle is even adorned with a Crown – a particularity which has been 'doffed and donned' by various regimes.[15] The Communists removed it, but it has been reinstated after 1989 and now appears on all Polish currency bills and on a number of other images celebrating the (new-found) Polish sovereignty, e.g. on the following one commemorating the centenary of Polish independence in 2018 (Image 2).

This is not true for the Hungarian Turul, which nevertheless comes across as a virulent, determined and aggressive defender of Hungarian-ness, culturally, historically and politically. The entrance to the Castle District in Buda, to the east of the so-called Habsburg Steps, sports a totemic Turul on one pillar.

---

15 In the Middle Ages we find the eagle without the crown (Piast dynasty). The eagle with the crown is the emblem of the Polish Lithuanian Commonwealth (Jagiellonian dynasty): Rzeczpospolita Obojga Narodów. See also Hałas 2016, 134–39, for a discussion of the debate about 'crowning the eagle' in Sejm, the Polish parliament, following the fall of communism. It is worth noting that also in Hungary there is a connection between the Turul and the Holy Crown, which is mentioned in the Fundamental Law of Hungary of 2011, embodying "the constitutional unity of Hungary's statehood and unity of the nation." The Turul monument in Tatabanya is portrayed with a Holy Crown on the Turul's head. The link has also been made by Viktor Orbán himself, as pointed out in Kürti 2015. See also the main text below. On the generic history and symbolics of the Holy Crown, see László 2003.

Image 2: The Crowned Eagle of Poland

It symbolizes not only present-day Hungary, but the continuity of Magyar history, stretching far back as it does to the advent of the seven Magyar tribes and their commander, Arpád, who is said to have led them into the Carpathian Basin more than a 1000 years ago (Image 3).

It can even be found hawkishly protecting memorials dedicated to the humiliating experience of Trianon (Image 4)[16].

The warrior-like image of Hungary is also present in the statue of the first King of Hungary, Szent István (Saint Stephen), in Heroes' Square in Budapest, equipped as he is there with a sword, a crown and, with his left hand, holding the typically Magyar double-bar cross up high. The statue perfectly depicts the union of royalty, religion and armed resistance.

---

16 I thank my research student, Bendegúz Barna, for permission to use the following private photo. The text reads: "Always stay faithful to your native country, O Hungarian! (Renovated on the occasion of the 11th centenary of the conquest 1996, August 20). The Tragedy of the Nation, Trianon 1920. 'We shall never forget!' (Erected by the citizens of Emöd, 4 June 2008)." The first sentence is a direct reference to the opening lines of the *Szózat*, Hungary's second but unofficial national anthem, written in 1836 by Mihály Vörösmarty.

Image 3: The Hungarian Turul

As might be expected, the Turul has been put to use by Viktor Orbán. András Bózoki mentions one of these instances as follows:

> The concept of political nation gave way to the ethnic idea of national consciousness. When inaugurating the monument of 'National Togetherness,' Viktor Orbán voiced his conviction that the Turul bird is the ancient image into which the Hungarians are born. Echoing Jobbik, he stated that 'from the moment of our birth, our seven tribes enter into an alliance, our king Saint Stephen establishes a state, our armies suffer a defeat at the Battle of Mohács, and the Turul bird is the symbol of national identity of the living, the deceased, and the yet-to-be-born Hungarians' (Bózoki 2016).

Thus, the Turul is invoked as the quasi-religious symbol gluing all Hungarians together across generations and protecting them from the threat of outside aggression.

What is interesting about this imagery in Poland and Hungary is how closely aligned it seems to be. Not only are both nation-states symbolized by birds, but by birds of prey, which are pictured in much the same way, as defenders, protectors and potential aggressors if the countries and their cultures are attacked. In addition, they have been reinstated to new and more foregrounded positions in the imagologies of the nation-states (Beller and Leerssen 2007) relatively

Image 4: The Turul and the Fourth of June

recently and concurrently with the rise to prominence and power of PiS and Fidesz, respectively. Connotations are different, though. In Poland, the White Crowned Eagle proudly represents the obstinate refusal of Poland to succumb to outside aggression and invasions and is totally in line with the modality of the national anthem. In Hungary, on the other hand, the Turul is a constant reminder of the struggle of Hungarians against the menace of imminent defeat, but also of their will to survive, their belief in future successes, and recently of a new-found national spirit of self-confidence. Waving goodbye to victimization is the current path of the Hungarian nation, riddled though it is with paradoxes of the past and injected with memories of defeat. The Turul is a predatory bird, but it is also a bird of dreams, a fantasy. Hungary still has not managed to put its injured past behind it and create a culture not just of survival, but optimism and progress too.

Conclusions: symbolization and the populist context

The symbolization of identity is, as I have tried to show, not a new phenomenon in either nation-state, but an integral part of the national imaginaries. However, it has taken on a new, more intense meaning in the age of populism (broadly speaking the last 15 years) and has followed much the same time sequence of turning points. Both countries entered the EU in 2004. The first PiS Government was between 2005 and 2007. The breakdown of the Socialist-Liberal Hungarian Government, led by Ferenc Gyurcsány, de facto occurred in 2007, though the Government did not resign until 2009. The Polish Smolensk flight disaster, which like nothing else fueled the flames of anti-Russian feelings in Poland and provided the decisive moment for the PiS takeover in 2015, took place in 2010. This was also the year of the Fidesz election victory; since then, the party and Viktor Orbán have ruled Hungary and experienced further successes in 2015 and 2018. Developments have thus run largely in parallel, aided and abetted by the collaboration of the four Visegrád countries and occasional meetings of the two heads of government/state (one formal, Orbán; the other real, Kaczyński).[17] They are both EU skeptical. They are both intent on strengthening the sovereignty and national identity of their countries. And they both use the history and histrionics of national myths and symbols in order to mobilize their people against liberalism, foreign 'conspiracies' and inside threats – though the backcloth, connotations and popular *habitus* are decidedly different and their personal charisma rests on very different public appearances and rhetorical performances.[18]

What is most remarkable, however, is the difference between the relationship of populist mentalities and economic interests in the two Central European countries. In this regard, Orbánism on the face of its makes more 'sense' than the Polish populist variation. Based on the many instances of victimization that Hungary has experienced, it is somehow understandable that there is a desire to

---

17 See for instance jmr 2018; Bayer 2018.
18 Orbán being full of rhetorical pomp, energy and bombast, while Kaczyński comes across as confident, but diffident and introvert.

Image 5: Two populist leaders, Viktor Orbán and Jarosław Kaczyński

stabilize the state, its sovereignty, the confidence and loyalty of the people, and its economic performance at the same time – though the forms and symbols of this 'illiberal democracy' can and should be criticized. Particularly significant is the fact that the transitional attempts to enter the world of normal European democracies following 1990 and the accession to the EU demonstrably failed (Hedetoft 2020, chapter 9). This to a very large extent accounts for the successes of Fidesz and for the relatively pragmatic approach of Orbánism to international cooperation, including membership of the EU. As long as it benefits Hungary, it is acceptable, it would seem, and Orbán's rhetorical adventurism – raging against the EU, Soros, and domestic liberal opponents – is balanced by instances of pragmatic, non-ideological adaptation and an astute eye for strengthening the economic and security foundation of the Hungarian nation-state through deals with many other countries, including Russia and China.[19]

Poland on the other hand presents a somewhat different picture. Not only is it not willing to make compromises with its Russian neighbors, but it is continuously and demonstrably hostile to any kind of interaction with Russia. It builds up its military capacity, cooperates with NATO and the USA, and strengthens its anti-Russian defenses and border vigilance. And like Hungary, it is highly

---

19 As an example, see Gorondi 2019 on the visit of Putin to Budapest in October 2019.

skeptical towards deeper EU collaboration and violates some of the liberal-democratic values of the Union to the extent that it has been excluded from voting in the European Council (pursuant to paragraph 7 of the EU Treaty, which the EU has activated). Some would argue that this populist recalcitrance is due to Poland's size and image of its own sovereign power capacity. For all its plausibility, this kind of explanation does not account for the abnormal feature of recent Polish history, ie that, unlike Hungary, Poland cannot be argued to have paid an economic price for membership, nor has it been subjected to anything similar to the domestic political problems that decisively strengthened Fidesz between 2007 and 2009. In fact, the Polish economy has been thriving due to EU membership; Poles are, by and large, supporters of EU membership; and the country did well on all economic parameters between 2006 and 2015, when PiS won their second political victory and took over from the liberal Civic Platform.[20] This is a riddle to many observers: how come a successful economic process should risk being thwarted mid-way by populist preferences?

I have tried to explain this paradox in my recent book (Hedetoft 2020). Briefly, populists tend to reverse the relationship between economics and identity/sovereignty, giving priority to the latter and treating the former as a dependent variable – unlike mainstream, 'normal' political thinking in liberal democracies, which prioritizes economics, growth and the interests of the private entrepreneur. It is this reversal of values and policies that we witness in Poland, strongly supported by the ecclesiastical community: the Catholic Church and its ideological spokespeople. The vociferous proclamations of and adherence to Polishness, the symbolic manifestations of identity and sovereignty that this article has reviewed, are all rooted in and find their explanation in this basic fact. Identity matters, nationalism matters, and it all trumps liberal preferences. This does not mean that people are not concerned with their material well-being; the populist reaction encompasses a critique of the globalist economy for creating greater divides and more inequality than ever before, thus neglecting the welfare of ordinary citizens. This is mirrored by the PiS policies for higher child benefits, lower taxes, medical screenings for people over 40, and earlier retirement age – all pledges which have been honored. Concurrently, it gives these new elites – which is what they are despite their rejection of the notion – the latitude to propagate their nationalist and religious policies of identity, history, sovereignty and, where necessary, abnegation and loyalty.[21] This

---

20 See BBC News 2015.

21 As clearly put in this *DW* article dating back to the October 2019 Elections: "But there's more at stake than just money. 'PiS has restored the people's dignity,' says a taxi

the real paradox and the ultimate *cul de sac* of these new nationalists: the symbolic politics of populism returns the people to the nation-state, its identity, its myths and symbols, as if they were a solution to problems that were originally created by the same entity.

References

Anderson, Benedict (1983) *Imagined Communities*. London: Verso.

Applebaum, Anne (2012) *Iron Curtain. The Crushing of Eastern Europe 1944–1956*. New York: Doubleday.

Atkin, Albert (2010) "Peirce's Theory of Signs." First published 2006; substantive revision 2010. Stanford Encyclopedia of Philosophy. See https://plato.stanford.edu/entries/peirce-semiotics/. Accessed December 18, 2019.

Bayer, Lili (2018) "The new communists." *Politico*, May 5. See https://www.politico.eu/article/new-communists-hungary-poland-viktor-orban-jaroslaw-kaczynski/. Accessed February 18, 2020.

BBC News (2015) *Poland elections: Conservatives secure decisive win*. October 26. See https://www.bbc.com/news/world-europe-34631826. Accessed December 18, 2019.

Beller, Manfred and Joep Leerssen (2007) *Imagology: The Cultural Construction and Literary Representation of National Characters: a Critical Survey*. Amsterdam: Rodopi.

Béni, Alexandra (2016) "Turul, the mystical Hungarian mythological bird." *Daily News Hungary*, April 4. See https://dailynewshungary.com/turul-the-mystical-hungarian-mythological-bird/. Accessed November 30, 2019.

Billig, Michael (1995) *Banal Nationalism*. London: Sage.

Bózoki, András (2016) "Mainstreaming the Far Right. Cultural Politics in Hungary." *Revue d'études comparatives Est-Ouest,* no 47, 87–116. See https://www.cairn.info/revue-revue-d-etudes-comparatives-est-ouest1-2016-4-page-87.htm. Accessed December 6, 2019.

Dabrowski, Patrice M. (2011) "Uses and Abuses of the Polish Past by Józef Piłsudski and Roman Dmowski." *The Polish Review* 56(1): 73–109.

---

driver from a village in eastern Poland. 'Symbols' is a key word here: national pride, heroism, sacrificing one's own advantages for the benefit of others — it's that kind of rhetoric that keeps cropping up in Jarosław Kaczyński 's party, and apparently it is in line with the zeitgeist. Even many people who don't have children of their own praise the introduction of publicly-funded child benefits" (Gwóźdź-Pallokat 2019).

Dittmar, Pia (2019) "Right-wing Populism and National Identity in Central and Eastern Europe." See https://hybridneighbourhood.com/2019/05/08/right-wing-populism-and-national-identity-in-central-and-eastern-europe/. Accessed December 19, 2019.

DW (no author) (2019) "Poland votes: PiS and its pact with the people." October 13. See https://www.dw.com/en/poland-votes-pis-and-its-pact-with-the-people/a-50804631. Accessed December 17, 2019.

Eröss, Ágnes (2016) "In memory of victims:" Monument and counter-monument in Liberty Square," *Hungarian Geographical Bulletin* 65(3): 237–254.

Gellner, Ernest (1983) *Nations and Nationalism.* Ithaca & London: Cornell University Press.

Gorondi, Pablo (2019) "Hungary's Orban: Good relations with Russia are a necessity." AP News. See https://apnews.com/e62669c80b9f4c43a3362c0891467c1a. Accessed December 18, 2019.

Gwozdz-Pallokat, Magdalena (2019) "Poland votes: PiS and its pact with the people." *DW*, 13 October. See https://www.dw.com/en/poland-votes-pis-and-its-pact-with-the-people/a-50804631. Accessed December 17, 2019.

Hałas, Elżbieta (2016) "Symbolic Transformations: State Symbolism and the Fall of Communism in Poland" in Elżbieta Hałas, (ed.), *Life-World, Intersubjectivity and Culture. Contemporary Dilemmas,* pp. Berne: Peter Lang.

Hedetoft, Ulf (1995) "Signs of Nations." Aldershot: Dartmouth.

_____ 2020. *Paradoxes of Populism. Troubles of the West and Nationalism's Second Coming.* New York and London: Anthem Press.

jmr (2018) "Memorial to Smolensk crash victims unveiled in Budapest," *Poland in Politics*, 6 April. See https://polandin.com/36693696/memorial-to-smolensk-crash-victims-unveiled-in-budapest. Accessed February 18, 2020.

Koper, Anna and Kacper Pempel (Reuters) (2019) "Polish far-right groups march on independence anniversary." November 11. See https://www.reuters.com/article/us-poland-independence-march/polish-far-right-groups-march-on-independence-anniversary-idUSKBN1XL22R. Accessed December 13, 2019.

Kossert, Andreas (2011) "Founding Father of Modern Poland and Nationalistic Antisemite: Roman Dmowski," in Rebecca Haynes and Martyn Rady, eds, *In the Shadow of Hitler: Personalities of the Right in Central and Eastern Europe.* London: I.B. Taurus, 89–105.

Kotwas, Marta & Jan Kubik (2019) "Symbolic Thickening of Public Culture and the Rise of Right-Wing Populism in Poland," *East European Politics & Societies* 33(2), 435–471. First published online April 16. Issue published May 1. See https://www.researchgate.net/publication/332460537_Symbolic_Thickening_of_Public_Culture_and_the_Rise_of_Right-Wing_Populism_in_Poland. Accessed December 13, 2019.

Kürti, László (2015) "Neoshamanism, National Identity and the Holy Crown of Hungary," Journal of Religion in Europe, 8:20, 235–260.

László, Peter (2003) "The Holy Crown of Hungary, Visible and Invisible," Slavonic and East European Review, 81(3): 421–510.

Lewis, Simon & Magdalena Waligórska (2019) "Introduction: Poland's Wars of Symbols," East European Politics and Societies, 33(2): 423–434. Article first published online: April 16. Issue published May 1. See https://journals.sagepub.com/doi/full/10.1177/0888325418821418. Accessed December 14, 2019.

Maryniak, Irena (2019) "Remembering to forget. Memory politics in Poland and Hungary." Eurozine, 21 May. See https://www.eurozine.com/remembering-to-forget/. Accessed November 11, 2019.

Müller, Jan-Werner (2016) What Is Populism? Philadelphia: University of Pennsylvania Press.

Peirce, Charles Sanders (1977) Semiotics and Significs, ed. Charles Hardwick. Bloomington, Indiana: Indiana University Press.

Pikulicka-Wilczewska, Agnieszka (2017) "Thousands of Nationalists, Fascists March in Warsaw," Al Jazeera, News Europe, 12 November. See https://www.aljazeera.com/news/2017/11/thousands-fascists-march-warsaw-171111052813155.html. Accessed December 20, 2019.

Sebeok, Thomas A. (1994) An Introduction to Semiotics. London: Pinter.

Sebestyen, Victor (2006) Twelve Days. Revolution 1956. London: Weidenfeld & Nicolson (Phoenix).

Short, Thomas L. (2007) Peirce's Theory of Signs. Cambridge: Cambridge University Press.

Wandycz, Piotr S. (1990) "Poland's Place in Europe in the Concepts of Piłsudski and Dmowski," East European Politics & Societies, 4(3): 451–468.

Website of the Hungarian Government (2019) "Viktor Orbáns Rede am Tag der Nationalen Zusammengehörigkeit" [Viktor Orbán's Speech on the Day of National Unity]. June 4, 2019, Sátoraljaújhely. See https://www.kormany.hu/en/the-prime-minister/the-prime-minister-s-speeches/viktor-orbans-rede-am-tag-der-nationalen-zusammengehorigkeit. Accessed December 15, 2019.

Anna Pless and Dick Houtman

Moral Traditionalism and Authoritarianism in Post-Communist Easter Europe: Converging Cultural Value Divides?

Abstract: Moral traditionalism-progressiveness and authoritarianism-libertarianism are often regarded as highly correlated and thus interchangeable value divides. Recent studies, however, suggest that the overlap between them is only typical of the most secularized societies of Western Europe and is an outcome of processes of secularization. In this chapter, we use the data from the EVS (1990–1999–2008) to study the link between the two value divides across 44 European countries. Our findings suggest that the two divides are virtually unrelated in societies with high levels of contextual traditionalism, as exemplified by Post-Communist Eastern Europe where the two represent different cultural-political dimensions.

Keywords: authoritarianism, cultural cleavage, Eastern Europe, moral traditionalism, secularization

Introduction

Despite the many differences between political cultures of countries in the East and West of Europe that attracted serious scholarly attention in recent decades, national political agendas all across Europe have in the same period become increasingly captured by cultural issues (Kriesi 2010; Norris, Inglehart 2019). Heated debates on such topics as justifiability of abortion and same-sex marriage, or immigration and ways to deal with it have been seen to polarize both political parties and the public at large in different societies all across Europe (Kiss 2016; Król, Pustułka 2018; McGraw 2018; Norris, Inglehart 2019; Rivkin-Fish 2018).

The aforementioned cultural issues are part and parcel of two different cultural value divides, referred to as authoritarian-libertarian and morally traditional-progressive in this chapter. The authoritarian-libertarian value divide is all-out secular and pertains to matters of law and order and immigration. It pits those who accept, or even embrace, cultural and ethnic diversity against those who understand the latter as a cause of major social problems (Flanagan, Lee 2003; Stubager 2008; Houtman 2003). The moral traditionalism-progressiveness value divide, on the other hand, refers to cultural, religious and political conflicts about the legitimacy of religiously inspired traditional moral values pertaining to sexuality, life and procreation, and the family (e.g. gay and lesbian rights, sexual freedom, abortion, euthanasia, and women's roles).

Many a political sociologist nowadays treats moral traditionalism-progressiveness and authoritarianism-libertarianism as largely equivalent value divides and blend them into one single value dimension that is central to a "new cultural cleavage" in politics (Kriesi 2010; Bornschier 2010). Recent findings, however, suggest that the overlap between the two divides is in fact a consequence of secularization and as such is only typical of the most sec-ularized and most culturally progressive societies of Western Europe (Pless, Tromp, Houtman 2020; De Koster, Van der Waal 2007). Given its apparent widespread support for both types of rightist stances (e.g. traditionalist and authoritarian), Post-Communist Eastern Europe, in comparison with the West, rather represents an opposite case that so far has not been studied.

In this chapter, we thus add Post-Communist Eastern Europe into the equation and study cross-national variation in the overlap between these two value divides across Europe, i.e. in the extent to which they are interre-lated or remain separate. Besides contributing theoretically and empirically to the existing literature on the so-called cultural cleavage across Europe, this chapter also highlights whether moral traditionalism-progressiveness and authoritarianism-libertarianism do at all overlap in Post-Communist Eastern Europe or rather tend to represent distinctive value dimensions.

In the remaining part of the chapter, we first discuss the two value divides in greater detail and then elaborate on how secularization has shaped the link between them. In the empirical part, we study how European countries differ in terms of both moral traditionalism and authoritarianism, and then analyze the overlap between the two value divides by means of statistical analysis of the survey data from the three waves of the European Values Study (1990, 1999, and 2008) for a pool of 44 European countries.

The cultural turn in politics

Two value divides: one religious and one secular

The first of the two value divides central to this chapter, *moral traditionalism–progressiveness*, pertains to the contrast between morally traditionalist and morally progressive stances about matters of life and death, family and gender roles, and sexuality, with attitudes towards abortion and homosexuality arguably standing out as most typical nowadays (McGraw 2018; Adamczyk, Pitt 2009). The traditionalist pole of this first value divide is closely linked to Christian religion (De Koster, Van der Waal 2007; Laythe, Finkel, Kirkpatrick 2001), with those concerned embracing religiously inspired "normative guiding standards that prescribe appropriate behavior and proscribe inappropriate behavior" in daily life (Storm 2016: 113). Those standards are understood as pre-given by a higher divine authority, as having proven their efficacy over centuries, and as more fundamental than man-made secular laws (De Koster, Van der Waal 2007).

The contrasting pole is represented by moral progressivists who tend to be non-religious and endorse the liberty to make individual lifestyle choices. They do as such not ground their moral principles in religion and do indeed reject the latter's notion of predefined social roles as well as its claims to unquestionable divine authority (Brown 2009; Houtman, Aupers, De Koster 2011). Such moral progressiveness sparks electoral support for the political parties of the New Left that have since the 1970s advocated individual liberty and opposed institutional coercion, be it by the churches, the state or corporations. Moral traditionalists, on the contrary, are triggered by the moral permissiveness this implies, which leads them to unite around Christian-Democratic or similar morally conservative parties (Knutsen 1989).

The second relevant value divide pertains to *authoritarianism–libertarianism*[1] and deals with the strictly secular matters of immigration and law and order. This divide is rooted not so much in religion, but rather in education (Stubager 2008; Houtman 2003; Van de Werfhorst, De Graaf 2004). The less educated are more likely to be authoritarian and are less likely to embrace immigration and the ethnic and cultural and diversity brought by it, since they tend to value order and control over individual freedom (Stubager 2010). This is why the less educated have become the happy hunting ground for New-Rightist political parties that boast anti-immigrant sentiments and populist zeal (Betz, Johnson 2004; Steenvoorden, Harteveld 2018). The more educated, on the contrary, tend

---

1   While there is a plethora of understandings of authoritarianism in the literature, most studies associate it with a preference for cultural sameness and cohesion that leads to unwillingness to accept cultural diversity. The other pole, represented by libertarianism, is associated with individual freedom in social and political sense but has nothing to do with the economic understanding of libertarianism (Stenner 2005; Lipset 1959; Flanagan, Lee 2003).

to be libertarian, i.e. to embrace ethnic and cultural diversity and to foreground individual liberty (Flanagan, Lee 2003; Stenner 2005).

A transformation of cleavage politics

The value divides of moral traditionalism versus progressiveness and authoritarianism versus libertarianism are typically understood as basically interchangeable, because they both reflect a more general opposition between cultural conservatives and cultural progressives (e.g. Flanagan, Lee 2003; Houtman 2003). The two are as such held to be jointly central to a newly emerged 'cultural cleavage' that has since the 1960s transformed Western politics.[2]

Traditionally, most research has been devoted to the so-called class cleavage, which pits a leftist-leaning working class against rightist-voting privileged classes in a political struggle that revolves around redistributive politics, i.e. the desirability of state intervention in matters of economic distribution between classes (Dalton 1996). In most Western democracies, however, the dominance of this class cleavage has shattered from the 1970s onwards due to cultural issues capturing Western political agendas, causing a steady decline of the traditional relationship between class and voting (Clark, Lipset 1991; Nieuwbeerta 1996; Elff 2007; Kriesi 2010).

According to Inglehart (1977), this transformation of cleavage politics is due to the coming of age in the 1960s of a new, so-called postmaterialist generation that has brought cultural issues pertaining to personal liberty, strengthening of democracy and acceptance of cultural diversity to the forefront of democratic politics. This coincided with the emergence of new types of political parties, from the 1970s onwards those of the New Left and from the 1980s onwards those of the New Right – parties that do not so much engage in conflict about economic distribution between classes, but foreground different, albeit contrasting, types of cultural values instead (Elff 2007; Kriesi 2010).

Unlike traditional 'old' left versus right class voting, class does not explain voting for these new types of parties. For while the middle class is indeed markedly more culturally progressive than the working class, this is not due to its class-based economic position, but rather to its education, which here operates as an indicator for cultural capital rather than class in an economic sense (Achterberg, Houtman 2006; Houtman 2003; Houtman, Achterberg 2010). In

---

2   Cleavage politics generally conceived refers to the prevalence of (1) structurally embedded social groups with (2) opposing values and/or interests that are (3) reflected in distinctive voting patterns (Lipset, Rokkan 1967).

combination with the increased political significance of cultural issues since the 1970s, this has led to a transformation of cleavage politics in the West, more specifically a proliferation of a new cultural cleavage with leftist-voting well educated pitted against rightist-voting low educated (Achterberg 2006; Van der Waal, Achterberg, Houtman 2007).

Where and why are the two value divides most strongly connected?

Because many empirical studies have demonstrated positive correlations between moral traditionalism–progressiveness and authoritarianism-libertarianism, the two value divides have often been combined to distinguish between cultural conservativism and cultural progressiveness more generally conceived (e.g. Flanagan, Lee 2003; Houtman 2003). Stenner (2009, 2005) has, however, demonstrated that the two can and should be distinguished theoretically and empirically, principally due to the fact that moral traditionalists are specifically triggered by violations of religiously inspired norms, while authoritarians are triggered by threats to sameness and conformity more generally. Indeed, the oft-found overlap between moral traditionalism and authoritarianism does at a closer and more critical look in fact stem from an overlap between their respective counterparts, i.e. moral progressiveness and basically secular libertarianism (De Koster, Van der Waal 2007). This is because moral progressiveness and secular libertarianism alike foreground individual liberty and oppose institutional coercion, be it by religious institutions or otherwise.

Based on the data from the Netherlands, one of the most secularized and morally progressive countries in the world (Norris, Inglehart 2004), De Koster and Van der Waal claim that the relationship between the two value divides is identical across national contexts. A recent study, however, suggests otherwise: it demonstrates that secularization has sparked a dual rejection of moral traditionalism and authoritarianism in the name of personal liberty, which leads the two value divides to coalesce (Pless, Tromp, Houtman 2020). Processes of secularization, understood as a decline both in religion's social significance and in numbers of religious individuals, thus erode the dominance of religiously informed moral traditionalism and increase the appeal of individual liberty and personal authenticity (Brown 2009; McLeod 2007).

The turn to moral progressiveness spawned by secularization therefore strengthens the overlap between our two value divides because it increases the numbers of those who oppose moral traditionalism and authoritarianism alike. This is why the most secularized Western European countries display the strongest overlaps between both value divides, while the correlation between the two is only weak or even completely absent in massively religious ones: because the former countries are less morally traditionalist than the latter (Pless, Tromp, Houtman 2020).

While secularization has thus been shown to make the two value divides overlap, existing studies tend to focus exclusively on Western Europe since Post-Communist Eastern European countries are quite different from the West in terms of secularization. Some of them have experienced religious revivals after the end of Communism, others have remained as secular as they were back then, and yet others have much like Western Europe been exposed to secularization (Norris, Inglehart 2004; Northmore-Ball, Evans 2016; Kulkova 2015).

In this chapter, we thus bring Post-Communist Eastern European countries into the equation and study whether this theory also holds for this region, more specifically, whether, how and why the two value divides are related there. In what follows, we first explore *whether* and *how* European countries from various regions differ in terms of levels of both moral traditionalism and authoritarianism, and also in terms of the overlap between the two value divides. We then move to study whether the two value divides do indeed show more overlap in more secular societies due to lower levels of contextual traditionalism there.

Moral traditionalism and authoritarianism across Europe

Measuring the two divides and their overlap

In the empirical part, we begin by studying how European countries differ in terms of both the two relevant value domains and the overlap between them. To do so, we use survey data from the 2008 wave of the European Values Study for 52,000 respondents from 44 European countries.

Moral traditionalism–progressiveness is measured through a scale constructed from the five questions that indicate whether a respondent finds homosexuality, abortion, euthanasia, divorce, and suicide justifiable.[3] These questions reflect respondent's moral stances on matters of life and death, procreation and family life. The resulting scale ranges from 0 to 10, with 10 indicating strongest moral

---

3   All items within the scale for moral traditionalism range from 0 (never justifiable) to 10 (always justifiable). Only those who responded to at least four of these five questions were assigned a score for moral traditionalism. The items were first standardized and then combined with equal weights. The scale is highly reliable with an overall Cronbach's Alpha of 0.81.

traditionalism. For each country, we then average individual scores to compute a measure of *contextual moral traditionalism*.

Authoritarianism–libertarianism is measured through one's attitudes towards immigration, and law and order. To construct a scale for it, we use five questions. Four of them measure one's opposition to having 1) immigrants, 2) people of different race, 3) Muslims, and 4) ex-criminals as neighbors, while an additional fifth one measures whether one thinks the native born should have priority in getting a job.[4] The scores were then transformed to range from 0 to 10, with 10 indicating strongest authoritarianism. *Contextual authoritarianism* is computed by averaging individual levels of authoritarianism within each country.

To measure how strong the link between the two value divides is (i.e. how much the two overlap), we compute zero-order correlations between the individual scales of moral traditionalism-progressiveness and authoritarianism-libertarianism for each of the countries separately.

National and regional differences in traditionalism and authoritarianism across Europe

Figure 1 visualizes mean moral traditionalism and authoritarianism in 2008 for all 44 European countries separately, as well as the correlation between these two cultural divides in a given country.[5] The countries are grouped into regions. The bars in Figure 1 represent mean traditionalism and mean authoritarianism for each country (see the ax on the left for the values), while the circles represent correlations between the two in a corresponding country (see the ax on the right for the values). Table 1 provides summary statistics for the

---

4   The first four items within the for authoritarianism scale are binary, while the fifth one (whether one thinks the native born should have priority in getting a job) is measured on a 3-point scale. All items were standardized and then taken with equal weights to compose the scale. The resulting scale is fairly reliable with an overall Cronbach's Alpha of 0.64.

5   *Northern Europe*: Denmark, Finland, Iceland, Norway, Sweden. *Western Europe*: Austria, Belgium, France, Germany, Ireland, Luxemburg, Netherlands, Northern Ireland, Switzerland, UK. *Southern Europe*: Albania, Bosnia, Croatia, Cyprus, Greece, Italy, Kosovo, Macedonia, Malta, Montenegro, Portugal, Serbia, Slovenia, Spain. *Eastern Europe*: Armenia, Belarus, Bulgaria, Czech Republic, Estonia, Georgia, Hungary, Latvia, Lithuania, Moldova, Poland, Romania, Russia, Slovakia, Ukraine.

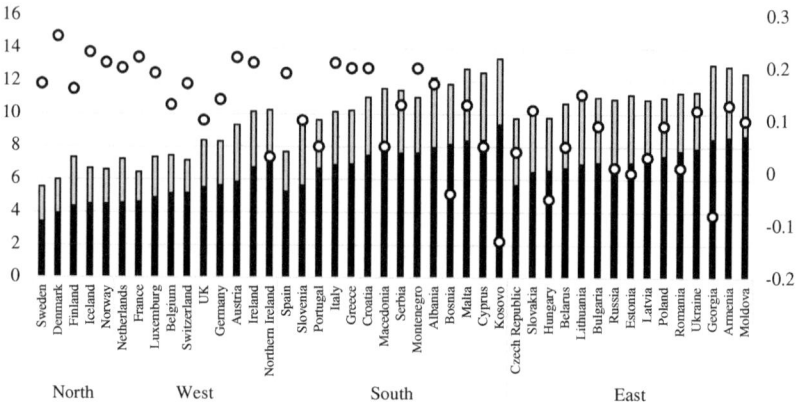

Fig. 1. Mean levels of moral traditionalism and authoritarianism, and mean traditionalism-authoritarianism correlations per country of Europe, 2008 (EVS wave 4)

Tab. 1. Mean levels of moral traditionalism and authoritarianism, and mean traditionalism-authoritarianism correlations per region of Europe, 2008 (EVS wave 4)

Region of Europe	Mean Moral Traditionalism	Mean Authoritarianism	Traditionalism-Authoritarianism Correlation
North	4.15	2.28	0.21
West	5.51	2.7	0.16
South	7.43	3.65	0.11
East	7.3	3.91	0.05
Europe in total	6.61	3.39	0.24

four European regions (Northern, Eastern, Southern and Western Europe), and for Europe as a whole.

From both Figure 1 and Table 1, it is clear that the Northern European countries feature the lowest levels of moral traditionalism (all countries score below 4.52 with an average of 4.15 for Northern Europe as a whole) and authoritarianism alike (all below 3.00 with a Northern European average of 2.28). It is also clear that the link between the two value divides is strongest in this region: the correlation is 0.21 on average, never falls below 0.16 (Finland) and reaches a maximum of 0.26 (Denmark). The second group of countries in Figure 1 represents Western Europe. These countries are more morally traditionalist (5.51 on average) as well as more authoritarian (2.70) than the Northern European ones. The link between the two value divides is also slightly weaker here: 0.16 for the region as a whole, ranging from 0.03 (Northern Ireland) to 0.22 (Austria and France).

Southern Europe is the most morally traditionalist part of Europe with mean moral traditionalism levels around 7.43, which is hardly surprising given the high number of massively religious countries in this region (e.g. deeply religious Malta with an average score of no less than 8.38). The countries in the south of Europe do also feature higher levels of authoritarianism than either Northern or Western Europe (3.65 on average), while the link between the two value divides is weaker in this region (0.11 on average, but with sizable differences between countries). These differences pertain especially to a contrast between two groups of countries within the region. On the one hand, older Southern European democracies like Spain, Italy, Portugal, and Greece, all demonstrate lower levels of traditionalism and authoritarianism and stronger links between the two (around 0.2 and higher). On the other hand, former Yugoslavian Post-Communist countries rather boast variegated combinations of traditionalism, authoritarianism, and relationships between the two, the latter ranging from negative in Bosnia and Kosovo, to weakly positive in Slovenia (0.10) and Serbia (0.13) and more strongly positive in Montenegro (0.20).

The Eastern European countries, finally, are only slightly less traditionalist than the Southern European ones yet more authoritarian than the rest of Europe. The average level of moral traditionalism within this group of countries is 7.30, ranging from 5.67 in the Czech Republic to 8.66 in Moldova. In all countries within this category, mean authoritarianism is as high as 3.91, ranging from 3.23 in Hungary to 4.40 in Lithuania and 4.54 in Georgia. The two value divides are also less strongly correlated in Eastern Europe, with an average correlation of no more than 0.05. Ten out of the fifteen countries in this region feature (typically insignificant) correlations below 0.10, with the lowest ones – that even turn out to be negative – recorded for Georgia (-0.08) and Hungary (-0.05). Only five Eastern European countries show correlations higher than 0.10, with none of these being higher than 0.15 (e.g. Moldova, Slovakia, Ukraine, Armenia, and Lithuania).

On the overall, the link between the two value divides appears to be stronger in those countries where both traditionalism and authoritarianism are at the lowest. As levels of traditionalism and authoritarianism increase, the link between the two divides becomes weaker. The Eastern European countries feature levels of moral traditionalism that are among the highest in Europe, only slightly below massively religious Southern Europe, and they stand out as more authoritarian than the rest of Europe. Moreover, the link between the two value divides is decidedly weaker in Eastern Europe than elsewhere in Europe, even though there are substantial differences between the various countries within this cluster.

Secularization and the overlap between the Two Divides

Exploring the link between the two value divides

In the previous subsections, we have shown some clear regional differences not only in terms of mean levels of moral traditionalism and authoritarianism but also in terms of the overlap between the two value divides. Our theory, however, suggests that the strength of the link between the two (i.e. whether they overlap or remain separate) depends on how secularized a given society is. In this part of the analysis, we thus explore how the strength of the link between the two divides varies across European societies characterized by different levels of religiosity and moral traditionalism.

To ensure that we have enough societies with both high and low levels of contextual religiosity and moral traditionalism, we add observations from the two previous waves of the EVS (1990 and 1999) into analysis.[6] This gives us 100 country-year combinations that are referred to as *contexts*. The same measure of the overlap between the two divides as in the previous part of the analysis is used here: zero-order correlations between moral traditionalism-progressiveness and authoritarianism-libertarianism calculated for each of the contexts in the sample. We measure *contextual religiosity* for each of the country-year combinations as the mean score of an individual-level religiosity scale. It consists of attending religious services at least once a month and believing in god, heaven, hell, sin, and life after death.[7] The least religious context is Bulgaria in 1990 (1.97

---

6   The overall dataset includes more than 108,000 individuals nested within 100 contexts (44 countries nested in three waves). The average number of respondents per context is 1,119 (EVS 2011).

7   All of the six variables within the individual religiosity scale are binary, yet strongly correlated and loading heavily on one factor with an Eigenvalue of 4.8 that explains 91 % of the variance. The resulting scale (mean standardized scores) is highly reliable with a Cronbach's Alpha of 0.86 and is recoded to range from 0 (least religious) to 10 (most religious).

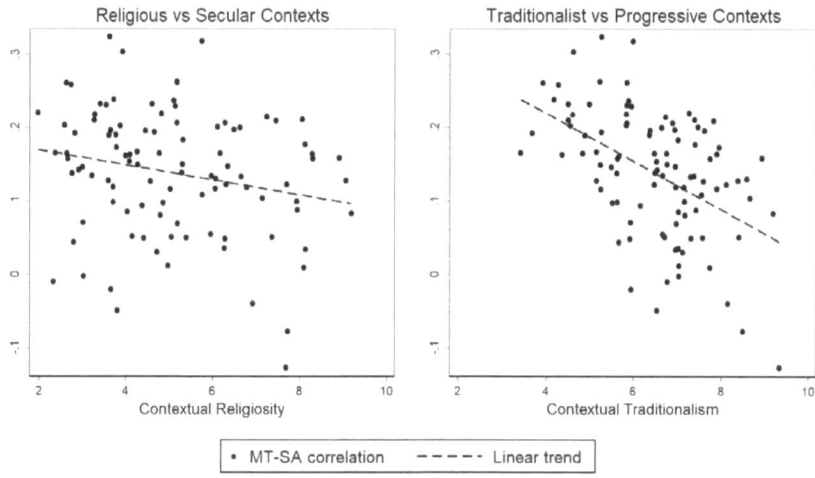

Fig. 2. The link between moral traditionalism and authoritarianism across Europe (zero-order correlations, EVS 1990, 1999, 2008)

out of 10) and the most religious one Malta in 1990 (9.18 out of 10). Contextual moral traditionalism was described in the previous section.

Figure 2 displays the strength of the link between the two divides across contexts with different levels of religiosity on the one hand and contexts with different levels of moral traditionalism on the other. The left-hand side of Figure 2 demonstrates that the most secular countries of Western Europe boast the strongest connections between our two value divides, even though the pattern is quite weak. If we plot the same correlations against contextual moral traditionalism rather than contextual religiosity (see the right-hand side of Figure 2), however, the pattern is considerably more pronounced. The strongest overlap between the two divides is observed for the least traditionalist societies whereas in the most traditionalist contexts the link between the two appears to be considerably weaker.

Explaining the link between the two value divides

While the link between our two value divides is definitely stronger in the more secular and especially in less traditionalist countries, the question now is whether these observed differences between the countries occur actually due to secularization and are not connected to some regional specifics of Europe?

To test this, we perform multilevel statistical analysis and study *why* the link between the two value divides is stronger in some countries than in others.

In multilevel regression analysis, we use the strength of the link between the two divides as the dependent variable.[8] The 100 contexts are treated as units of analysis, with countries serving as a second-level grouping variable. The explanatory variables are *contextual religiosity* and *contextual moral tradition-alism*. Control variables are region of Europe, time,[9] and contextual authoritar-ianism. We control for time in all models and, because the two value divides have so often been found to be interconnected, we also control for contextual authoritarianism in models that include contextual moral traditionalism.

We introduce the variables in the model in a stepwise fashion, starting with an exploration of regional differences in the strength of the link between the two divides, with a special focus on Post-Communist Eastern Europe. Model 1 in Table 2 shows that the link between the two value divides is considerably weaker in countries in Southern and Eastern than in Western Europe. On average, the correlation between the two is by 0.053 lower in the South than in the West, and by 0.094 weaker in the East than in the West. The link between the two is thus strongest in the North and the West, followed by the South, and then the East.

We then enter contextual religiosity into the equation, which enables us to see whether the initially recorded differences between the European regions can be attributed to contextual differences in religiosity. In Model 2, contex-tual religiosity has a weak negative effect on the strength of the link: countries that are more secular do indeed demonstrate a slightly stronger link between moral traditionalism and authoritarianism. At this point, Southern contexts no

---

8   This approach is typically referred to as two-stage multilevel regression modeling. In the first stage, we use individual-level observations to calculate zero-order corre-lation scores between the two value dimensions for each context under study. In the second stage, these correlation scores are used as the dependent variable in regres-sion models. This approach does not only provide computational benefits (e.g. we fit models with two levels instead of adding the individual level as a third one), but also prevents the problem of obtaining statistically significant results with negligible effect sizes at the individual level (a problem caused by extremely large samples at the individual level) (Fairbrother 2014). The intra-class correlation (ICC) of 0.53 suggests that multilevel modeling is required in the second stage of analysis to account for country-level variation in the dependent variable.

9   *Time* is measured as the respective wave of the EVS (1990, 1999, 2008) and is included in all models as a continuous predictor.

longer differ from Western ones, which means that contextual religiosity actually accounts for the weaker correlations between the two divides in Southern Europe. Even controlling for contextual religiosity, however, Eastern Europe still differs from Western Europe.

Tab. 2. The link between traditionalism and authoritarianism across Europe: multilevel regression analysis results (EVS 1990, 1999, 2008)

	(1)	(2)	(3)	(4)
Contextual traditionalism			-0.029***	-0.036***
			(0.009)	(0.012)
Contextual religiosity		-0.009*		0.006
		(0.005)		(0.007)
European region (reference=West)				
North	0.010	0.003	-0.017	-0.018
	(0.034)	(0.035)	(0.033)	(0.033)
South	-0.053**	-0.043	0.001	0.002
	(0.025)	(0.026)	(0.029)	(0.029)
East	-0.094***	-0.090***	-0.045	-0.041
	(0.024)	(0.024)	(0.030)	(0.031)
Time (wave)	-0.015*	-0.014*	-0.022***	-0.024***
	(0.008)	(0.008)	(0.008)	(0.008)
Contextual authoritarianism			-0.006	-0.004
			(0.018)	(0.018)
Constant	0.228***	0.268***	0.435***	0.447***
	(0.030)	(0.039)	(0.066)	(0.067)
Random Effects (variances):				
Country	0.002	0.002	0.002	0.002
	(0.001)	(0.001)	(0.001)	(0.001)
Country-year	0.004	0.004	0.003	0.003
	(0.001)	(0.001)	(0.001)	(0.001)
Number of contexts	100	100	100	100
Number of countries	44	44	44	44
Snijders/Bosker R2 (level 1)	0.25	0.26	0.34	0.34
Snijders/Bosker R2 (level 2)	0.33	0.32	0.41	0.42

Standard errors in parentheses; unstandardized coefficients reported.
*** p<0.01, ** p<0.05, * p<0.1

Model 3 then demonstrates that bringing contextual traditionalism into the equation eliminates all regional differences whatsoever. Contextual moral traditionalism has a strong and substantial negative effect on the strength of the link under study: with one unit increase in contextual moral traditionalism, the correlation between the two divides decreases by 0.029. This translates into a difference in the correlation of no less than 0.172 between the least and most traditionalist contexts, with all other variables held constant.

The link between the two divides is in effect stronger in the most secular European countries, but is this *because* these countries are the least morally traditionalist ones? Model 4 proves that this is indeed the case: it is contextual traditionalism that accounts for the strength of the link between the two divides, not contextual religiosity or regional specifics. The effect of contextual traditionalism even increases, while that of contextual religiosity and region loses its statistical significance. All regional dummies are insignificant here, which means that the previously recorded differences between Eastern and Western Europe actually occur due to differences in levels of moral traditionalism. In short, our two value divides do indeed overlap less in Eastern Europe, because countries in this region are more morally traditionalist.

Discussion

In this chapter, we have studied whether and how Post-Communist Eastern European countries differ from the rest of Europe in terms of religiously informed moral traditionalism-progressiveness and basically secular authoritarianism-libertarianism, and in terms of the overlap between these two divides.

Our first principal finding is that Post-Communist Eastern European countries do indeed differ from the rest of Europe when it comes to both value dimensions. These countries feature levels of moral traditionalism that are among the highest in Europe, indeed only slightly below those of the massively religious Southern European countries, and they stand out as more authoritarian than the rest of Europe. Post-Communist Eastern European countries do as such boast political cultures that are less cosmopolitan and less open to acceptance of cultural diversity and individual liberty than those in the rest of Europe.

We have also studied variations in the strength of the overlap between the two value divides across Europe. Confirming a previous analysis that remained confined to Western European countries, the two value divides do only coalesce in the wake of processes of secularization, because the latter spark a dual rejection of moral traditionalism and authoritarianism in the name of personal liberty (Pless, Tromp, Houtman 2020). The two value divides thus tend to overlap in the more secular societies *because* they are the least traditionalist.

The other way around, moral traditionalism-progressiveness and authoritarianism-libertarianism tend to remain distinct value divides in the most religious parts of Europe *because* those societies are the most traditionalist. These findings are especially important for the countries of Post-Communist Eastern Europe that fall into this category: our analysis shows that the two divides there are virtually unrelated because the population remains comparatively traditionalist, and *not* due to some regional specifics (or even Post-Communist legacy).

This leads us to the conclusion that, even though often suggested otherwise, the two value divides do not necessarily blend into one single, more generally defined value divide between cultural conservatives and cultural progressives. Moreover, in the case of Post-Communist Eastern Europe, blending the two value divides into one broad cultural dimension in politics is especially misleading since the two divides there rather refer to separate cultural discussions.

References

Achterberg, Peter (2006) *Considering Cultural Conflict: Class Politics and Cultural Politics in Western Societies*. Maastricht: Shaker.

Achterberg, Peter, Dick Houtman (2006) "Why Do so Many People Vote "Unnaturally?" A Cultural Explanation for Voting Behaviour," *European Journal of Political Research* 45(1): 75–92.

Adamczyk, Amy, Cassady Pitt (2009) "Shaping Attitudes about Homosexuality: The Role of Religion and Cultural Context," *Social Science Research* 38(2): 338–351.

Betz, Hans-Georg, Carol Johnson (2004) "Against the Current — Stemming the Tide: The Nostalgic Ideology of the Contemporary Radical Populist Right," *Journal of Political Ideologies* 9(3): 311–327.

Bornschier, Simon (2010) "The New Cultural Divide and the Two-Dimensional Political Space in Western Europe," *West European Politics* 33(3): 419–444.

Brown, Callum G. (2009) *The Death of Christian Britain: Understanding Secularisation, 1800–2000*. London: Routledge.

Clark, Terry Nichols, Seymour Martin Lipset (1991) "Are Social Classes Dying?" *International sociology* 6(4): 397–410.

Dalton, Russell J. (1996) "Political Cleavages, Issues, and Electoral Change" in Lawrence LeDuc (ed.), *Comparing Democracies: Elections and Voting in Global Perspective*, pp. 319–342. Thousand Oaks (Calif.): Sage.

Elff, Martin (2007) "Social Structure and Electoral Behavior in Comparative Perspective: The Decline of Social Cleavages in Western Europe Revisited," *Perspectives on Politics* 5(2): 277–294.

EVS (2011) *European Values Study 1981–2008, Longitudinal Data File*. Cologne, Germany: GESIS Data Archive.

Fairbrother, Malcolm (2014) "Two Multilevel Modeling Techniques for Analyzing Comparative Longitudinal Survey Datasets," *Political Science Research and Methods* 2(1): 119–140.

Flanagan, Scott C., Aie-Rie Lee (2003) "The New Politics, Culture Wars, and the Authoritarian-Libertarian Value Change in Advanced Industrial Bemocracies," *Comparative Political Studies* 36(3): 235–270.

Houtman, Dick (2003) *Class and Politics in Contemporary Social Science: 'Marxism Lite' and Its Blind Spot for Culture*. New York: Routledge.

Houtman, Dick, Peter Achterberg (2010) "Two Lefts and Two Rights: Class Voting and Cultural Voting in the Netherlands, 2002," *Sociologie*(1): 61–76.

Houtman, Dick, Stef Aupers, Willem De Koster (2011) "Introduction: The Myth of Individualization and the Dream of Individualism" in *Paradoxes of Individualization: Social Control and Social Conflict in Contemporary Modernity*, pp. 1–24. Farnham: Aldershot.

Inglehart, Ronald (1977) *The Silent Revolution: Changing Values and Political Styles among Western Publics*. Princeton: Princeton University Press.

Kiss, Eszter (2016) "The Hungarians Have Decided: They Do Not Want Illegal Migrants:" Media Representation of the Hungarian Governmental Anti-Immigration Campaign," *Acta Humana*(6): 45–78.

Knutsen, Oddbjørn (1989) "Cleavage Dimensions in Ten West European Countries: A Comparative Empirical Analysis," *Comparative Political Studies* 21(4): 495–533.

De Koster, Willem, Jeroen Van der Waal (2007) "Cultural Value Orientations and Christian Religiosity: On Moral Traditionalism, Authoritarianism, and Their Implications for Voting Behavior," *International Political Science Review* 28(4): 451–467.

Kriesi, Hanspeter (2010) "Restructuration of Partisan Politics and the Emergence of a New Cleavage Based on Values," *West European Politics* 33(3): 673–685.

Król, Agnieszka, Paula Pustułka (2018) "Women on Strike: Mobilizing against Reproductive Injustice in Poland," *International Feminist Journal of Politics* 20(3): 366–384.

Kulkova, Anna (2015) "The Interaction between Religiosity and Social Conservatism: Russia and Europe Compared," *Social Sciences and Modernity* 3: 141–154.

Laythe, Brian, Deborah Finkel, Lee A. Kirkpatrick (2001) "Predicting Prejudice from Religious Fundamentalism and Right-Wing Authoritarianism: A Multiple-Regression Approach," *Journal for the scientific study of Religion* 40(1): 1–10.

Lipset, Seymour Martin (1959) "Democracy and Working-Class Authoritarianism," *American Sociological Review* 24(4): 482–501.

Lipset, Seymour Martin, Stein Rokkan (1967) "Cleavage Structures, Party Systems, and Voter Alignments: An Introduction" in Seymour Martin Lipset, Stein Rokkan (eds.), *Party Systems and Voter Alignments: Cross-National Perspectives*, pp. 1–63. New York: Free Press.

McGraw, Sean (2018) "Multi-Dimensional Party Competition: Abortion Politics in Ireland," *Government and Opposition* 53(4): 682–706.

McLeod, Hugh (2007) *The Religious Crisis of the 1960s.* New York: Oxford University Press.

Nieuwbeerta, Paul (1996) "The Democratic Class Struggle in Postwar Societies: Class Voting in Twenty Countries, 1945–1990," *Acta Sociologica* 39(4): 345–383.

Norris, Pippa, Ronald Inglehart (2004) *Sacred and Secular: Religion and Politics Worldwide.* Cambridge: Cambridge University Press.

_____ (2019) *Cultural Backlash: Trump, Brexit, and the Rise of Authoritarian Populism.* Cambridge, United Kingdom: Cambridge University Press.

Northmore-Ball, Ksenia, Geoffrey Evans (2016) "Secularization versus Religious Revival in Eastern Europe: Church Institutional Resilience, State Repression and Divergent Paths," *Social Science Research* 57: 31–48.

Pless, Anna, Paul Tromp, Dick Houtman (2020) "The "New" Cultural Cleavage in Western Europe: A Coalescence of Religious and Secular Value Divides?" *Politics and Religion* 13(3): 445–464.

Rivkin-Fish, Michele (2018) "Fight Abortion, Not Women:" The Moral Economy Underlying Russian Feminist Advocacy," *Anthropological Journal of European Cultures* 27(2): 22–44.

Steenvoorden, Eefje, Eelco Harteveld (2018) "The Appeal of Nostalgia: The Influence of Societal Pessimism on Support for Populist Radical Right Parties," *West European Politics* 41(1): 28–52.

Stenner, Karen (2005) *The Authoritarian Dynamic.* Cambridge: Cambridge University Press.

_____ (2009) 'Three Kinds of "Conservatism," *Psychological Inquiry* 20(2–3): 142–159.

Storm, Ingrid (2016) "Morality in Context: A Multilevel Analysis of the Relationship between Religion and Values in Europe," *Politics and Religion* 9(1): 111–138.

Stubager, Rune (2008) "Education Effects on Authoritarian–Libertarian Values: A Question of Socialization," *British Journal of Sociology* 59(2): 327–350.

_____ (2010) "The Development of the Education Cleavage: Denmark as a Critical Case," *West European Politics* 33(3): 505–533.

Van der Waal, Jeroen, Peter Achterberg, Dick Houtman (2007) "Class Is Not Dead — It Has Been Buried Alive: Class Voting and Cultural Voting in Postwar Western Societies (1956–1990)," *Politics & Society* 35(3): 403–426.

Van de Werfhorst, Herman, Nan Dirk De Graaf (2004) "The Sources of Political Orientations in Post-Industrial Society: Social Class and Education Revisited," *British Journal of Sociology* 55(2): 211–235.

Nicolas Maslowski

The Symbols of the Dissent in Central European Politics since 1989

Abstract: The post 1989 transformation should be considered, to a large extent, as a period of post-dissent. The post-dissent, group using the dissent legitimacy in politics, defines indeed, symbolically, the new national discourses. Its divisions or its enemies are together structuring the political conflict in the post-1989. To be a former dissident becomes a resource, even though it was sufficient to be elected only in 1989. The logics of distinction pushes the post-dissent to spread into various groups, using their symbolic capital. The manipulation of history and the control of the past begin to be an element of the political conflict in the whole central European region and this, for many years.

Keywords: Central Europe, dissent, post-communism, post-dissent, symbolic transformation

Until today, the concept of post-communism is widely used to define and explain contemporary Central and Eastern Europe, even though we can observe its relative decline (Roberts 2010: 1–12). Nevertheless, it should be quoted that there are various debates considering that the whole world is in a post-communist period and that the fall down of the Eastern bloc had changed also the Western bloc (Balibar 2001: 133–162). There was indeed a so called "normal" and rich world, the Western bloc, considered as an ideal, serving as a model to transform the Eastern societies distorted by the communist period (Kaminski & Kurczewska 1995: 131–152). The consequences of this dominating paradigm were often described with concepts underlining the specificity of the region. This specificity was resulting from an unfinished transformation and a non-consolidated democracy and leading to the emergence of hybrid systems (Fagan, Kopecký et al., 2000: 315–317).

All these concepts were criticized, but no other relevant alternative has been widely accepted or used. They are certainly problematic for many reasons that cannot be addressed wholly within the limited scope of this chapter. However, the main question that we have to address and discuss here is the idea of a mental heritage of communism. The modernization or the transformation paradigms underlines the negative weight of this past, comparing Central and Eastern Europe's situation to what could have been if it had been in the

Western Bloc. The post-1989 is then analyzed as a period of Westernization/ Europeanization, of catching up. But these approaches lose a major aspect of the symbolic transformation: the aspect deriving from the marginal group of the dissidents and their destinies, the heart of the story of the nations.[1] And this last transformation was present in all the former soviet-type countries, within a huge or smaller scale. We will see that it is clearly a major phenomenon in Central European countries.

In this chapter, we will defend the thesis supporting that the symbol of the dissent, managed by what we call the **post-dissent** (Maslowski 2011: 123 and next), constituted one of the structuring elements of politics in Central Europe and therefore, largely influenced the shape of post-1989 democracy. This transformation was related to the symbol of dissent and to the new interpretation of history.

Post-dissent after 1989

1989 was a moment of a radical Copernican revolution in political symbolism. The national symbols, the international collaborations as well as the politics of memory were deeply transformed. Indeed, if some political forces criticized the brutality of the change, the general direction stayed similar during the following decades.[2]

This change within the symbol of the State was resulting from the change of the political staff. In 1989, when the communist regimes fell, some intellectuals, artists, dissidents are coming to power in Central Europe, with a wide influence. They are bringing their memory(-ies), interpretation(s) of history, their perception of the symbolic hierarchies in the societies, and all these elements that will have a major influence on the symbolic systems within the Central European Region. From this point of view, we can consider that we are not in a symbolic post-communist period, but rather in a period symbolically structured by these new rulers. Thus, post-1989 is not only made up of a specifically post-communist legacy, but also is unevenly and complexly coupled with a post-dissident legacy, that we call the *post-dissent period*. The post-1989 rulers used alternatives to the communist symbols. Therefore, they used cultural resources, coming from the symbolic systems from the interwar period or even earlier, using culture as a tool kit (Swidler 1986). They also used largely the more

---

1 With some exceptions like Gil Eyal (2000: 49–92) or Mirosława Grabowska (2004).
2 And about the fact that culture matters, see Piotr Sztompka (2004: 481–496).

actual symbolic systems developed by the dissident movements from each different country.

Despite a progressive economic and political transformation during the transition period, the symbolic transformation was quite quick. The medals, the honorable guests of the Presidents, the discourses on history, the values exposed by the new rulers were presenting a radical discontinuity in each of the Central European country. The symbols from the dissidents' repertories (that were different in each country) were used by officials. It began with the V made by Tadeusz Mazowiecki's fingers in the *Diet*, after the vote choosing him as a Prime minister. The most pictorial was in Czechoslovakia, with the President Havel integrating the values of the *cultural underground*, that played a particularly important role in the structuration of the Czechoslovak dissent. Indeed, Havel organized underground rock concerts in the Prague castle, received Frank Zappa in 1990, and later, the Rolling Stones in Prague (Žantovský 2014: 345–567). These aspects, as well as the politics resulting from the reflections of the dissidents were not always very well understood by the whole population. But years passing, they convinced a certain part of the citizens.

These symbolic politics, developed by the former dissidents, were concerning their own group as well, which resulted in some mixed feelings of conflict of interests (Eröss 2009). But there was a recognition for jailed persons, for activities from the dissident time like samizdat editions or other resistance activities, according to hierarchies resulting from the history of the dissident worlds (Bolton 2012: 239–265). The competition between different dissident groups and the conflicts within the dissident groups created sometimes opened conflicts.

But the dissidents were very different from country to country, despite their similarities. Certain similarities, that we can observe in the post-dissent groups, come directly from history: the dissidents' movements appeared in reaction to the communist dictatorship and inspired one another. But on the other side, the dissents were structured mainly nationally. They have individual characteristics as they constitute modes of actions, communities with specific codes, whose norms and hierarchies can be explained by endogenous processes (internal logics of changes in the communities) as well as by exogenous ones, therefore external to these communities (result of State's repressions, for example). Poland is here exceptional for the massive support received by the Solidarity movement, as well as for its pioneer activity in the fall of communism. Dissents' movements were not monolithic but constituted by a variety of networks having a multiplicity of codes and references. These networks as well as the divisions were partly institutionalized and were, to a certain extent, changing regularly until the 1989 revolution.

The first governments, after 1989, were composed of intellectuals and artists, generally attached to the dissent's movement. The new State's recognition for the dissident movement brings then to the constitution of a new group: the **post-dissent**. The group is constituted by people having obtained a political capital for the legitimacy of their dissident action. The post-dissent beneficiates more or less openly from a dissident glorious past. It differs from the community of the former dissidents, as not all the dissidents wanted or succeeded to use this legitimacy for capital gaining. This phenomenon is strengthened by the role of the networks. Three phenomena are directly related to this: first, the history of the role of different dissident groups in the communist period and of old alliances plays a role in the structuration of the field. Secondly, the interpretation of this history, its distortions and manipulations began to play a role and to be an instrument and a source of political conflict. Thirdly, the relationships between different dissident's groups before and after 1989: there were indeed some alliances or competitions between dissidents' groups. Some periods were bringing to more unity while others were facing exclusions from the main-stream post-dissent or divisions between brothers in arms. . . All this situation which was existing before 1989, was continuing in the new context of democracy, within this post-dissent worlds. The post-dissent inherited from the complex structures of the national dissent movements and also from their divisions. We will see that it creates as well a new chapter in the reconciliations and new conflicts in a new context.

Defining the borders of this *post-dissent* group is not obvious, as the limits of the dissidents' group were not clear. The sociologist and former dissident Jiřina Siklová tempted to theorize the problem, defining the *grey zone* (Šiklová 2004: 135–148), constituted by the part of the population that supported dissidents, without necessarily being part of the movement. Often, being recognized for important dissidents' activities or beneficiating from the caution of a famous dissident was sufficient to be a "recipient" of this post-dissident capital. For instance, since the first fully democratic election in Poland[3] in 1989, a photo with Lech Walesa is from far the first factor explaining the success of each candidate to the Senate elections (Codogni 2012). This political logic of the transformation period was a transfer of the confidence of the majority of the voters

---

3   but it was fully democratic only for a part of the Parliament: 35 % of the Sejm, and
    the whole Senate.

to the dissident (later on post-dissent group) representing the alternative and the transformative force. The post-dissent will lose some influence but will play an important role during a very long period.

The symbol of dissent and new memories

Having rulers from the post-dissent engenders many symbolic consequences. They are bringing a new memory to the nation. Large movements of protests, like 1956 in Hungary, 1968 in Czechoslovakia or the Solidarność Movement in Poland, help to interpret communism as a geopolitically imposed regime, without any legitimacy. But the soviet-type communist regime, as it was a totalitarian regime, was largely based on unclear elements of support within the population. For Václav Havel (1990), in his first new-year discourse as a Czechoslovak President, the regime was based upon the participation of all the citizens in its every-day functioning.

> For I am talking about all of us. We have all got used to the totalitarian system and accepted it as an unchangeable fact and thus actually maintained it. In other words: we are all – although of course each to a different extent – responsible for the running of the totalitarian machinery, no one is just a victim of it, but we are all also its co-creators…; Few of us were able to call out aloud…; A better government, the best Parliament and the best President cannot do much on their own. And it would be deeply wrong to expect a general remedy only from them. Freedom and democracy means the participation and therefore the co-responsibility of all.[4]

If the reflexive personalities from the post-dissent, like Václav Havel, Tadeusz Mazowiecki, János Kis could easily have such discourses at the beginning of the transformation (that helped the population to understand its own compromises), it was not the case of all the dissidents. The existence of a differentiated dissident movement and its complex relation to the past brought the Central European countries to a fractured memory regime. It created situations

---

4 "Mluvím o nás všech. Všichni jsme si totiž na totalitní systém zvykli a přijali ho za nezměnitelný fakt a tím ho vlastně udržovali. Jinými slovy: všichni jsme – byť pochopitelně každý v jiné míře – za chod totalitní mašinérie odpovědni, nikdo nejsme jen její obětí, ale všichni jsme zároveň jejími spolutvůrci…; Jen málokteří z nás dokázali nahlas zvolat…; Sebelepší vláda, sebelepší parlament i sebelepší prezident toho sami mnoho nezmohou. A bylo by i hluboce nesprávné čekat obecnou nápravu jen od nich. Svoboda a demokracie znamená přece spoluúčast a tudíž spoluodpovědnost všech"Novoroční projev prezidenta ČSSR Václava Havla, Praha, Pražský hrad, 1. ledna 1990, translated from Czech by Nicolas Maslowski 06/08/2020.

where important groups were cultivating parallel, non-official memories, con-stituting as well a variety of mnemonic actors (Bernhard & Kubik 2014). But very quickly, for many Central Europeans, having dissidents ruling after the fall of the regime allowed some "normal" citizens who have lived in a regime without questioning it (some would have said by "collaborating"), feeling like part of a tradition of dissent, of suffering. Underlining the jails and suffering of the dissidents becomes a source of a new national martyrology[5] (Głowacka-Grajper 2018: 924–935). We can compare the phenomenon to the French recon-struction of identity after the Second World War, that allowed French citizens to consider themselves as a country of the resistance, thanks to the new memory brought by De Gaulle and his colleagues, although this was not necessarily the case (Wieviorka 2005). France had to wait for an American historian Robert Paxton to rediscover that there was an important phenomenon of collabora-tion during the war, and not only a heroic martyrium (Paxton 1972). Similarly, in Central Europe, the memorial museums constituted a transnational space (Zombory 2017:1030). According to Máté Zombory, "The "first wave" of memo-rial museums of Communism, . . . were initiated by sub-state political activist forces, composed of anti-Communist political diaspora, and domestic dissi-dence. Early promoters of Communism memory made direct references to the Holocaust from the beginning," entering the paradigm of a national martyr-ology (Zombory 2017:1030). What is not underlined by Máté Zombory and many others, is the fact that this memorial evolution has consequences not only on the historical memory of communism, but also, on the specific memory of the dissidents, giving them a special role.

Dissidence as a Political and Social Resource

For some parts of the local Central-European population or even for western intellectuals or some western media or politicians, the dissidents were admi-rable. Their activity was considered therefore as heroic. The abnegation of the dissent was impressive, and it would be superficial to believe that they were acting just for the glory. But the fact is that a side-effect of their actions and

---

5   In parallel to other kind of martyrdom, like the religious ones, the WWII ones, lost-territories ones. . .This symbolic aspects are not questioning the reality of the trauma of large social groups, from the war, soviet invasions, assassinations, political trials. We want here mainly to underline the fact that we have a totally new interpretation of history of communism, partly dissent-based. Their suffering is becoming a source of explanation of their special position.

sufferings was that special position in the society. During the communist time, some people were avoiding them as much as possible, not to have problem with the regime, but some other were attracted by this prestigious group. And a large part of the population was not interested at all in these persons neither by their activities.

After the change of regime, the risks of problem with the regime disappeared. The ostracization disappeared as well. And the dissidents were becoming the new heroes, playing a new role after 1989 (Falk 2003: 354–364). Movies and documentary films were spreading information and legends about them.[6] Many of them reintegrated their legitimate position in their professional group of origin, with a particular aura. Some received honorific medals. In the Czech Republic, the concept of third resistance emerged, giving to the dissidents a kind of military financial support, equivalent to the financial recognition for the resistance during war (Sommer 2012). And if not all important dissidents become ministers or politicians and if many of them remain in modest positions, they know personally members of the government. Indeed, they are sometimes invited to the presidential palace or to the castle and argue as equals with the top of the State. During the first years of transformation, these former dissidents begin getting the identity of the voice of the civil society as well. They are particularly often invited to speak in newspapers or on TV, even if their quality of former dissident is not always emphasized. One calls them public intellectuals, for example.

This group is unified by their past and by some particular moments: some burials, a commemoration, birthdays… For example, some meet until today, every year, to have a beer in the memory of Olga Havel, for her birthday. If they are diverse in their political opinions, get upset, argue between themselves, the former dissidents are regularly meeting and communicating with one another, etc. (Benetková 2018).

The political dimension interacts with this phenomenon described above. The post-dissent world, using this legitimacy, participates in these meetings but is also making a political career at the same time (Jørgensen 1990). Some former dissidents are not participating to this community. They left it in 1989 but have an unwritten right to come "back." Indeed, during my researches, I have heard

6   There is a wonderful project, DOKEST 1989, in France, to gather all documentary references concerning the communist past, but maid after 1989 (https://dokest89.wordpress.com/). They are concerning to a large extent the dissent world. See as well the Nadège Ragaru, Ania Szczepanska's publication (2016)

such confidence as "I was not making the revolution / the communism falling down, to get this." The quality of former dissidents can give to some of them a paternalist feeling. It opens the possibility to be in a critical posture towards politicians.

The social resource brings many of them to create their own movement, in politics, in the media, with a smaller or larger success. The newspaper *Gazeta Wyborcza* directed by Adam Michnik is a famous example of media success and actually the only important one. It will create many legacy conflicts around the use of the Solidarność logo in the frontpage of the newspaper. But the success of the micro-parties, societies and media had to be confronted to the democratic game, the free market. In parallel, the competition for this resource brought up conflicts and manipulations. Groups, in competition for the allocation of resources, are occupying or creating positions in the civil society: Soros/Bathory foundation, Institute 56, the Václav Havel Library, some positions in science. All these institutions are understood as important and the personal CV of a candidate for the direction plays a role. . . They are helped and supported by people that were never former dissidents, but respect them or some of them particularly.

In general, a beatification is easier after death.

Worlds of Disunities in politics: the economy of the political worth of dissent[7]

The arrival of the dissidents in politics brings to competitions and conflicts. These were often already existing during the communist period, but pressure and danger due to the regime were creating a centripetal force that limited the divisions (Szulecki 2019: 207–229). This force disappeared mainly in 1989.

This phenomenon was described in Poland as the war on the top ("wojna na górze" (Nalewajko 1997)), a war between the post-dissidents, divided between groups trying to keep a pluralist unity, within a centrist compromise (Democratic Union directed by Tadeusz Mazowiecki in Poland) and the ones trying their chance on the electoral free market, but also using a post-dissident legitimacy, like Lech Wałęsa in the first free presidential elections. In a similar way, the democratic Forum in Czech lands got divided already in the 1990 and the Public against Violence in the Slovak case fell into pieces. In Hungary, the dissident politicized movement was already divided since the first elections, but

---

7   We refer here to the conceptions of the French pragmatic sociology (Boltanski, Thévonot 2006)

the logics of distinction (SzDSz, FIDESZ, Democratic Forum) was bringing to an always greater opposition between the organizations as well (Bernhard 1993).

Besides the typical ideological or strategic opposition, arguments and critics against political competitors were organized around the question of the symbol of the dissent, in general and in particular.

The political roles of the dissidents were the main cause of the fights concerning history of communism. Some interpretations, more in the interest of political actors, were instrumentally favored. There were concerning the role of concrete dissidents, of groups of dissidents in competition, or the question of the role of the dissent in the history. Since the very beginning of the political competition, in the Central European nations, if a dissident's heroic past is a political resource, it gets naturally attacked by competitors. This phenomenon took a variety of forms:

- The relativization of the importance of someone's historical role, his/her heroism,
- the "revelation" of secret aspects of his/her past,
- the denunciations of compromises.

The publications of more or least official lists of collaborators of the secret services, including many dissidents, became an importance source of attacks (Williams, Fowler, Szczerbiak 2005). The generalization of the so-called Institutes of National Memory (referring to the Polish institution), between ten and twenty years after the regime changed, became a source of political conflicts and institutionalized the use of history as a political tool (Mink 2013). As a typical example, we can notice that in all the publications of the Polish IPN, there is no book or monograph concerning the role of the leader of the Solidarność movement, Lech Wałęsa, in the democratic opposition. In this institution supposed to organize the national memory and having a budget larger than the total of all the departments of history from all Polish universities, Lech Wałęsa is present only in a book supposing to prove his collaboration with the secret services of the regime. In each political party, some people attack the other parties' dissidents and defend "their" ones (Atwood 2003). There are many other examples deriving from the Polish political scene and concerning the symbols of Solidarność, beginning with, a huge conflict on the use of the symbol of Solidarność on *Gazeta Wyborcza*'s frontpage and finishing with the question of deciding who is legitimate to control the European Solidarity Center in Gdansk. And similar conflicts are existing in other countries.

In parallel, to these personal attacks, there are, in the political world but as well in the intellectual background debates, attacks concerning the whole dissident movement and its role in history. These attacks were different from countries to countries and between different parties.

In Poland, the politician and academic professor Jerzy Wiatr, a former communist activist, will regularly present an interpretation of history (Wiatr 1999) where the main actors of the democratization were the reforming communists. To simplify, without the communists, there wouldn't be any way out from communism. A similar point of view will be presented by the Hungarian French historian Péter Kende, director of the Institute 1956 (Kende 1990). For Václav Klaus, the dissidents played no role in the fall of communism. The regime fell on its own (Klaus, Martinek 2019).

A particular way to get around the legitimacy of the dissident mainstream, from a more right-wing perspective, is to underline the heroism of the fighters in the forties-fifties. This vision was developed particularly in the 21st century. In Poland, there is a new state of recognition for the so called "cursed soldiers" (Kończal 2020), that were supposed to fight heroically against the soviet occupier. In the Czech Republic, there is a similar model of heroization of the brothers Mašín (Sveda 2010). In Hungary, the debates concentrated more on the military victims from 1956. In each case, in this type of arguments, underlining this type of national anti-communist heroes, the politicians could relativize the worth of the mainstream post-dissident groups. In similar ways, underlining the victims of the Stalinist period or of 1956, using associations of victims from this period, can be a technique to over-pass symbolically the post-dissents.

Any long-term consequences?

The first consequence of the emergence of the specific type of worth, the status of former dissident, had an extra-advantage, in the electoral competition, for the latter. This advantage was clear and important in 1989 and seems to reduce with time. Later, the electoral competition gave more and more importance to political parties and there is less and less place for "personalities." A second reason of the decrease of this demography is that former dissidents are getting older and older. For demographic reasons, they are leaving us.

What will stay from these dissident worlds in political symbols? The death of Václav Havel in 2011 can be a representative example. Václav Havel was such a symbol that his death had an international echo. In the Czech Republic, people from all ages gathered in an important moment of national emotion, despite the fact that the younger never lived the communist regime (Skovajsa 2012). Václav Havel entered definitively in the history of the Czech Nation. It is not possible to separate what is due to his status of former dissident from his attitude of moral

Tab. 1. Forms of attacks on the political symbols of the dissent

	targeted attack	Symbolic murder	Rejections of the symbol of dissents
Argumentation	Relativization of the role played by a dissident or a concrete group	Withdrawal of the benefit from belonging to the dissent movement by denouncing collaboration with the secret services	Relativization of the role played by the dissent
Instruments	Role of politicized historians or historian journalists supporting this or that group – control of archives	Questionable lists of collaborators, takeover of archives	Substitute topics, or a critic of the hidden personal interest of the dissidents in their activities (trips, money. . .)

President. Havlism became a kind of political option having many friends and some enemies as well, where many reflections, attitudes, networks, symbols come directly from the dissident times. Vaclav Havel beneficiated from the symbol of the dissent, as much as the Czech (and Central European) dissent beneficiated from his symbol.

The deaths of Bronislaw Geremek in 2008 and Tadeusz Mazowiecki in 2013 in Poland, György Konrad in 2019 in Hungary and to a certain extent, Miroslav Kusý in 2019 in Slovakia were related to national and international signs of recognitions. But the death is not closing the chapters.

The younger generations were socialized to those symbols and heritages. In protest movements against Orbán in Hungary, against politics of the Law and Justice Party in Poland, against Babiš in Czech Republic, against murders and corruption in Slovakia, there are explicit references to the dissent's tradition. These protests represent the democratic forces facing the democratic fatigue (Rupnik 2007). Some members of the post-dissent are denunciating here a manipulation. We should rather interpret this as the entrance of these repertories of actions and symbols within the national, cultural tool kit.

References:

Atwood, Sarah (2003) "Transition Pains: Hungary's Uncertain Dissidents," *Georgetown Journal of International Affairs* 4(1): 147–154

Balibar, Étienne (2001) "L'Europe après le communisme" in Étienne Balibar *Nous, citoyens d'Europe?*, pp. 133–162. Paris: La Découverte

Benetková, Eva (2018) *Disent po roce 1989, Využití teorie změny habitu Pierra Bourdieu na příkladu, vybraných organizací postdisentu*, Diplomová práce. Prague: FHS- Karlova univerzita.

Bernhard, Michael (1993), "Civil Society and Democratic Transition in East Central Europe," *Political Science Quarterly* 108(2): 307–326.

Bernhard, Michael, Jan Kubik (eds.) (2014): *Twenty Years after Communism: The Politics of Memory and Commemoration*. Oxford: Oxford University Press.

Boltanski, Luc, Laurent Thévenot (2006) *On Justification: Economies of Worth*. Princeton: Princeton University Press.

Bolton, Jonathan (2012) "Dreams of a dissent," in Jonathan Bolton, *Worlds of Dissent: Charter 77, The Plastic People of the Universe, and Czech Culture Under Communism*, pp. 239–265. Cambridge: Harvard University Press.

Codogni, Paulina (2012) "Rozdział IV: Anatomia zwycięstwa – kampania wyborcza obozu solidarnościowo-opozycyjnego" in Paulina Codogni, *Wybory czerwcowe 1989 roku. U progu przemiany ustrojowej*. Warsaw: Monografie IPN.

Eröss, Gábor (2009) "Pour le meilleur et pour le pire: L'étonnante constance des (ex-)dissidents hongrois depuis trente ans," *Tumultes* 32/33: 265–285.

Eyal, Gil (2000) "Anti-Politics and the Spirit of Capitalism: Dissidents, Monetarists, and the Czech Transition to Capitalism," *Theory and Society* 29 (1): 49–92

Fagan, Adam, Petr Kopecký, Lenka Bustikova & Andrea L. P. Pirro (2020) "Anniversary Symposium, "1989 at 30 years," *East European Politics*, 36(3): 315–317.

Falk, Barbara J. (2003) "Marginalization or Public engagement: The Role of Central European Intellectuals in the Post-Communist Era," in Barbara J. Falk, *The Dilemmas of Dissidence in East-Central Europe: Citizen Intellectuals and Philosopher kings*, pp. 354–364. Budapest: Central European University Press.

Głowacka-Grajper, Małgorzata (2018) "Memory in Post-communist Europe: Controversies over Identity, Conflicts, and Nostalgia," *East European Politics and Societies and Cultures* 32(4): 924–935.

Grabowska, Mirosława (2004) *Podział postkomunistyczny: społeczne podstawy polityki w Polsce po 1989 roku*. Warszawa: Wydawnictwo Naukowe Scholar.

Havel, Vaclav (1990) "Novoroční projev prezidenta ČSSR Václava Havla" available at http://old.hrad.cz/president/Havel/speeches/index.html. Prague: Pražský hrad.

Jørgensen, Knud Erik (1990) "The End of Anti-politics in Central Europe" in *Democracy and Civil Society in Eastern Europe Selected Papers from the*

Fourth World Congress for Soviet and East European Studies, pp. 32–60. North Yorkshire: Harrogate.

Kaminski, Antoni Z., Joanna Kurczewska (1995) "Strategies of Post-communist Transformations: Elites as Institution-Builders" in Bruno Grancelli (ed.), *Social Change and Modernization*, pp. 131–152. Berlin: De Gruyter.

Kende, Peter (1990) "Hongrie: de la réforme à la transformation," *Politique étrangère* 55(1): 35–44.

Klaus, Vaclav, Jan Martinek (2019), "Disidenti komunismus nezbourali, sesypal se sám," available at www.novinky.cz/domaci/clanek/klaus-disidenti-komunismus-nezbourali-sesypal-se-sam-40302107 (accessed 12.6.2020)

Kończal, Kornelia (2020) "The Invention of the "Cursed Soldiers" and Its Opponents: Post-war Partisan Struggle in Contemporary Poland," *East European Politics and Societies and Cultures* 34(1): 67–95.

Maslowski, Nicolas (2011) *Manifester en République tchèque: société civile et protestation 1989–2009*. Saarbrücken: SVH.

Mink, Georges (2013) "Institutions of National Memory in Post-Communist Europe: From Transitional Justice to Political Uses of Biographies (1989–2010)." in: Georges Mink, Neumayer Laure. (eds) *History, Memory and Politics in Central and Eastern Europe*, pp. 155–170. London: Palgrave Macmillan.

Nalewajko, Ewa (1997) *Protopartie i protosystem? Szkic do obrazu polskiej wielopartyjności*. Warsaw: ISP PAN.

Paxton, Robert O. (1972) *Vichy France: Old Guard and New Order 1940–1944*, New York: Knopf.

Ragaru, Nadège, Ania Szczepanska (2016) (eds.), *L'écriture documentaire de l'histoire: le montage en récit, actes du colloque DokEst89 organisé le 3 et 4 Novembre 2015*, Paris: HiCSA, available at https://hicsa.univ-paris1.fr/documents/pdf/CERHEC/DokEst89/Actes_dokest89_integral_3.pdf (accessed 12.06.2020)

Roberts, Ken (2010) "Is post-communism still a useful concept? Evidence from studies of young people's life stage transitions," *Annales, ser. Hist. soc.* 1: 1–12.

Rupnik, Jacques. (2007) "Is East-Central Europe Backsliding? From Democracy Fatigue to Populist Backlash," *Journal of Democracy* 18(4): 17–25.

Šiklová, Jiřina (2004) "Courage, Heroism, and the Postmodern Paradox," *Social Research* 71(1): 135–148.

Skovajsa, Marek, (2012) "Cultures of Civil Society in East Central Europe: Discourses, Codes, and Performances of Czech Civil Society," in John M. Carey and Lynn Vavreck APSA 2012 Annual Meeting Paper

Washington: APSA. Available at SSRN: https://ssrn.com/abstract=2104845 (accessed 10.6.2020)

Sommer, Vítězslav (2012) "Cesta ze slepé uličky "třetího odboje". Koncepty rezistence a studium socialistické diktatury v Československu – A Way Out of the 'Third Resistance' Cul de Sac: Concepts of Resistance and the Study of Socialist Dictatorship in Czechoslovakia," *Journal: Soudobé Dějiny* 19(1): 9–36.

Sveda, Josef (2010) *Narrative and ideological discourses in representations of the Mašín Brothers. MPhil(R) thesis.* Glasgow: university of Glasgow thesis. Available at http://theses.gla.ac.uk/2289/ (accessed 10.6.2020)

Swidler, Ann (1986) "Culture in Action: Symbols and Strategies," *American Sociological Review* 51 (2): 273–286.

Sztompka, Piotr (2004) "From East Europeans to Europeans: shifting collective identities and symbolic boundaries in the New Europe," *European Review* 12(4): 481–496.

Szulecki, Kacper (2019) "Conclusion: Can Dissidentism Explain Post-Dissident Politics?" in *Dissidents in Communist Central Europe Human Rights and the Emergence of New Transnational Actors*, pp. 207–229. Basingstoke: *Palgrave Macmillan.*

Wiatr, Jerzy (1999) *Socjologia wielkiej przemiany.* Warsaw: Krajowa Agencje Promocyjna.

Wieviorka, Michel (2005), "Les problèmes de la reconstruction identitaire," *Le Coq-héron*, 1 (180): 122–131.

Williams, Kieran, Brigid Fowler, Aleks Szczerbiak, (2005) "Explaining lustration in Central Europe: a 'post-communist politics' approach," *Democratization*, 12(1), 22–43.

Žantovský, Michael (2014) "Prezident Rock'n Roll," in Michael Žantovský, *Havel*, pp. 345–567. Prague: Argo.

Zombory, Máté (2017) "The birth of the memory of Communism: memorial museums in Europe," *Nationalities Papers* 45(6): 1028–1046.

THE SYMBOLIC POLITICS
OF EUROPEAN (DIS)UNIFICATION

Laure Neumayer

A Common Historical Narrative for Europe? Reappraising Communism in European Institutions

Abstract: Since the mid-1990s, an interpretation of history framed in the totalitarian paradigm and based on the alleged equivalence of Communism and Nazism has gained ground in European organizations. This chapter traces the mobilizations initiated by Central European members of European assemblies that shaped this memory regime. Drawing on the sociology of memory, a biographical approach highlights the national roots of the mobilizations carried out by anti-communist memory entrepreneurs. It also sheds light on the logic of specialization and professionalization of these newly elected representatives, which enabled them to overcome their tendential marginality and to redesign the hegemonic pan-European historical narrative.

Keywords: Communism, European Parliament, memory entrepreneurs, Parliamentary Assembly of the Council of Europe, remembrance policy

The European organizations, starting with the Council of Europe (CoE) and the European Union (EU) have since their inception celebrated the common past of their member states in order to root the European project in a historical ground and to increase its legitimacy. After the Cold War, Europe's "dark past" was included in this heritage and the Holocaust became the "negative founding myth" (Leggewie 2008) of the CoE and the EU. Both organizations imposed a soft "mnemonic accession criterion" on their future member states, which were required to critically evaluate their own complicity in this genocide and to give greater visibility to the commemoration of its victims. Meanwhile in the former Eastern bloc, a historical narrative centered on the equivalence of Nazism and Communism was gaining ground. From the mid-1990s onwards, numerous anti-Communist circles criticized the 'incomplete' character of the regime change, which they claimed had allowed former Socialist leaders to evade justice and to maintain comfortable positions in society (Mark 2010). In line with the paradigm of totalitarianism, a variety of politicians, academics and activists made crime the essence of the Communist ideology and stressed its structural proximity to Nazism.

Against this background, European organizations became venues where bilateral and domestic disputes over the past could be continued or amplified (Mink and Neumayer 2013). One of the most conflictual issues was the retrospective assessment of Communism, which sparked heated discussions in both the Parliamentary Assembly of the Council of Europe (PACE) and the European Parliament (EP). Representatives from the former Eastern bloc set out to renegotiate the boundaries of legitimate European historical narrative by seeking equal treatment of Nazi and Communist mass violence in terms of historical reckoning, collective remembrance and legal accountability. Their interpretation of "Nazism and Communism as equally evil" started to compete, in European-level debates, with the Western European narrative that made Auschwitz the standard of persecution and asserted the uniqueness of the Holocaust (Littoz-Monnet 2012).

Such an analysis of Communism became hegemonic in both assemblies, which adopted several official parliamentary resolutions centered on the equivalence of Stalinism and Nazism. The most outstanding of these texts are the 2006 resolution of PACE on the "need for international condemnation of the crimes of totalitarian Communist regimes" (PACE 2006) and the 2009 resolution of the EP on "European conscience and totalitarianism" which declared 23 August, the date on which the Molotov-Ribbentrop Pact was signed in 1939, the "Day of remembrance for the victims of totalitarian and authoritarian regimes" (European Parliament 2009).[1] The requests to use criminal law – to penalize denial of "Communist crimes"[2] and institute an international court headquartered in the EU to judge those responsible for these crimes – were not met. But remembrance served as a substitute for legal treatment of Socialist-era mass violence with the creation by the EU of a new policy called "Active European Remembrance," which sponsored projects that maintain "the main

---

1   With the treaty of non-aggression signed in August 1939, Nazi Germany and the Soviet Union pledged not to attack each other for 10 years. By signing the agreement, Hitler avoided the threat of a major two-front war. The treaty included a secret protocol which allowed these two countries to carve up spheres of influence in Eastern Europe. The German-Soviet Pact paved the way for the joint invasion and occupation of Poland that September. The Soviet Union was permitted subsequently to expand its rule over the Baltic states (Lithuania, Latvia, and Estonia) and parts of Romania and Finland.

2   Memory activists use this expression to lump together, across national contexts and historical periods, all the serious violations of human rights committed by Communist regimes after 1917.

sites and archives associated with deportations as well as the commemorating of victims of Nazism and Stalinism" (European Commission 2007: 7).

In the literature, these mobilizations have been analyzed as "claims for recognition" (Closa 2010; Mälksoo 2014) or attempts to set a "Gulag memory" against a "Shoah memory" (Droit 2007). Despite the indisputable "politics of recognition" involved in these demands, these interpretations may suggest a binary opposition between 'Western' and 'Eastern' readings of the past. This obscures the ideological dimension of the conflicting assessments of Socialist legacies throughout the continent, and the fact that the condemnation of Communism provides the Conservatives with a strong symbolic advantage over the Left not only in Eastern, but also in Western Europe. To bring ideology back, this chapter considers European-level debates about Communism as the result of the combined action of a multiplicity of social agents, who made specific claims and developed particular repertoires of contention in a variety of interconnected socio-political spaces (national political fields, European institutions and the interstitial spaces between them). It does not seek to measure the European institutions' capacity to conceive or pass on a hypothetical 'common memory' of Communism, nor to assess the legitimacy of the requests for an equal treatment of Communism and Nazism, but to analyze the political competitions and public policies related to the Socialist past, which developed in pan-European arenas.

Central European proponents of a totalitarian interpretation of Communism promoted their vision of history at PACE and in the EP. These newcomers, hence relatively sidelined in European assemblies, managed to strengthen their position in those institutions and obtained some consecration of an assessment of the Socialist era that altered the hegemonic European-level memory regime. In order to account for this implausible success, this chapter traces the mobilizations initiated after the Cold War by anti-Communist memory entrepreneurs,[3] most of them from Central European states, who have used their seats at PACE and the EP to shape the remembrance policy of European organizations. A biographical approach based on a prosopographical analysis highlights the national roots of their mobilizations as well as the logic of specialization and professionalization of these newly elected representatives,

---

3 Following Pollak (1993), the notion of memory entrepreneurs refers to actors interested in bringing the Socialist past to public attention and establishing common political and legal norms to commemorate the victims of gross human rights violations and to prosecute perpetrators.

which enabled them to overcome their tendential marginality and to reshape the dominant European historical narrative.

Analyzing anti-communist mobilizations in European Assemblies

The present chapter draws on a variety of studies under the theoretical and methodological influence of Pierre Bourdieu, that have sought to understand the formation of a distinct European 'field' of political action, specified the types of 'capital' thus valorized and the 'habitus' they incarnate. Whatever their divergences, the studies that use the concept of 'field' on a European scale refer to a partially autonomous space, the differentiation of which is related to processes of accumulation of specific capital, peopled by actors equipped with unevenly distributed resources who are competing for particular political goods (Georgakakis and Vauchez 2015). In this open and polycentric space, the structure of which is less firm and often much less autonomous than that of national political fields, agents exchange different forms of specifically European capital and renegotiate the value of resources previously acquired in national (political, bureaucratic, academic...) fields. This approach helps understand the formation of a European political space that is composed of both a transnational level and more established national units but constitutes nevertheless a single structure that constraints and enables political action.

This theoretical perspective determines the empirical scope of the analysis of the struggles to impose a totalitarian reading of Communism. Memory activism takes place in a complex configuration, made up of the main European institutions (PACE, the CoE's Committee of Ministers, the EP, the European Commission and the EU Council), as well as transnational political parties and anti-Communist networks. To grasp the moving contours of this European scale of history writing, the anti-Communist mobilizations are considered as multi-located processes, initiated by successive or simultaneous initiatives in the EP and PACE. These assemblies are seldom analyzed together, despite their historical proximity and the similarities in how they operate. Although national logics are more openly recognized at PACE, the work in both parliaments is structured around national delegations and mostly identical political groups, which constitute powerful co-ordination instruments for political competitions. The rivalry and co-operation between these organizations in the defense of fundamental rights and the chronological discrepancy in their enlargements, which led the anti-Communist memory entrepreneurs to invest PACE before moving their struggle to the EP, warrants a cross-analysis.[4]

The representatives at PACE and the members of parliament at the EP (MEPs) constitute the most relevant empirical entry to grasp how the criminalization of Communism, which originated in the political spaces of certain member states, was translated into the European political space. Elected under national frameworks but embedded in institutions governed by their own rationales, these representatives were placed at the interface between transnational and national political spaces (Beauvallet and Michon 2016). Their alignment of interests with a variety of social actors – academics, memory activists, administrators of European institutions – allowed for the active circulation of an anti-Communist grammar across the European political space, which shaped a common understanding of the 'proper way' for the CoE and the EU to manage the human rights violations of the Communist regimes.

From a methodological point of view, the analysis builds on an actor-centered political sociology (Rowell and Mangenot 2010) that is particularly suited to grasp the practical conditions of integration of newcomers into European assemblies in connection with their attempts to alter prevailing mnemonic norms. Focusing on their sociopolitical properties sheds light on the memory entrepreneurs' biographical, partisan and ideological motivations, but also on the constraints placed on their mobilizations. The calls for remembrance and justice launched by mainly conservative or liberal representatives can be considered as an extension of their struggles at national levels to impose their vision of Communism, disqualify their opponents or send a signal to Russia. However, most of these politicians were rather marginal members of PACE and the EP, and some of them experienced a discrepancy between a high level of national political resources and a lower position in European assemblies.

The new representatives from the former Eastern bloc, while often equipped with political capital and professional reputations built before their election at PACE or the EP, had to acquire resources specific to these arenas to be able to fully assume their role. In the 1990s, a tension existed at PACE between the principle of equality of the states and the 'student-teacher' quality of the relations between representatives from the longstanding member states and their peers from the nascent post-Communist democracies (Müller et al., 1999). At

---

4   The former satellite countries, a number of former Soviet Republics and Russia joined the CoE between 1990 and 1996, whereas the EU integrated eleven post-Communist countries between 2004 and 2013.

the EP, seniority has become a major determinant to access leading functions since the 1990s. To influence its work, specific know-how is needed in terms of capacity to build coalitions, command of admissible arguments and compliance with legitimate rules of interaction (Beauvallet and Michon 2013). After 2004, the enlargement intensified the struggles between dominant and contenders and the new representatives were tendentially marginalized (De Clerck-Sachsse and Kaczyński 2009; Hurka and Kaeding 2012). Integrating the rules of the parliamentary game was essential for acquiring European institutional credit, namely 'a knowledge, which has become intimate, of the formal and informal rules of the institutions and the policies or that of sociability and the proper behavior in a multicultural context' (Georgakakis and Rowell 2013: 319).

This chapter contends that marginality was one of the driving forces of a behavior meant to simultaneously strengthen individual positions within European Assemblies and reshape European historical memory. Anti-Communist mobilizations are therefore approached as a trial-and-error process characterized by a series of struggles and compromises with dominant Western conservative allies and left-wing opponents. This brings focus to the essential question of socialization in its capacity to structure practice through habitus, i.e. the internalization of meanings and compliance to social norms. The memory entrepreneurs' gradual command of European roles, acquired inter alia through their engagement in the anti-Communist cause, exemplifies a broader process of professionalization to which the newly elected PACE and EP members eager to acquire a 'sense of the European political game' were submitted. The European assemblies were consequently an echo chamber for demands, the rationales of which were related as much to the memory entrepreneurs' militant backgrounds and their political affiliations as to the modalities of their investment in a European career.

During the numerous historical debates held at PACE and in the EP after their respective enlargements to the East, two divergent ways of assessing Communism and its comparability with Nazism were defended by representatives with distinct biographical characteristics and ideological references.

The first interpretation underlined the singularity of the Holocaust and historicized the analysis of Communism. It distinguished several phases in the history of the Socialist regimes, characterized by variable degrees of violence and various ways of enacting Marxist ideology. This was the argumentative line of a group of representatives of the Left and the far Left from the S&D (Progressive Alliance of Socialists and Democrats) and the GUE (European United Left) groups, which rejected any similarity between Fascism and Nazism on the one hand and Communism on the other.[5] This discourse also prevailed in the Russian delegation at PACE, which defended a heroic vision of the 'Great Patriotic War' and victory over Nazism, as well as among the Communist representatives from southern European countries recently marked by dictatorships (Portugal and Greece).[6]

A second vision characterized Communism by what they saw as its essence, namely violence. It considered it an ahistorical project of brutality comparable with other outbursts of mass violence, notably genocidal, and demanded equal treatment of the victims of Nazism and of those of Communism. This interpretation was mainly advanced by Central European representatives from the conservative EPP (Europe's People Party) and the liberal ALDE (Alliance of Liberals and Democrats in Europe) wings, joined by some Green representatives. The group mixed former dissidents with younger representatives who had entered politics during the regime change. They particularly highlighted the 1939 Molotov-Ribbentrop Pact, by which these two dictatorships had shared out zones of influence between them. From their perspective, this alliance distinguished Stalinism and Nazism from the other twentieth-century dictatorships and proved equivalence between their crimes.

A closer look at anti-Communist memory entrepreneurs is necessary to understand the consecration of this particular interpretation of Communism in European assemblies.

Three types of memory entrepreneurs

Anti-Communist mobilizations were led by a small group of representatives who participated in historical debates at PACE and at the EP, initiated official texts condemning 'Communist crimes' and regularly contributed

---

5   In 2004, the most important groups in terms of numbers at the EP were the European People's Party (EPP) and the social-democrat group (PES, then S&D). These were followed by the Alliance of Liberals and Democrats for Europe (ALDE), the radical-left Group of the European United Left (GUE) and the Greens/European Free Alliance (Greens/EFA). There were also several small conservative groups, like the Union for a Europe of the Nations (UEN) in 2004–2009, and the European Conservatives and Reformists Group (ECR) set up in 2009.

6   PACE members are divided into 5 officially recognized political groups. The most important, numerically speaking, are the group of the European People's Party/ Christian Democrats (EPP-CD) and the Socialist Group (SOC). These are followed by the Alliance of Liberals and Democrats for Europe (ALDE), the Group of the European United Left (GUE) and the European Conservatives Group (EC).

to awareness-raising actions in European assemblies and in transnational networks.[7] Eighteen elected members, 17 of which represented states of the former Eastern bloc, acted as 'anti-Communist memory entrepreneurs' between 1992, when the first debate on Communism was held at PACE, and the start of the EP's 8th term in July 2014.

The European careers of these representatives varied depending on the types of office they held – some of them were elected only to PACE, to PACE then to the EP, or only to the EP. They also entered the European assemblies at different points in time. The terms at PACE are exclusively determined by national elections and thus depend on completely specific timetables. But even the MEPs did not have identical terms. Some were elected at the beginning of the 6th term in 2004 or at the beginning of 7th in 2009; others, like László Tőkés, when Romania joined in 2007; while the Estonian Katrin Saks entered the EP after the term had started to replace an outgoing MEP.

With a few exceptions, the memory entrepreneurs' investment in the European assemblies had begun as soon as their country joined the CoE or the EU. Some of these representatives – such as Saks, Tunne Kelam (from Estonia) and Vytautas Landsbergis (from Lithuania) – moved from PACE to the EP in the course of their career. Latchezar Toshev (from Bulgaria), Emanuelis Zingeris (from Lithuania) and Göran Lindblad (from Sweden) were in office only at PACE, for one or several terms. All the others also had a seat at the EP, where they concentrated their efforts starting in 2004.

The following table sketches out these European careers between 1992 and 2014.

At PACE and at the EP, the vast majority of the anti-Communist memory entrepreneurs (13 out of 18) were affiliated with the EPP. Only Katrin Saks and Marianne Mikko (Estonia) belonged to the S&D, while Bronisław Geremek (Poland) was a member the liberal group ALDE. Two Polish MEPs were part of small conservative groups: Wojciech Roszkowski belonged to the Union for Europe of the Nations group (UEN) and Marek Migalski to the European Conservatives and Reformists group (ECR).

Despite this ideological proximity, the anti-Communist memory entrepreneurs featured diversified socio-political properties depending on their previous national and European political trajectories. Although, as a whole, they tended to be dominated in European assemblies, the structure and volume

---

7   The most active of these networks is the 'Platform of European Memory and Conscience' created in Prague in 2011 (Neumayer 2019).

Tab. 1. Memory entrepreneurs' European terms of office

	PACE	EP's 6th term, 2004–2009	EP's 7th term, 2009–2014	Beginning of the EP's 8th term, July 2014
Latchezar Toshev (Bulgaria)	1992–2005; 2009–2013			
Tunne Kelam (Estonia)	1993–2000	2004–2009	2009–2014	2014–...
Vytautas Landsbergis (Lithuania)	1993–1997; 2000–2003	2004–2009	2009–2014	
Emanuelis Zingeris (Lithuania)	1994–2000; 2005–2008; 2009–...			
Göran Lindblad (Sweden)	2004–2010			
Katrin Saks (Estonia)	2003–2006	2006–2009		
Bronisław Geremek (Poland)		2004–2008		
Wojciech Roszkowksi (Poland)		2004–2009		
Jana Hybášková (Czech Republic)		2004–2009		
Marianne Mikko (Estonia)		2004–2009		
Bogusław Sonik (Poland)		2004–2009	2009–2014	
Inese Vaidere (Latvia)		2004–2009	2009–2014	2014–...
László Tőkés (Romania)		2007–2009	2009–2014	2014–...

(continued on next page)

Tab. 1.   Continued

PACE	EP's 6th term, 2004–2009	EP's 7th term, 2009–2014	Beginning of the EP's 8th term, July 2014
József Szájer (Hungary)	2004–2009	2009–2014	2014–...
György Schöpflin (Hungary)	2004–2009	2009–2014	2014–...
Marek Migalski (Poland)		2009–2014	
Milan Zver (Slovenia)		2009–2014	2014–...
Sandra Kalniete (Latvia)		2009–2014	2014–...

of political resources held when elected to their first European term defined their initial position at PACE and the EP, while their subsequent investment in their European term of office determined their degree of specialization in the anti-Communist cause. Based on these variations, three ideal typical categories of memory entrepreneurs are defined. Some of the historical figures of opposition to Communism, well equipped with national and sometimes European political capital, sat in the most sought-after parliamentary committees and occupied leadership positions in their political groups. They differed from the 'anti-Communist young guard' that had gone into politics when state socialism fell, who were less equipped with political capital but had some technical expertise, which gave them access to parliamentary committees with an important legislative role. Lastly, a few peripheral political actors began their European term of office with relatively little political capital and did not always manage to acquire European institutional credit.

Based on national careers before the first European mandate, the following table classifies memory entrepreneurs in these ideal typical categories.

The first category, that of 'historical opponents,' comprised some prominent political figures who had played a leading role during the 1989–1991 period in the Eastern bloc. All of them had a large amount of national political capital, and sometimes, international notoriety. When they entered the EP, four of them had already held EU-related functions as member of the Convention for

Tab. 2. Three categories of memory entrepreneurs

Historical opponents	'Young guard'	Peripheral actors
Tunne Kelam (Estonia, EPP): born in 1936, historian. One of the leaders of the independence movement in Estonia, member of the Estonian Committee (1990–1992) and of the Estonian Parliament (1992–. . .).	*Latchezar Toshev* (Bulgaria, EPP): born in 1962, Master's in biology (1991), environmental activist (1990–. . .), MP (1991–. . .).	*Göran Lindblad* (Sweden, EPP): born in 1950, city councilman (1991–1997), MP (1997–. . .).
Vytautas Landsbergis (Lithuania, EPP): born in 1932, musicologist. Leader of the pro-independence Sajudis movement (1988–1991), President of Lithuania (1990–1992).	*Emanuelis Zingeris* (Lithuania, EPP): born in 1957, Master's in philology (1981), Director of the State Jewish Museum (1989–. . .), member of the pro-independence Sajudis movement (1988–1991), MP (1990–. . .).	*Wojciech Roszkowski* (Poland, UEN): born in 1947, PhD in history (1978), Vice-Rector of Warsaw School of Economics (1990–1993), Director of the Institute of Political Science, Polish Academy of Sciences (1994–2000), Professor (1995–. . .).
Bronisław Geremek (1932–2008) (Poland, ALDE): PhD in history, Professor of history at the University of Warsaw (1955–1985), leading expert of Solidarność (1980–1981), participant in the Round Table Talks (1989), MP (1989–1997), minister of Foreign Affairs (1997–2000).	*Katrin Saks* (Estonia, S&D): born in 1956, degree in Journalism (1981), degree in International Relations (1993), journalist (1977–1997), head of NGO (1998–2000), minister of Population and Ethnic Affairs (1999–2000), MP (2003–. . .).	*Marianne Mikko* (Estonia, S&D): born in 1961, degree in Journalism (1984), journalist (1989–2004).
László Tőkés (Romania, Greens then EPP): born in 1952, bishop. Leader of the 1989 demonstrations in Timisoara, leading activist for national minority rights in Romania.	*Jana Hybašková* (Czech Republic, EPP): born in 1956, Master's in Arabic (1989), diplomatic career, ambassador to Slovenia (1997–2001) then to Kuwait and Qatar (2002–2004).	*György Schöpflin* (Hungary, EPP): born in 1939, refugee in the UK at age 11, LLB (1962), researcher at the Royal School of International Affairs (1963–1967), journalist at the BBC (1967–1973), lecturer then Professor of Political science at University College London.

(continued on next page)

Tab. 2. Continued

Historical opponents	'Young guard'	Peripheral actors
Sandra Kalniete (Latvia, EPP): born in 1952, art historian. One of the leaders of the Latvian Popular Front (1988–1991), diplomat (1990–2001), minister of Foreign Affairs (2002–2004), member of the Convention for the Future of Europe (2002–2003), EU commissioner for Agriculture (2004), MP (2006–2009).	*Bogusław Sonik* (Poland, EPP): born in 1953, Master's in law (1978), journalist in exile in France (1983–1989), minister plenipotentiary at the Polish Embassy in France (1990–1996), regional councilman in Poland (1998–2004).	*Marek Migalski* (Poland, ECR): born in 1969, PhD in political science (2001), Associate Professor at the University of Silesia (2000–...)
	Inese Vaidere (Latvia, UEN then EPP): born in 1952, PhD in economics (1992), Associate University Professor (1975–2003), political adviser (1996–1998), minister of the Environment (1998–1999), deputy to the mayor of Riga (2001–2002), MP (2002–2004).	
	József Szájer (Hungary, EPP): born in 1961, lawyer, president of the FIDESZ group at the Hungarian Parliament (1990–2002), president of the European Affairs Committee (1998–2002), vice-president of Parliament (2002–2004). Member of the Convention for the Future of Europe (2002–2003). Observer at the EP (2003).	

Tab. 2. Continued

Historical opponents	'Young guard'	Peripheral actors
	Milan Zver (Slovenia, EPP): born in 1962, researcher at the University of Ljubljana (1987–1992), political adviser (1992–2004), MP (1998–2003), minister of Education (2004–2008).	

the Future of Europe in 2002–2003 (Tunne Kelam from Estonia and Sandra Kalniete from Latvia), as 'observer'[8] at the EP (Vytautas Landsbergis) or as European commissioner (Sandra Kalniete). The former heads of state or foreign ministers were given a seat at the EP in the most prestigious parliamentary committees such as the Foreign Affairs committee. This 'biographical effect' was reinforced by an 'institutional effect' stemming from leading positions in political groups, such as membership in bureaus of the EPP for Landsbergis and of the ALDE for Geremek.

A second sub-group, the anti-Communist 'young guard,' included younger representatives whose political capital stemmed from a strong position within the EPP and/or close ties with their national political-bureaucratic apparatus. Their European political resources were sometimes combined with national resources that were party-based (József Szájer had been one of the main leaders of Hungarian party FIDESz since its creation), government-based (Inese Vaidere from Latvia and Milan Zver, from Slovenia, were former ministers) or of the diplomatic type (Jana Hybášková, from the Czech Republic, was a former ambassador). These belonged to parliamentary committees in line with their expertise: environmental protection for Latchezar Toshev (from Bulgaria) and Bogusław Sonik (from Poland), foreign affairs for Hybášková, law for Szájer and education for Zver. Several of them had long European careers during which they reached positions of responsibility within the EPP or in parliamentary committees, such as Toshev at PACE or Szájer at the EP.

---

8 Observers were delegated by acceding countries in 2003 to attend the work without taking part in the decision making.

The third category of memory entrepreneurs, dubbed 'peripheral political actors,' includes representatives who had entered PACE and the EP with lesser national and European political capital. Although some of them remained confined to minor political groups or to marginal parliamentary committees, others managed to secure a seat in a sought-after committee in the course of their terms at PACE or at the EP. For instance, Migalski and Mikko, associate university professor and journalist, respectively, belonged to the lower-profiled parliamentary Committee for Culture and Education, whose sphere of action reflected their professional skills. The university professors Wojciech Roszkowski (from Poland) and György Schöpflin (from Hungary) joined more prestigious committees, respectively charged with Foreign Affairs and with Budget issues. This group also includes the only memory entrepreneur who was not from Central and Baltic Europe, namely the Swede Göran Lindblad, dentist by training. Although nothing in his biography seems to have destined him to engage in the debates on Communism, he was selected as rapporteur for the resolution condemning the crimes of Communist regimes at PACE in 2006 and subsequently specialized in defending fundamental rights in the former Soviet Union (Neumayer 2019).

What these memory entrepreneurs had in common, whatever their former political trajectory, was engagement in the defense of human rights, particularly in the post-Soviet space. Several of them were members of the EP's Subcommittee on Human Rights or of parliamentary delegations in charge of relations with the former Soviet Republics. As summarized on the PACE and EP websites, the same concentration on human rights shows up in their parliamentary activities: tabling parliamentary questions, writing declarations and motions for a resolution, and even drafting reports. This positioning enabled memory entrepreneurs to 'denationalize' the anti-Communist cause and to embed it in a theme that is at the core of these assemblies' role, i.e. the protection of fundamental rights and freedoms.

There were however strong variations in the intensity and the forms of these representatives' engagement in the anti-Communist cause. These variations depended on the place in their career of their European office and on their possession of sectoral expertise, but also on their unequal access to the resources of parliamentary power offered by political groups. At PACE, Landsbergis and Kelam used their term of office mainly to discuss the bilateral disputes opposing their countries to Russia. The other memory entrepreneurs, whether they belonged to the anti-Communist 'young guard' or to the group of peripheral actors, were overall more active and defended human rights in the whole former Soviet Union. They also undertook more diversified activities, as testified by the topics of the reports that they prepared for the Assembly.[9]

At the EP, there were also marked variations between on the one hand the historical figures of the opposition to Communism, who were the least inclined to adopt the apolitical posture that characterizes European political games and favored plenary-meeting interventions, and on the other hand the 'young guard' who became involved in the daily task of government through reports or opinions on technical issues. The 'young guard' had acquired through their national career a form of expertise that structured their parliamentary activities to the same extent as their commitment to human rights. Anti-Communist mobilizations were not their only form of investment in European assemblies, and their knowledge in various fields of EU action enabled some of them to sit in prominent committees and to draft legislative reports on a variety of issues. This was particularly true of Szájer, a lawyer by training, who sit for ten years in the prestigious committee of Constitutional Affairs and stood out in terms of legislative work.[10] Regarding peripheral political actors, only some of the memory entrepreneurs who had been elected to the EP with little national political and bureaucratic capital managed to acquire enough peer recognition to be tasked with drafting parliamentary reports.

This brief group portrait highlights the plurality of motivations and of forms of anti-Communist engagement in European assemblies. Besides ideological motivations, investment in sensitive historical debates could help these newcomers define a distinctive parliamentary profile and acquire European institutional credit. This explains their uneven specialization in the anti-Communist cause, depending on whether memory activism was the basis of a European career and of the militant trajectory that preceded it, or whether it was considered an additional skill in a professionalization dynamics based on other forms of legitimacy valued in the European political space.

The limits of anti-Communist activism in European Assemblies

The partial success of the mobilizations for historical reckoning, collective remembrance and legal accountability for Socialist-era mass violence sheds

---

9 For instance, Toshev drafted reports and opinions on bioterrorism and on cooperation in transborder basins, while Lindblad signed reports on the situation in the Middle East and on migrations in Europe.

10 Just in the 6th term, Szájer prepared six reports.

light on three major constraints faced by anti-Communist memory activism in European assemblies.

First, it is worth noting that only those representatives initially equipped with considerable resources, such as well-known former dissidents, or those combining strong national political capital and relevant European expertise, managed to stay at the core of European parliamentary power and to be reelected as MEPs after their first mandate. This testifies to the additional character of mnemonic activism as a source of political capital, which was not sufficient to stabilize an EU career in the absence of the political skills that are crucial to the European political profession.

Second, the rationales of European-level political debates and policies for managing painful pasts diluted the anti-Communist cause into a broader condemnation of all types of dictatorships that have befell Europe in the twentieth century. The rules of European political competition entail euphemizing ideological conflicts and denationalizing issues, in order to build broad coalitions across parliamentary groups and national delegations. Anti-Communist representatives, who overwhelmingly belonged to the EPP, faced fierce ideological opposition from their peers in the S&D and in the GUE. In 2008, the Social-Democrats even established a History Working Group at the EP with the explicit goal of "countering any attempts to rewrite history" (Neumayer 2015).

Anti-Communist memory entrepreneurs were also forced to adjust their claims to the normative beliefs that underpinned existing EU policies for managing painful pasts. Yet their demands were at odds with the patterns of remembrance established in the Western World in the 1970s and consecrated by the EU in the 1990s. Their request to acknowledge their own suffering presented as wrongfully ignored differed from the "politics of regret" favored by Western governments (Olick 2007) that recognize past wrongs and ask for the victims' forgiveness. The will to impose a single narrative as historical truth on the whole continent also collided with the 'multi-perspective' history promoted by the European organizations, which admits the plurality of points of view on the past as long as they are founded on an objectively established factual basis. Moreover, including historical episodes other than World War II among the common pasts of Europe indirectly questioned the significance of the Holocaust as founding event of the continent's history. This led anti-Communist memory entrepreneurs to be regularly accused by their political competitors and by militants of the Jewish cause of trivializing Nazism and of minimizing the complicity of Eastern European societies in the extermination of the Jews. Last but not least, their mobilizations also prompted calls for recognition of other dictatorships, such as the regimes established by Mussolini, Franco, Salazar and the Greek military junta.

To comply with these many constraints, anti-Communist memory entrepreneurs adjusted their cause to the human-rights paradigm that structures European-level mnemonic politics. They requested that European institutions assess Socialist legacies with the same criteria as the ones used for other dictatorships, which would entail denouncing the crimes that they perpetrated and commemorating their victims. However, moving to this level of generality diluted to some extent the anti-Communist cause in a blanket condemnation of 'all forms of totalitarianism' having existed on the European continent (EP 2009), thereby tempering the Communism-Nazism equivalence.

Third, the existing European remembrance policy and the segmentation of the European political space demonetized the parliamentary resolutions outside of PACE and the EP. This diminished the legal and judicial implications of the anti-Communist grammar endorsed by these Assemblies. Remembrance policies drawn up by the EU and the CoE in the 1990s had left the member states free to manage their painful pasts by means of law, without imposing any legally binding instruments regarding the fight against historical denial or the prosecution of perpetrators. Moreover, it was difficult to convert parliamentary resolutions into European-level public policy and legal action because of the fragmented nature of the European political space. At the CoE, the Council of ministers did not act upon the 2006 resolution on the "[n]eed for international condemnation of the crimes of totalitarian Communist regimes." In the EU, although the remembrance strand of the program 'Europe for Citizens' encompassed Stalinist mass violence, it fell short of the ultimate goal of most anti-Communist memory entrepreneurs: the adoption of EU-level legal steps to prosecute former high-ranking Communist leaders (Neumayer 2019).

The anti-Communist cause undoubtedly lost its salience in European organizations after the adoption of the resolution on 'European conscience and totalitarianism' by the EP in 2009.

In 2013, the own-initiative report on "Historical memory in culture and education in the EU" tabled by Marek Migalski was rejected by the EP Committee on Culture and Education even before it could be discussed in plenary session. When the program "Europe for citizens" was renewed in 2013, its remembrance strand was extended to include initiatives that 'reflect on the causes of totalitarian regimes in Europe's modern history (especially but not exclusively Nazism which led to the Holocaust, Fascism, Stalinism and totalitarian Communist regimes) and commemorate the victims of their crimes, but also "activities concerning other defining moments and reference points in recent

European history" (EU Council 2013: 10). This broader scope attenuated the sole focus on Stalinism and Nazism that had initially shaped the EU's remembrance program. This highlights the contraction of the memory entrepreneurs' room for maneuver: the controversy over Communism had lost its intensity in European assemblies, while the European Left had taken the opportunity of the condemnation of Communism to obtain the same for an ideology against which it was primarily defined, namely Fascism.

In order to keep the issue of 'Communist crimes' on the EU's agenda, anti-Communist representatives still carry out awareness-raising activities such as exhibitions, film screenings, conferences and hearings at the EP. However, their impact in the assembly is limited to a very specific segment – the Central European Conservatives -, while their symbolic resonance in the general public is mostly restricted to the former Eastern bloc (Neumayer 2017). In Western Europe, the visibility of the remembrance actions dedicated to the victims of Soviet-era mass violence remains far lower than that of the tributes to the victims of Nazi atrocities. It is very telling that 23 August, established in 2009 as 'Day of Remembrance for the victims of all totalitarian and authoritarian regimes' in the EU, has failed to gain the same symbolic significance as the 'International Day of Commemoration in memory of the victims of the Holocaust' on 27 January.

To conclude, 30 years after the demise of Socialism, European-level historical debates remain structured around two diverging accounts of the past. In the first, the Holocaust is seen as a unique form of mass violence and as the negative symbol of a 'new Europe' based on protecting human rights, while the second demands, in the name of the universality of human rights, that the gravity of gross violations of human rights in the former Eastern bloc be recognized as equivalent. In an attempt to find a middle ground between these two narratives, the EU and the CoE have produced a historical memory based on a broad denunciation of all forms of totalitarianism and on the commemoration of their victims. The very fact that this under-specification was necessary to evade controversies over the rankings of different painful pasts confirms that the European-level discussions did not put an end to the hefty debates on the comparison of the Holocaust with other mass violence. On the contrary, the controversy over Communism, which engages the European institutions' capacity to produce a consensual historical narrative while integrating new states, illustrates the persisting difficulties of establishing common grounds for a shared culture of memory on the European continent.

References

Beauvallet, Willy, Michon, Sébastien (2016) "The changing paths of access to the European Parliament for French MEPs (1979–2014)," *French Politics* 14: 101–125.

Beauvallet, Willy, Michon, Sébastien (2013) "MEPs: towards a specialization of European work" in Didier Georgakakis, Jay Rowell (eds), *The Field of Eurocracy. Mapping EU actors and professionals*, pp. 16–34. Houndmills, Basingstoke: Palgrave Macmillan.

Closa, Carlos (2010) "Negotiating the Past: Claims for Recognition and Policies of Memory in the EU," Working Paper 08. Madrid: Instituto de Politicas y Bienes Publicos, CCHS-CSIC.

De Clerck-Sachsse, Julia, Kaczyński, Piotr Maciej (2009) "The European Parliament: more powerful, less legitimate? An outlook for the 7th term," *CEPS Working Paper*, 34/2009.

Droit, Emmanuel (2007) 'Le Goulag contre la Shoah. Mémoires officielles et cultures mémorielles dans l'Europe élargie,' *Vingtième siècle* 94: 101–120.

European Commission (2007) *Europe for Citizens Programme 2007-2013. Programme Guide*. https://ec.europa.eu/citizenship/pdf/programme_guide_fr.pdf

EU Council (2013) "Council Regulation establishing for the period 2014–2020 the programme "Europe for Citizen," Doc. 12557/13, https://register.consilium.europa.eu/doc/srv?l=EN&f=ST%2012557 %202013 %20COR%204.

European Parliament (2009) "Resolution of 2 April 2009 on European conscience and totalitarianism,' available at https://www.europarl.europa.eu/sides/getDoc.do?pubRef=-//EP//TEXT+TA+P6-TA-2009-0213+0+DOC+XML+V0//EN (accessed 22 April 2020).

Georgakakis, Didier, Vauchez, Antoine (2015) "Le concept de champ à l'épreuve de l'Europe" in Johanna Siméant (ed.) *Guide de l'enquête globale en sciences sociales*, pp. 197–217. Paris: Editions du CNRS.

Georgakakis, Didier, Rowell, Jay (eds) (2013) *The Field of Eurocracy. Mapping EU actors and professionals*. Houndmills, Basingstoke: Palgrave Macmillan.

Hurka, Steffen, Kaeding, Michael (2012) "Report allocation in the European Parliament after Eastern enlargement," *Journal of European Public Policy* 19(4): 512–529.

Leggewie, Claus (2008) "A Tour of the Battleground: The Seven Circles of Pan-European Memory," *Social Research* 75: 217–234.

Littoz-Monnet, Annabelle (2012) "The EU politics of remembrance: Can Europeans remember together?" *West European Politics* 35(5): 1182–1202.

Mälksoo, Maria (2014) "Criminalizing Communism: Transnational Mnemopolitics in Europe," *International Political Sociology* 8: 82–99.

Mark, James (2010) *The Unfinished Revolution: Making Sense of the Communist Past in Central-Eastern Europe.* New Haven: Yale University Press.

Mink, Georges, Neumayer, Laure (2013) *History, Memory and Politics in East Central Europe. Memory Games.* Houndsmills, Basingstoke: Palgrave Macmillan.

Müller, Birgit, Ditchev, Ivalyo, Filipova, Olga, et al (1999), "The Council of Europe after Enlargement: An Anthropological Enquiry," *Document de Travail du CEFRES*, 18, available at halshs-00137949v1 (accessed 22 April 2020).

Neumayer, Laure (2015) "Integrating the Central European Past into a Common Narrative: the mobilizations around the "crimes of Communism" in the European Parliament," *Journal of Contemporary European Studies* 23(3): 344–363.

_____ (2017) "Advocating for the cause of the "victims of Communism" in the European political space: memory entrepreneurs in interstitial fields," *Nationalities Papers* 45(6): 992–1012.

_____ (2019) *The criminalisation of Communism in the European political space after the Cold War.* London and New York: Routledge.

Olick, Jeffrey (2007) *The Politics of Regret, On Collective Memory and Historical Responsibility.* London: Routledge.

PACE (2006), "Need for an international condemnation of the crimes of the totalitarian Communist regimes," doc 10765.

Pollak, Michael (2000) *L'expérience concentrationnaire: essais sur le maintien de l'identité sociale.* Paris: Métailié.

Rowell, Jay, Mangenot, Michel (eds.) (2010) *A Political Sociology of the European Union. Reassessing Constructivism.* Manchester: Manchester University Press.

Valentin Behr

From Anticommunism to Antiliberalism. Polish Conservative Intellectuals' Involvement in the Transnational Circulation of Ideas

Abstract: Referring to Europe mainly as a Christian civilization, the Polish Law and Justice Party (PiS) takes part in the current struggle over the definition of European values. This chapter focuses on the narrative about European values that has been shaped by Polish conservative intellectuals. The transnational perspective adopted permits to emphasize the circulation of ideas within transnational networks of conservative intellectuals. First, the group of Polish intellectuals that have contributed to shape PiS's political offer is described. Second, the Polish case is situated in the broader context of the reconfiguration of the European Right. Finally, this chapter takes a closer look at the ideology that is promoted by Polish conservative intellectuals, both in Poland and within transnational circles.

Keywords: conservative ideas, European values, intellectuals, Poland, transnational circulation of ideas

Introduction

During Spring 2020, the *Stowarzyszenie Tworców dla Rzeczypospolitej* [Association of Creators for the Republic], a Polish NGO founded by a Polish Member of the European Parliament from the *Prawo i Sprawiedliwość* [Law and Justice, PiS] party – Zdzisław Krasnodębski – released on social media a "Preamble for the Constitution of a Federation of European Nations." Advocating for a "confederation of Nation States," this constitutional project relies on an allegedly common Western European culture. That culture would have been

> shaped by various sources, out of which we have to particularly underline the teaching of the Old Testament, Greek thought, Roman State art, the Christian revelation and the heritage of the Romanic, Germanic and Slavic people, and saw the light in an institutionalised form since the formation of the spiritual sovereignty of the Church and of the political authority of the imperial dignity restored in 800.[1]

---

1   Available at: https://www.davidengels.be/preamble (accessed 20 August 2020).

Far from being a solely Polish project, the Preamble was drafted by David Engels, a Belgian historian, professor at the Université libre de Bruxelles and, since 2018, at the *Instytut Zachodni* [Western Institute] in Poznan.

Far from isolated, this example of East-West cooperation is part of a broader phenomenon: in recent years, right-wing conservative projects attempting at thinking Europe anew, understood not only as the European Union (EU) but also more generally as European civilization, have emerged: Visegrad States, with Poland and Hungary's "illiberal democracy" at the forefront, tried to challenge the Paris-Berlin axis in EU politics; Donald Trump's former adviser Steve Bannon settled *The Movement*, a Brussels-based organization which ambitioned – and failed – to rally European populists and nationalists in the prospect of the 2019 European election; European intellectuals from several EU States made an attempt to outline the tenets of a European conservative renewal.[2] Engels' "Preamble for the Constitution of a Federation of European Nations," together with his book *Renovatio Europae* (Engels 2019), is part of that latter attempt.

These projects are not ideologically homogeneous. However, they are signs of a work of ideological production, or a metapolitical[3] work, realized by loose and partly overlapping transnational networks. These networks bring together a few politicians, but mainly scholars and intellectuals. They contribute to the "democratic backslide" to which many research works have been dedicated recently, however the ideological dimension of that phenomenon remains under researched so far.

Indeed, the flourishing scholarly literature devoted to the rise of illiberal or authoritarian governments throughout the world has been focusing on party politics, voters' support and institutional change (Csillag and Szelenyi 2015; Rupnik 2017; Eatwell and Goodwin 2018; Blokker 2019; Vachudova 2019). Political parties such as PiS in Poland and Fidesz in Hungary have often been labelled as "populist" (Mudde 2007; Pankowski 2010; Minkenberg 2017;) and/ or "Eurosceptic" (Neumayer 2008; Dakowska 2010). Nonetheless, the academic

---

2 See the "Paris Statement," signed by intellectuals participating in the activities of the Center for European Renewal, a conservative pan-European think tank to which I shall come back later in this chapter, available at: https://thetrueeurope.eu/ (accessed 20 August 2020).

3 By metapolitical work, I mean political reflection produced by "intellectuals rejecting direct and activist parliamentary or extra-parliamentary political interventions and focusing their energies on changing hearts and minds and the 'conquest' of civil society." See Bar-On (2013, 3).

literature dedicated to populism and Euroskepticism is rarely preoccupied with ideology. It seldom questions the societal blueprint supported by these political groupings. An exception is the literature devoted to the ideational dimension of the democratic backslide, often inspired by political economy and/or discourse analysis (Bluhm and Varga 2019). As Buzogány and Varga, put it, "the contestation of liberalism is not reducible to political parties and instead should be approached as a broader phenomenon," namely by tackling its ideological dimension (Buzogány and Varga 2018).

While populism has often been labelled as a "thin" ideology, I would argue that "conservative" is a more appropriate label when it comes to describing the worldview of the Polish intellectuals I deal with in this chapter, for at least two reasons. First, they claim the conservative label for themselves, so even if we should put into question the way social actors define themselves, it seems to be a good starting point in the case of political thinkers. Second, this label permits to free oneself from certain preconceptions conveyed by other labels such as populism, illiberalism or Euroskepticism. All too often, such labels implicitly convey assumptions that tend to "exoticize" Central Europe as a region that would be *a priori* undemocratic. The notion of conservatism, on the contrary, permits us to situate the PiS party and its intellectual backers within a broader phenomenon, that of the ideological reconfiguration of European right-wing parties, in their diversity (Christian-democracy, neo-conservatism, neo-liberalism, nativism, etc.). I thus follow Frédéric Zalewski's proposal to consider the "democratic backslide" in Hungary and Poland as "conservative revolutions," that is, as variants of the conservative shifts that occurred in the United States and Great Britain in the 1980s (Zalewski 2016).

Hence, it is important not to reduce the "democratic backslide" to a Central European or post-communist problem. The puzzle at stake is that of an emerging transnational cooperation between European conservatives. The "National Conservatism Conference" organized in Rome in early 2020, which brought together intellectual and political figures such as Ryszard Legutko – Polish PiS MEP and philosopher) –, Marion Maréchal (from the French National Rally) and Viktor Orbán, among other speakers from all over Europe, was just another example of that potential cooperation.

Thus, there is a need for in-depth studies of what has been described as a "cultural backlash" that would bear similarities between Donald Trump's election as President of the United States, Brexit and the rise of "authoritarian populism" (Norris and Inglehart 2019). The uses of "gender ideology" and the "refugee crisis" in the context of electoral campaigns in Poland has already been emphasized (Korolczuk and Graff 2018; Lewis and Waligórska 2019).

"Culture wars" seem to be particularly intense in Central Europe, where since 1989 political divides have been articulated around cultural rather than social issues (Kubik 2003; Ost 2005; Brier 2009).

Since political ideas are social constructs, it is necessary to look at the actors – mainly intellectuals – who produce them and therefore foster the cultural divides. Kubik emphasizes the role of "cultural entrepreneurs" (i.e. political and cultural elites) to underline the fact that cultural legacies are "transmitted," not "received from:" they are not just a "weight" of the past, they are constructed, shaped, used, by these entrepreneurs (Kubik 2003: 318). As demonstrated by Bourdieu, intellectuals have the power of preserving or transforming the social world by preserving or transforming the categories of perception of that world (Bourdieu 1992, 2001). Bourdieu's field theory constitutes a particularly relevant methodological framework to study the political role of the Polish intelligentsia which, due to historical reasons and Poland's positions as a "semi-periphery" of Western Europe, appears more autonomous from the State than in most Western countries. That would explain the rather favored position of members of the intelligentsia and the domination of cultural capital over political capital within the Polish field of power (Zarycki, Smoczyński, and Warczok 2017; Smoczyński and Zarycki 2017).

Thinking in terms of differentiated social fields permits to grasp the multipositionality of Polish conservative intellectuals, which is indeed considerable: Legutko and Krasnodębski are both scholars and Members of the European Parliament at the same time. They also have been quite successful as columnists in the press and media for a while. At the crossroads between the political, intellectual and media fields, they enjoy a genuine multipositionality that permits them to cumulate resources, such as political, social and symbolic capital. The biographic approach adopted in this chapter permits to highlight the successful career of such intellectual entrepreneurs, who have had some success in the field of ideological production, both in Poland and abroad. Indeed, their social and intellectual trajectories should not be isolated from the dynamics of the transnational exchanges in which they participate.

Focusing on Polish actors, but willing to resist any form of methodological nationalism, this chapter seeks to show how the work of ideological production by Polish conservative intellectuals resonates with developments elsewhere in Europe (and beyond). The aim is not to set up Central Europe as a model or a warning to the world (Krastev and Holmes 2019), but to treat it as a vantage point from which to grasp reconfigurations of the European Right.

To do so, I will focus on the way European values are tackled by Polish conservative intellectuals. Defined by Article 2 of the Treaty on European Union,

European values are subject to conflicting uses, in the absence of a consensus on their meaning (Foret and Calligaro 2018; Coman and Leconte 2019).[4] While article 7 has been triggered against Poland's reforms of the judiciary that would threaten the rule of law, the conflict is not just about diverging understandings of European values, but about the very definition of European identity and, therefore, of the course of the European Union.

This chapter is divided into three parts. First, the group of Polish intellectuals that have contributed to shape PiS's understanding of European values is described. Second, they are situated in the broader context of the reconfiguration of the European Right, by examining transnational networks to which they have contributed so far. Finally, I take a closer look at the ideology that is promoted by Polish conservative intellectuals, both in Poland and within transnational circles.

Between academia, media and politics: The conservative fraction of the Polish Intelligentsia

It has already been noticed that intellectuals have directly contributed not only to the elaboration of Law and Justice's political offer, but also to the concrete exercise of power by that Party, as members of parliament or as experts and policy advisers (Dąbrowska 2019). Conservative intellectuals seem to have been particularly efficient in creating a set of think tanks that have greatly contributed to design Law and Justice's manifestos. While this has been well established in the case of economic policies (Dąbrowska, Buzogány, and Varga 2019), I focus here on values and morality issues.

Among Polish conservative think tanks, Ośrodek Myśli Politycznej [Center for Political Thought, OMP] deserves special attention. Established in the early 1990s, the OMP has been one of the hotbeds of conservative political philosophy in Poland. Other think tanks, journals and magazines have contributed to the development of conservative ideas since the 1990s (Matyja 2015), however it is striking how several scholars that took part in the metapolitical work of the OMP (mainly conferences and publications) have subsequently held leading political positions with the support of PiS. To name just a few, among the most illustrative of multipositionnality and among the most active in the public

---

4 The Treaty on European Union identifies human dignity, freedom, democracy, equality, the rule of law and respect for human rights as EU values.

debate are Andrzej Nowak, Wojciech Roszkowski, Krzysztof Szczerski and the abovementioned Zdzisław Krasnodębski and Ryszard Legutko.[5]

Krasnodębski, born in 1953, graduated in sociology at the University of Warsaw (1976), where he defended a PhD in 1984. He lectured at the University of Warsaw. Since the early 1980s, he made a few stays in German universities. From 1991 to 1995, he was a professor at the universities of Kassel and then Bremen. When he returned to Poland he was, next to his academic career, a columnist for several newspapers and magazines of a conservative and/or catholic orientation, such as *Znak*, *Rzeczpospolita*, *Gazeta Polska* and *W Sieci*. After the creation of the PiS party in 2001, he progressively became a close adviser to that party. In 2010, the President of the Republic of Poland Lech Kaczyński appointed him a member of the National Development Council, an advisory body to the President. In 2014, he became a member of the PiS Program Council before being elected a Member of the European Parliament (MEP) following the European elections held the same year. Between 2018 and 2019, he served as vice-president of the European Parliament and was re-elected as MEP in 2019. In his essays and press articles, Krasnodębski has been a strong advocate of the PiS party and criticized on many occasions the so-called liberal-left opposition. In 2016, he became a co-host of *Konfrontacje Idei* [Confrontation of Ideas], a program displayed every second week on Polish public radio.

Born in 1949, Legutko graduated at Jagiellonian University in Krakow, in English philology (1973) and in philosophy (1976). He became a member of the academic staff in the same university, as a specialist of ancient Greek philosophy. An English-speaking academic, interested in conservative political thought, he had the opportunity to travel to the West as visiting scholar to the University of Chicago at the beginning of the 1980s. When he came back to Poland, Legutko joined the editorial team of the underground magazine *Arka*, published in Krakow since 1983. Legutko was its chief editor from 1987 to 1991. From 1992 to 2005, he was the chairman of the Center for Political Thought (OMP). In 2005, following PiS victory in both presidential and legislative elections, Legutko stepped into professional politics. He was elected senator and resigned from his position of chairman of the OMP. He was then briefly minister of Education in 2007 and failed to be re-elected as senator after the early legislative elections held in the fall of 2007. Then, he joined

---

5   The biographical information provided here has been collected online (institutional websites, media websites, *Wikipedia*) and during two interviews I conducted with Ryszard Legutko and Zdzisław Krasnodębski.

the Cabinet of the President of the Republic of Poland, before being elected as MEP in 2009. He has been re-elected twice, in 2014 and 2019. In the European Parliament, Legutko is the co-chairman of the European Conservatives and Reformists group (ECR), that associates the PiS representatives with the British conservatives, among others. His book *The Demon in Democracy: Totalitarian Temptations in Free Societies*, published in 2016 as the English translation of a book previously published in Polish, enjoyed a genuine echo in European conservative circles (Legutko 2016).

Next to Krasnodębski and Legutko, many PiS politicians and political advisers have been involved in the OMP's activities. To name just a few, among them are Ryszard Terlecki, professor of history, currently chairman of the PiS parliamentary caucus in the lower house of the Polish parliament; Andrzej Nowak, professor of history, a well-known public intellectual and adviser of the President of the Republic of Poland, who replaced Legutko as chief editor of the *Arka* magazine in 1991; Wojciech Roszkowski, also a historian, who was a PiS MEP between 2004 and 2009 and recently published a political essay devoted to the "fall of Western civilization" (Roszkowski 2019); and Krzysztof Szczerski, professor of political science, currently Head of the Cabinet of the President of the Republic of Poland and his adviser for European Affairs. Such multipositionality is not peculiar to conservative intellectuals. Rather, it is a structural feature of the Polish intelligentsia (Zarycki, Smoczyński, and Warczok 2017). It clearly distinguishes Polish intellectuals – for whom the metapolitical work is directly linked with personal political careers – from most of their counterparts in the transnational networks I will present in the next section.

I will deal with Krasnodębski and Legutko in the first place, as they are particularly relevant for the purpose of this chapter. Indeed, they both are allegedly close advisers of Jarosław Kaczyński, the head of the PiS party (*Gazeta Wyborcza*, 2018). Besides, they co-authored the opening chapter on "values" in the party's program for the 2019 electoral campaign in the legislative election.[6] Finally, they are the most active in conservative transnational networks, due to their academic background and thanks to their positions as MEPs.[7]

These intellectuals' multipositionality, at the crossroads between the academia, the media and politics, is a social resource: it permits some ubiquity,

---

6   Interview led by Valentin Behr with Ryszard Legutko, Brussels, 15 October 2019.
7   Here it is worth recalling that academic degrees and expertise are key resources for political careers at the EU level (Beauvallet and Michon 2010; Neumayer 2010).

which is a distinctive feature of members of the elite (Boltanski 1973). Multipositionality results in the blurring of frontiers between scholarly work and political involvement, between the academic and the intellectual fields (Pinto 1986). One can assume that such blurring favors intellectuals' influence, on both the definition of the public debate (via conferences and publications) and the definition of the political offer (through positions of advisers). Taking part in the "struggle for the imposition of the dominant worldview," intellectuals make a key contribution to the definition of the realm of the "politically thinkable." Their work of ideological production contributes to the shaping of what Bourdieu calls "doxa," i.e. "the set of beliefs that form the basis of the worldview and make the world go without saying" (Sapiro 2007).

Conferences gathering various members of the elite such as scholars, journalists, politicians or clergymen, constitute important *"lieux neutres"* (neutral spaces) which favor the rapprochement and collusions between different fractions of the field of power (Bourdieu and Boltanski 1976). Since its creation, the OMP has played a key role in the organization of such events, contributing to provide political leaders with new catchwords and ideas. The conferences Polska Wielki Projekt [Poland's Great Project], organized each year since 2011 by the OMP together with other conservative NGOs and think tanks, consisted initially in an attempt at shaping a cultural counter-hegemony in the Gramscian sense. Since PiS came to power in 2015, it has become a major event organized under the patronage of the President of the Republic of Poland and sponsored by big public compagnies. It gathers members of governments, CEOs of big public companies, intellectuals and politicians from across Europe, who meet to discuss various issues such as economic policies, challenges of EU integration and of course, morality issues. Hence, I agree with Trencsény when he points at

> the profound ambiguity of the notion of civil society, which, in the context of the East European transitions, has been perceived as a key agent of democratization. To the contrary, what the last decade has shown is the immense power of a profoundly antiliberal civic mobilization that has created an antidemocratic and often ethno-nationalist "parallel polis" ... (Trencsényi 2014, 151)

Decentring the focus of analysis from political parties to the work of ideological production that takes place primarily within civil society, invites to reflect on the social forces that support the so-called illiberal regimes, be it business interests or NGOs such as Ordo Iuris which, in Poland, lobbied for a total ban on abortion. By looking at the field of ideological production, it is therefore not a question of considering that a party like PiS would be more ideological and less pragmatic than another, but of considering the configurations of actors that support this party and contribute to setting its agenda.

The social space in which Polish conservative intellectuals operate, i.e. the field of ideological production, is also dependent on transnational intellectual exchanges. Ideas are products that circulate internationally, although this circulation goes hand in hand with differentiated appropriations and translations, depending on the characteristics of the national and transnational spaces between which ideas circulate (Bourdieu 2002). The following section examines some transnational spaces in which conservative ideas circulate.

From the Cold War to EU accession: Polish contributions to right-wing transnational networks

Among the rich scholarly literature devoted to the transnational circulation of ideas, the dissemination of hegemonic ideas produced in the United States or Western Europe has dominated the field so far. This is the case with studies on the diffusion of neo-liberalism, through transnational think tanks such as the Mont-Pèlerin Society (Mirowski and Plehwe 2009). However, little is known of transnational conservative networks.

Based on my ongoing research, I have been able to identify at least three distinct networks. This is by no means exhaustive, but it permits to highlight the diversity of the meeting spaces and their progressive evolution over time. These networks were indeed constituted at different times and invite us to consider the ideological evolution of the Right since the end of the Cold War.

First of all, Cold War anti-communist networks have been channels of circulation of conservative ideas. The already mentioned *Arka* magazine – whom Legutko was chief editor in the 1980s – hosted contributions from Western authors, mostly French, British and US conservatives, neoconservatives and libertarians. Many Western authors were contributors of anti-communist and conservative publications such as *Encounter*, the *Salisbury Review* or *Commentary*. Contacts between *Arka*'s editorial staff and Western scholars are also illustrated by the international "Patronage Council" that was made of prominent Western intellectuals, who were supposed to constitute a symbolic protection for the underground magazine. All of them had links with anti-communist Cold War organizations such as the Congress for Cultural Freedom (1950–1967) – which became the International Association for Cultural Freedom (1967–1978) after it was revealed that the organization had been financed by the CIA[8] – and the Committee for the Free World, a neocon-servative anti-communist think tank in the United States.

Next to the criticism of soviet-style regimes, communism and totalitar-ianism, contributors to the magazine shared their concerns about Western "culture wars" and "political correctness," thus contributing to the diffusion of Western conservative thinking in Poland, already before 1989. As a result, criticism towards Western liberal democracy was a quite common topic in *Arka* even before the fall of the communist regime.

Besides *Arka*'s international connections, it is worth mentioning the Jagiellonian Trust Foundation, an NGO established in the early 1980s by the late British conservative philosopher Roger Scruton and Caroline Cox, a member of the British House of Lords. Designed on the model of the Jan Hus Educational Foundation, set up earlier to operate in Czechoslovakia, the Jagiellonian Trust supported anti-Communist dissent in the former Soviet bloc, supplying con-servative circles with books and magazines. Regular lectures by foreign guests were also held in private apartments. Legutko and Krasnodębski were the Foundation's contact persons in Poland, in Krakow and Warsaw respectively (Krasnodębski, 2016).

Eurosceptic political networks established already in the 1990s constituted another space of circulation of conservative ideas between East and West. A closer cooperation between British conservatives and their Central European counterparts emerged in the 1990s (Slobodian and Plehwe forthcoming). Indeed, British conservatives have taken the EU enlargement to the East as an opportunity to consolidate a Eurosceptic right-wing that would counter-balance the French-German axis and advocate in favor of an intergovern-mental conception of the EU. This ultimately led to the creation of the Alliance of European Conservatives and Reformists (AECR), launched in March 2009 with the Prague Declaration, spearheaded by the British Tories and members of Vaclav Klaus's ODS (Neumayer 2010). The Prague Declaration linked neolib-eral and conservative thinking. In 2010, the AECR launched its own think tank, *New Direction* whose patron was Margaret Thatcher until her death in 2013.

Even if that East-West cooperation was primarily stimulated by the Czech ODS rather than the Polish Law and Justice, PiS has become, next to the British Tories, the most numerous delegations in the European Conservative and Reformists parliamentary group (ECR), that succeeded to AECR following the 2014 European election. Legutko – as president of the PiS delegation in the

---

8   See Scott-Smith and Lerg (2017).

European Parliament and vice-president of the ECR group since 2017 – and Krasnodębski – as vice-President of the European Parliament between 2018 and 2019 – became thus prominent actors of the European Right. However, the ECR group appears weakened after the departure of the British MEPs following Brexit.

The third space of transnational circulation of conservative ideas is that of the Center for European Renewal (CER), a pan-European think tank bringing together scholars and intellectuals from across Europe. The CER was established in 2007 by participants to the Vanenburg meetings that take place each year since 2006. It publishes a monthly magazine, *The European Conservative*, which is

> committed to contributing to a renewal of Western culture, and seeks to promote conservative and Christian thinkers and ideas from Europe, the Americas, and other areas of the world. It thus serves as an outlet for many varieties of 'conservatism' — including but not limited to agrarianism, classical liberalism, constitutional monarchism, distributism, libertarianism, radical localism, and traditionalism.[9]

Roger Scruton has been a major figure of the CER until his death in January 2020. Among the participants to the Vanenburg meetings and contributors to *The European Conservative* are Ryszard Legutko, David Engels, Hungarian philosopher and Fidesz adviser András Lánczi, British writer and political commentator Douglas Murray, and French philosopher Chantal Delsol. The CER, which is formally hosted by the Edmund Burke Foundation in the Netherlands, draws inspiration form the Intercollegiate Studies Institute (ISI), an organization dedicated to the diffusion of conservative political thought on American campuses, which has sponsored the first Vanenburg meetings. Just as the ISI but with meagre means, the CER targets primarily higher education and culture, with an explicit reference to anti-communism. On the first Vanenburg Conference, Douglas Murray stated that: "We may have won the Cold War, but we've lost the universities."[10]

These three distinct networks also correspond to different but partly overlapping historical moments, as do the actors to be found in several of these networks, such as Legutko. The role of the British conservatives in the constitution of an intergovernmentalist coalition opposed to a federal Europe and defending a classic neo-liberal political agenda appears today as one intermediate step. This

---

9   Available at: https://europeanconservative.com/about/ (accessed 20 August 2020).

10 Summary of the first Vanenburg meeting, available at: https://europeanrenewal.org/ history/ (accessed 20 August 2020).

step may have helped the newcomers from post-communist Europe to learn the rules of the political game at the EU level and to diversify their international connections, towards the political field rather than academia. It now appears to have come to an end, both as a result of Brexit and the contestation of the neo-liberal consensus in Poland and Hungary, which resulted in the implementation of heterodox economic policies, marked by a form of social redistribution and the desire to support, through State intervention in the economy, a national capitalism.

The creation of the CER is more of a metapolitical work, in which the question of European values has a prominent place. However, one should not overestimate the ideological homogeneity of the actors brought together in this initiative, who come from different tendencies – intellectual and political – of the Right. Similarly, the 2019 European elections have shown that despite the increase in seats of right-wing political groups opposed to a federal Europe and their willingness to broaden their alliances, there is currently no consensus between these political forces, either in terms of agenda or of leadership (Camus and Lebourg 2019).

However, at the metapolitical level, we note the existence of meeting spaces between different fractions of the Right. The Polska Wielki Projekt conferences are one such place, where intellectuals such as Eric Zemmour, David Engels, or György Schöpflin join the discussions with representatives from Hungarian, Czech, French, or Italian political parties. Such transnational *lieux neutres* even reveal connections between fractions of the Right and the Far Right that are otherwise in competition in their respective countries: for instance, members of the French National Rally and Les Républicains, or of the Italian Lega and Fratelli d'Italia, took part in the Polska Wielki Projekt conferences, albeit on different panels.

It remains to be seen what the political agenda of this prospective pan-European conservative Right might be. The question is even more important as the metapolitical work is above all a way to mobilize voters and to strategically distinguish one's political camp from its opponents. The work of ideological production is indeed part of the work of political mobilization, by producing catchwords and worldviews.

From anti-communism to anti-liberalism

Looking at the writings of Polish conservative intellectuals, one can easily note a strong adequacy between their discourse and that of the PiS party on a set of "morality issues" such as LGBTIQ rights, gender, immigration, etc., of which the civilizational conception of Europe is an important aspect. To understand how scholars such as Krasnodębski and Legutko became politicians at the forefront of PiS, it is worth coming back to 1989 and its aftermath. As Brier puts it, "The origins of the culture cleavage of the 1990s and 2000s undeniably lie in the social conflict of the 1980s" (Brier 2009, 68). In Poland, right-wing anticommunist narratives describe 1989 as a "false" or "stolen" revolution. They have fuelled Law and Justice's rhetoric and legitimized its strengthening control of the Polish State institutions, judiciary and media since 2015. Questioning the "Round Table Agreements" is at the heart of the "Fourth Republic" project advocated by the PiS (Brier 2009). The belief that 1989 did not mark a genuine break with the communist regime fuels the speeches of the party's leaders, according to which a "liberal left-wing" establishment defending its own interests has been dominating Polish political life for the past thirty years. Thus, the "conservative revolution" led by the PiS since 2015 is legitimized by historical arguments.

If the Polish conservative Right has been rather marginal on the political scene until the 2000s, the anti-communist narrative of post-1989 transformations was actively cultivated by conservative intellectuals. Thus, since the 1990s, OMP and the *Arka/Arcana* magazine have been developing core ideas to be found in the worldview proposed by PiS nowadays. It is worth recalling that the strategy that led to the Round Table Agreements of 1989 was disputed among dissent in the late 1980s already. Fractions of the dissidence movement were hostile to the idea of power sharing between Solidarity and the Communist Party. In 1988 already, Legutko published an article in *Arka* titled "So that the opposition would be the opposition," in which he criticized what he called the "partnership strategy" (Legutko, 1988).

The lack of consensus in Poland on the meaning of dissent and the political transition of 1989 fueled political cleavages. The narrative of the political capture by the "liberal-left" was thus reactivated at the time of the debates on the 1997 Constitution, but also during the discussions on EU accession and the European constitution, because the conservative and ethno-religious Right remained durably distant from power and these important texts were for the most part negotiated and adopted by majorities from the post-communist Left (Blokker 2019).

A reactivation of the dissident spirit is reflected in Legutko's book, *The Demon in Democracy*. In this book, Legutko claims that liberal democracy constitutes a danger similar to Soviet-style communism, as both would be ideological projects aiming at destroying "traditional values" (i.e. family, the nation) in order to build a new political social order, defined as secular and post-national. Beyond communism, it is therefore any political project based on the promotion of individual rights that is perceived as threatening the political community. Hence the repeated criticism of the French revolution by Polish conservative intellectuals.

Opening Law and Justice's political program for the 2019 electoral campaign, the chapter on "values" co-authored by Legutko and Krasnodębski defines "Polish Europeanness" with references to the Christian, Greek and Roman heritage (*Prawo i Sprawiedliwość*, 2019). While that heritage is presented as part of a common European identity, the two authors advocate for a "Europe of diversity," "including different political cultures" (p. 19). Thus, they reject any form a cultural unification that would be encouraged by the EU and present their "Eurorealism" as follows:

> For us, the European Union is primarily a union of states. We are in favor of a 'Europe of homelands.' We want the treaties to be respected and respect for the principle of subsidiarity. We reject political correctness, that is, restrictions on freedom of speech and opinion that are hitting many more and more painfully of Europeans, imposed today not only by cultural violence, but also through administrative action and criminal repression. We do not accept the uncontrolled erosion of the sovereignty of European homelands (p. 20).

This ideological corpus is not specifically Polish. *The European Conservative* regularly reports on the progress of perceived threats to the "natural order" across Europe, such as gay marriage, sexual education and gender studies, next to post-colonial issues or immigration. The consequence is a promotion of a conservative vision of European values, best illustrated by the "Paris Statement," a common declaration released by intellectuals of the Center for European Renewal in May 2017.[11] Titled "A Europe we can believe in," the statement is made of 35 points that form a kind of manifesto. It distinguishes between a "false" Europe, incarnated by the European Union, and a "true Europe," understood as "a community of nations." It criticizes the "denial of Christian roots of Europe," while Muslims would be tolerated. The authors consider that:

> The true Europe is in jeopardy. The achievements of popular sovereignty, resistance to empire, cosmopolitanism capable of civic love, the Christian legacy of humane and dignified life, a living engagement with our Classical inheritance – all this is slipping away. As the patrons of the false Europe construct their faux Christendom of universal human rights, we are losing our home.

---

11   Available at: https://thetrueeurope.eu/a-europe-we-can-believe-in/ (accessed 20 August 2020).

Finally, the Paris Statement ends with a declaration in support of "populism:"

> There is great anxiety in Europe today because of the rise of what is called 'populism' . . .. We acknowledge that much in this new political phenomenon can represent a healthy rebellion against the tyranny of the false Europe, which labels as 'antidemocratic' any threat to its monopoly on moral legitimacy. The so-called "populism" challenges the dictatorship of the status quo, the 'fanaticism of the center,' and rightly so. It is a sign that even in the midst of our degraded and impoverished political culture, the historical agency of the European peoples can be reborn.

Here we see how transnational networks brought together thanks to the CER, among others, can serve as advocates of the "illiberal regimes" of Central Europe facing stronger critiques coming from the EU and some member States. Among the signatories of the Paris Statement are conservative intellectuals from France, Germany, Belgium, the Netherlands, Spain, Hungary, the Czech Republic and Poland. Next to Legutko are Roger Scruton, Chantal Delsol, David Engels, Czech conservative politician Roman Joch and András Lánczi, a political philosopher who has been the chairman of *Századvég Foundation*, the principal think-tank of the Fidesz party.

Conclusion

Understanding these transnational networks' impact on the ongoing reconfiguration of the European Right remains a research agenda. Nonetheless, Central European intellectuals have provided a key contribution to both the shaping of such networks and their ideological equipment. In an interesting move, the Central European "conservative revolutions" appear as references to some of the Western conservatives. Considering themselves as the true defenders of "European values," understood mainly as Christian, PiS and Fidesz challenge the European values as they have been defined in the European treaties, mainly the rule of law and fundamental rights. Or, to put it like Holly Case: "We are the real Europeans, Orbán and Kaczyński claim, and if the West wants to save itself, it will have to imitate the East" (Case 2019). The examination of transnational conservative networks from the perspective of ideological production invites to formulate the hypothesis of a reconfiguration of the European Right on the basis of a cultural agenda, in connection with migration issues (multiculturalism) and family policy (LGBTIQ rights, abortion, etc.). The apparent success of the rhetoric of "traditional values" in the political competitions of the member States – not only in Central Europe – raises the question of the contours of a political Europe: on which political values should European integration be based?

References

Bar-On, Tamir (2013) *Rethinking the French New Right: Alternatives to Modernity*. London: Routledge.

Beauvallet, Willy, Sébastien Michon (2010) "L'institutionnalisation Inachevée Du Parlement Européen," *Politix* 89 (1): 147–72.

Blokker, Paul (2019) "Populist Counter-Constitutionalism, Conservatism, and Legal Fundamentalism," *European Constitutional Law Review* 15 (3): 519–43.

Bluhm, Katharina, Mihai Varga (eds.) (2019) *New Conservatives in Russia and East Central Europe*. New York: Routledge.

Boltanski, Luc (1973) "L'espace Positionnel : Multiplicité Des Positions Institutionnelles et Habitus de Classe," *Revue Française de Sociologie* 14 (1): 3–26.

Bourdieu, Pierre (1992) *Les Règles de l'art : Genèse et Structure Du Champ Littéraire*. Paris: Seuil.

——— (2001) *Langage et Pouvoir Symbolique*. Paris: Seuil.

——— (2002) "Les Conditions Sociales de La Circulation Internationale Des Idées," *Actes de la recherche en sciences sociales* 145 (1): 3–8.

Bourdieu, Pierre, Luc Boltanski (1976) "La Production de l'idéologie Dominante," *Actes de la recherche en sciences sociales* 2 (2): 3–73.

Brier, Robert (2009) "The Roots of the "Fourth Republic:" Solidarity's Cultural Legacy to Polish Politics,' *East European Politics and Societies* 23 (1): 63–85.

Buzogány, Aron, Mihai Varga (2018) "The Ideational Foundations of the Illiberal Backlash in Central and Eastern Europe: The Case of Hungary," *Review of International Political Economy* 25 (6): 811–28.

Camus, Jean-Yves, Nicolas Lebourg (2019) "Les Droites Extrêmes En Europe, Du Scrutin Européen de 2019 à La Pandémie de Covid-19," *Chaire Citoyenneté, Sciences Po Saint-Germain-en-Laye*, June.

Case, Holly (2019) "The Great Substitution," *Eurozine*, March.

Coman, Ramona, Cécile Leconte (2019) "Contesting EU Authority in the Name of European Identity: The New Clothes of the Sovereignty Discourse in Central Europe," *Journal of European Integration* 41 (7): 855–70.

Csillag, Tamás, Ivan Szelenyi (2015) "Drifting from Liberal Democracy. Neo-Conservative Ideology of Managed Illiberal Democratic Capitalism in Post-Communist Europe," *Intersections. East European Journal of Society and Politics* 1 (1).

Dąbrowska, Ewa (2019) "New Conservatism in Poland. The Discourse Coalition around Law and Justice," in Katharina Bluhm and Mihai Varga (eds.), *New Conservatives in Russia and East Central Europe*, pp. 92–112. New York: Routledge.

Dąbrowska, Ewa, Aron Buzogány, Mihai Varga (2019) "The "Budapest-Warsaw Express:" Conservatism and the Diffusion of Economic Policies in Poland and Hungary," in Katharina Bluhm and Mihai Varga (eds.), *New Conservatives in Russia and East Central Europe*, pp. 178–197. New York: Routledge.

Dakowska, Dorota (2010) "Whither Euroscepticism? The Uses of European Integration by Polish Conservative and Radical Parties," *Perspectives on European Politics and Society* 11 (3): 254–72.

Eatwell, Roger, Matthew J. Goodwin (2018) *National Populism: The Revolt against Liberal Democracy*. London: Pelican.

Engels, David (2019) *Renovatio Europae: Plädoyer Für Einen Hesperialistischen Neubau Europas*. Manuscriptum.

Foret, François, Oriane Calligaro (eds.) (2018) *European Values: Challenges and Opportunities for EU Governance*. Abingdon: Routledge.

Gazeta Wyborcza (2018) "Salonik pani Bieleckiej na zapleczu PiS. Tu się spotyka nowa elita," 14 April.

Korolczuk, Elżbieta, Agnieszka Graff (2018) "Gender as "Ebola from Brussels:" The Anticolonial Frame and the Rise of Illiberal Populism," *Signs: Journal of Women in Culture and Society* 43 (4): 797–821.

Krasnodębski Zdzisław (2016) "Parę słów o Jagiellonian Trust," *Wszystko co najwazniejsze*, 9 June: https://wszystkoconajwazniejsze.pl/prof-zdzislaw-krasnodebski-pare-slow-o-jagiellonian-trust/ (accessed 20 August 2020).

Krastev, Ivan, Stephen Holmes (2019) *The Light That Failed: A Reckoning*. Londres: Allen Lane.

Kubik, Jan (2003) "Cultural Legacies of State Socialism: History Making and Cultural-Political Entrepreneurship in Postcommunist Poland and Russia" in Grzegorz Ekiert and Stephen E. Hanson (eds.) *Capitalism and Democracy in Central and Eastern Europe: Assessing the Legacy of Communist Rule*, pp. 317–351. Cambridge: Cambridge University Press.

Legutko, Ryszard (1988) "Żeby opozycja była opozycją," *Arka*, n° 23.

———(2016) *The Demon in Democracy: Totalitarian Temptations in Free Societies*. New York: Encounter Books.

Lewis, Simon, Magdalena Waligórska (2019) "Poland's Wars of Symbols," *East European Politics and Societies: and Cultures* 33 (2): 423–34.

Matyja, Rafał (2015) "Songs of Innocence and Songs of Experience. Polish Conservatism 1979–2011" in Michal Kopeček and Piotr Wciślik (eds.) *Thinking through Transition. Liberal Democracy, Authoritarian Pasts, and*

Intellectual History in East Central Europe after 1989, pp. 201–236. Budapest and New York: Central European University Press.

Minkenberg, Michael (2017) *The Radical Right in Eastern Europe: Democracy under Siege?* New York: Palgrave Macmillan.

Mirowski, Philip, Dieter Plehwe (eds.) (2009) *The Road from Mont Pèlerin: The Making of the Neoliberal Thought Collective*. Cambridge and London: Harvard University Press.

Mudde, Cas (2007) *Populist Radical Right Parties in Europe*. Cambridge: Cambridge University Press.

Neumayer, Laure (2008) "Euroscepticism as a Political Label: The Use of European Union Issues in Political Competition in the New Member States," *European Journal of Political Research* 47 (2): 135–60.

_____ (2010) "Mobiliser la "science" en investissant l'arène européenne : les ressources paradoxales de l'euroscepticisme du parti civique démocratique tchèque (ODS)," *Societes Contemporaines* 80 (4): 113–32.

Norris, Pippa, Ronald Inglehart (2019) *Cultural Backlash: Trump, Brexit, and Authoritarian Populism*. Cambridge: Cambridge University Press.

Ost, David (2005) *The Defeat of Solidarity: Anger and Politics in Postcommunist Europe*. Ithaca: Cornell University Press.

Pankowski, Rafal (2010) *The Populist Radical Right in Poland: The Patriots*. London: Routledge.

Pinto, Louis (1986) "Une science des intellectuels est-elle possible ?" *Revue de Synthèse* 107 (4): 345–60.

Prawo i Sprawiedliwość (2019) *Program Prawa i Sprawiedliwości 2019, Polski model Państwa dobrobytu.*

Roszkowski, Wojciech (2019) *Roztrzaskane Lustro. Upadek Cywilizacji Zachodniej*. Krakow: Biały Kruk.

Rupnik, Jacques (2017) "La démocratie illibérale en Europe centrale," *Esprit* June (6): 69–85.

Sapiro, Gisèle (2007) "Pour une approche sociologique des relations entre littérature et idéologie," *COnTEXTES. Revue de Sociologie de La Littérature*, No. 2.

Scott-Smith, Giles, Charlotte A. Lerg (eds.) (2017) *Campaigning Culture and the Global Cold War: The Journals of the Congress for Cultural Freedom*. London: Palgrave Macmillan.

Slobodian, Quinn, Dieter Plehwe (forthcoming) "Neoliberals Against Europe" in William Callison and Zachary Manfredi (eds.) *Neoliberal Remains Market Rule and Political Ruptures.*

Smoczyński, Rafał, Tomasz Zarycki (2017) *Totem Inteligencki. Arystokracja, Szlachta i Ziemiaństwo w Polskiej Przestrzeni Społecznej*. Warszawa: Scholar.

Trencsényi, Balázs (2014) "Beyond Liminality? The Kulturkampf of the Early 2000s in East Central Europe," *Boundary2*, No. 1: 135–52.

Vachudova, Milada Anna (2019) "From Competition to Polarization in Central Europe: How Populists Change Party Systems and the European Union," *Polity* 51 (4): 689–706.

Zalewski, Frédéric (2016) "Révolutions conservatrices en Europe centrale et orientale," *Revue d'études Comparatives Est-Ouest* 47 (4): 7–27.

Zarycki, Tomasz, Rafał Smoczyński, Tomasz Warczok (2017) "The Roots of Polish Culture-Centered Politics: Toward a Non–Purely Cultural Model of Cultural Domination in Central and Eastern Europe," *East European Politics and Societies* 31 (2): 360–81.

Rok Zupančič, Faris Kočan, Iris Ivaniš

Symbolic Power of the European Union in Bosnia-Herzegovina: The Bourdieusian Approach to Post-Conflict Societies

Abstract: If the European Union (EU) has lost some credibility in world affairs due to several challenges this organization in recent years has not been able to find adequate answers to (migration; rise of illiberalism etc.), how is it then possible that the EU is still perceived as a dominant power-symbol in some post-conflict countries? Using Bourdieusian approach and drawing on empirical evidence collected during fieldwork in Bosnia-Herzegovina (BiH), the authors argue that for the majority of people in BiH *the* EU – despite all its flaws – still primarily symbolizes different sorts of freedom (political, economic, cultural etc.), stability, prosperity, and, overall, better life opportunities. However, these positive notions constantly, in a dialectic manner, clash with the negative perceptions of the EU, allegedly symbolizing also hypocrisy, injustice, double standards and a threat to ethnic identity.

Keywords: Bosnia-Herzegovina, Bourdieusian approach, European Union, post-conflict societies, power

Introduction: Symbolic power as the fourth dimension of EU's power

Among many scholars, there is a tacit assumption that the EU's attractiveness and the power arising from it have diminished (Bouris 2011; Schwarzer 2017; Šlosarčik 2015; Wagnsson and Hellman 2018; Webber 2016). The notion of the EU's power, which is predominantly understood through the lens of civilian, soft, transformative and normative power (Belloni, 2009; Gross and Juncos 2011; Noutcheva 2009; Patalakh; 2017; Shepherd 2009; Zupančič and Pejič 2018), began being questioned because of internal and external challenges: lack of coordination among EU member states in addressing the corona-virus and migration issues effectively; rise of illiberalism, nationalism and populism in and outside of the EU; the EU's ineffective response to the armed conflicts in the neighborhood etc. Many of these issues directly concern Southeast European countries, which have been expecting to join the EU in the upcoming years. However, recent political developments, in particular the French *non* to the further EU expansion voiced in 2019, decreased political optimism to join the EU in prospective Southeast European countries. Surprisingly, the above-outlined challenges have not translated directly into this region's distrust toward this international organization. On the contrary, the EU still enjoys relatively high credibility and seems to be an appealing symbol there. To explain why this is the case is the central aim of this chapter.

In our chapter, we follow Lukes' (2004) conceptualization of the third dimension of power – *shaping the preferences and behavior of others*[1] – while focusing on Bosnia-Herzegovina (BiH) as an example of a post-conflict country, which strives toward the EU membership and where the EU's role has been a significant factor in the last 25 years. While acknowledging the contributions of soft, civilian, transformative and normative power scholarship, we analyze the EU's ability to shape the preferences and behavior of others – in our case, BiH – which is underpinned by the EU's symbolic power in this country. Hence, the EU does not influence BiH only directly through economic, military and political incentives, but also in more subtle ways through *the power of domination* – a theoretical concept entrenched in the political sociology inspired by Pierre Bourdieu (Lukes 2005: 139–144; Schwartz 2013: 44; Vangeli 2018: 675). In particular, we aim to contribute to the understanding of the EU's symbolic position as it is seen in the minds of BiH's citizens, by employing the notions of EU symbolic power/domination in BiH through the lens of Lukes' third dimension of power.

To complete our aim, we rely on the data collected in the Horizon2020 project RePAST – Revisiting the Past, Anticipating the Future. As one of the methods, we conducted focus groups in different regions of BiH. In the process, while one author was moderating the focus group, the other employed participant observation as a supportive method; such an approach fits the *Bourdieusian* approach well (Bourdieu 2003: 281–294). Additionally, we also conducted in-depth interviews with the locals – or what we call 'ordinary people' (people not holding any important political or economic posts) – and moreover relied on the analysis of media reports and secondary literature to acquire a big picture.

---

1 Following the conceptualization of Steven Lukes (2004: 104–107), power has three dimensions, namely: a) winning conflicts and influencing decision-making (decision-making); b) limiting the alternatives and setting the agenda (non-decision-making); c) shaping the preferences and behavior of others (ideological).

Symbolic power or symbolic dominator Europe: theoretical framework

Even though Lukes' pivotal work in *Power: A Radical View* (2004) has made a durable mark on a number of scholars, his analytical insights have never been discussed systematically in the context of the EU (Robinson 2006: 1). One reason for this lies in the fact that researchers, when focusing on the EU, operate with either social constructivism or Neo-Gramscian analysis, which have a clear resonance with Lukes' work. If the parallels between social constructivism and Lukes' third dimension of power can be drawn from the way in which real and perceived interests can be shaped by factor(s) external to an actor, the similarities between neo-Gramscian analysis and Lukes' third dimension are even more vivid. This luminosity can be found in the studies of particular constellation of social forces and dominant ideational configuration that defines and sustains (world) order (Bieler 2005; Bieler and Morton 2001; Cowles 2003; Robinson 2006).

However, if the third dimension of power, understood as an ability to shape the preferences and behavior of others, is theorized within the concept of symbolic power as proposed in this chapter, then the academic literature broadens. Here, we should emphasize that the literature on the symbolic power and symbolic domination of the EU remained predominantly focused on the symbolic power in European diplomacy (cf. Adler-Nissen 2014; Kuus 2015) up until 2016 when Gstöhl and Schunz (2016) argued that the EU's promotion of reforms through the adoption of norms and rules constitutes key symbolic capital in EU's neighborhood policy. The debate on the symbolic power in the EU was further deepened in 2018 in a Special issue of academic journal *Österreichische Zeitschrift für Soziologie* that addressed processes of European integration and disintegration in times of crisis, where the authors explored how the before-mentioned processes can alter the social status and symbolic power of social groups (Pernicka and Lahusen 2018: 4). For the purpose of this chapter, the argumentation provided by Gstöhl and Schunz (2016) regarding the EU's symbolic power manifestation through norms and rules fits the most. The latter is, as we argue, becoming a part and parcel of an institutionalized symbolic domination of the EU *via* stabilization and association processes – the EU-driven set of requirements and standards in various domains Southeast European countries have to fulfil as a precondition to join the EU.

Symbolic domination refers to power relationships where conflict is not perceptible; this means that power is not only exerted over those that are 'only' subjects of that power, but is exercised prolifically, as a power to shape views and preferences with the subordinated objects being implicitly compliant, and not fully aware of the essence of the process (Bourdieu 1990: 52–53; Vangeli 2018). Symbolic power is the power to distress the thinking and behavior of other using language itself, as well as through speaking from a particular position within the constellation of power, in a way that muddles the nature of power relationship (Bourdieu 1984: 64–65; Vangeli 2018).

Symbolic domination 'occurs,' according to Eagelton-Pierce (2012: 3), in the realm of doxic claims, doxic relationships and doxic subordination. Doxa, in its most rudimentary understanding, is understood as a set of beliefs and viewpoints of the dominant actor that defines a particular arena and appears natural to the other (Bourdieu 1990: 60). Furthermore, when EU's presence is understood through the 'common-sense' discourse, it can underpin power relations by forming the so-called axiomatic consensus. Here, we should also note that doxa – exercised through words and positions – is not static and can be transformed as a result of changes in the power balances (Vangeli 2018: 676).

In analytical terms, symbolic power as a concept supplements the existing approaches in the literature on the third dimension of EU's power in at least two ways. First, it broadens the discussion on Neo-Gramscian hegemony, as the EU is not automatically becoming a hegemon in its vicinity, but it is rather establishing new perspectives in order to (re)shape the existing socio-political processes in the region through a process of symbolic domination. Second, it objectifies the notion that structure of the international sphere, which is built upon and defined by ideas, influences the identities and interests of an actor and highlights the actorness of the EU beyond structure with power to influence behavior and preferences (Barnett 2001; Bieler 2006; Risse, Ropp and Sikkink 1999; Williams 2014). Based on this, the EU's symbolic power does not simply derive from its economic resources, but rather from the language and discourses, e.g. the discourse on Economic Europe and Social Europe (Manners and Murray 2016: 188).

Furthermore, the Economic Europe and Social Europe narratives, for example, are based on the fact that the EU has managed to institutionalize highly competitive social market economy for almost 30 European states, which in turn implicitly legitimizes EU's policymaking, and situates it as one of the most important actors in the global political economy (Rudloff and Laurer 2016; Strezhneva 2018; Tonra 2005). Indeed, the EU has accumulated prestige through a variety of social and economic statistics that show that the EU is not just the second largest economy in the world but also an organization where the expenditure on all types of social protection of its member states is equivalent to 28 % of GDP (Amadeo 2019; Eurostat 2020).

This symbolic power has also taken on a visual form through economic means, namely through EU-funded projects. The projects are, when talking about large infrastructure developments such as roads, bridges and other public facilities, always accompanied with signs emphasizing the financial support by the EU and marked with an appropriate flag emblem. In line with this logic, the transitional democracies in the EU vicinity are, through the pre-accession financial assistance and several programs, mobilized by the EU into an asymmetrical relationship; they are facing a (dominant) actor that speaks from the position of power with capacities to generate meanings. Likewise, the countries where the EU projects its (symbolic) power are, due to their membership 'aspirations,' adjusting to the EU's discourse and policies. They are changing behavior due to the process of EU's symbolic domination.

The EU as a versatile power-symbol in Bosnia-Herzegovina

A multidimensional approach of the EU towards BiH since the end of the war in 1995, ranging from imminent humanitarian assistance in the first after-war years, to the more sophisticated programs for establishing good governance in various domains of political, socioeconomic and cultural life in BiH, turned the EU into a versatile symbol for Bosnian-Herzegovinians. Based on the analysis of focus groups and interviews collected in BiH in 2018 and 2019, and the analysis of secondary and primary sources revealing the "European discourse" in and on BiH, we structure our argument around five points. We demonstrate that the EU, as a versatile power-symbol, is nowadays perceived in BiH as a symbol of 1) *economic power,* 2) *stability and order,* 3) *freedom,* 4) *hypocrisy and injustice,* 5) *threat to ethnic identity.*

The EU as a symbol of economic power

Comparing relative wealth of the EU with economic characteristics of BiH, the EU, unsurprisingly, soon became recognized as a symbol of economic power, wealth and prosperity in BiH. This comes as no surprise, taking into account the immense discrepancies in economies of Bosnia-Herzegovina and the EU. For instance, EU's GDP per capita in 2000 equalled €22,960, and €27,780 in 2017 (Eurostat 2020a). In comparison, BiH's GDP per capita in 2000 was €1,594 only, while in 2017 it was €4,700 (European Commission 2011: 60; European Commission 2019: 177e). Furthermore, while the unemployment rate in the EU was 7.6 % in 2017, in BiH the rate was 20.7 % (Eurostat 2020b). As it can be seen, the differences in basic economic provisions are remarkable, which further supports the claims from the people in BiH that the EU offers better standards and opportunities.

For Bosnian-Herzegovinians, the extent of the perceived economic power of EU goes further – the notion of the economic power seems to be an umbrella term for myriad of possibilities. For many of them, EU's economic power is largely a symbol of attainable opportunities for overall higher living standards, better employment opportunities and better business opportunities (UNDP 2017: 51). Moreover, in this UNDP study, "55.8 % of respondents entirely agree with the statement that the BiH membership in the EU would mean a better standard of living." Hence, the population's need for improvement of living standards and opportunities for growth are principally manifested in their perception of EU's economic power.

Similarly, multiple interviewees in our study have concurred with this view. For instance, in an interview with a group of young students from Banja Luka (average age >22), the perception of EU as a symbol of economic power was predominant: "Well, now, there are different perceptions. First, cradle of the culture and civilization. Then, a better life, 'the West.' Everyone keeps leaving from here to go to Europe, looking for better life conditions" (Focus group 7 2019). Another example of such stance is given by an interviewee: "Whatever you're interested in, you can find in Europe, jobs as well. Here, people do whatever they can for 200, 300 convertible marks, just to survive, whereas there, that would be paid much, much better. There are more jobs. Here, there are not enough firms and employers" (BA_M_P_5 2018). Any form of improvement is something that people in BiH seem to be striving for, as stated: "I believe that Europe has a well-established standard for progress and development" (BA_F_T_11 2018).

Such opinions resonate with the recent study by Akmedir (2018: 13), who demonstrated that a significant proportion of Bosnian-Herzegovinians "regarded the EU as a force that could overcome the economic and political problems of the state." This study also shows that people in BiH believe that economic development is the most important value of the European identity and culture. The analysis insinuates that the narrative template of 'Economic Europe,' which postulates on the idea of 'homogenous (and wealthy) internal economic area' (Manners and Muray 2016), is becoming a part and parcel of the doxa among the ordinary citizens of BiH. In Bordieu(s)ian language, we could argue that the Economic Europe narrative is becoming an important dimension of the symbolic power of the EU, which in turns determines the trajectories of asymmetric (doxic) relationship between the EU and BiH.

The EU as a symbol of stability and order

Political, economic and social state of the country seems to be stagnating in many people's eyes since the end of the war in 1995. Due to the troubled past of BiH, especially in the more recent history, national discourse oftentimes focuses on issues related to the war. For many people, BiH is still 'stuck in the 1990s,' or remained in the state of conflict: "I cannot understand the people. Simply, it seems as if majority just hates others for no reason, and is just waiting for someone to say something, just so they could express their bottled-up hatred. As if they've been holding it in for many years, and are just waiting for a trigger, to break" (BA_M_P_5 2018).

This statement demonstrates that Bosnian-Herzegovinians believe that their country is always at the brink of a new war. In addition to the lack of social and economic progress in BiH, the perception of EU as a symbol of stability remains strong.

Stability in this sense also refers to democracy, or better said, to the stability of political systems; this is, as Bosnian-Herzegovinians generally believe, the quality the EU supposedly has. In 2019, 32.6 % of BiH's citizens in 2019 supported the EU membership of BiH because the EU supposedly symbolizes "peace and political stability" (Directorate for European Integration 2019). One of our interviewees said that the EU countries are "well-ordered in every possible sense, more orderly than other states that are not in the EU, and safer as well" (BA_F_T_6 2018). Along the same lines, this notion extends to people's perception of EU as a symbol of civilization, thus, an added face symbolizing stability. The perceived stability within the EU further establishes an additional level of social sophistication and order that is appealing to people. In the words of our interviewee (BA_M_T_2 2018):

> the very basic rules and order is what I consider 'Europe;' etiquette, sophistication. Actually, it has little to do with mere civilization. There is a saying in the Balkans: "When they (in Europe) ate with hands, we (in the Balkans) already used forks." I like things that are orderly, being educated properly, being fairly paid for your work, and that's the issue of today's brain drain.

The EU was able to convey the message that it has an ability to maintain all levels of society and organization under high level of control; this contributes to its identity of a symbol of order and stability. The oscillating political systems, constant inter-ethnic conflicts and overall stagnation in the country have become omnipotent issues, where the perceived power of the EU is even more intense. For instance, in Akmedir's study, almost half of the respondents (46 %) considered the EU as a place of social safety (2018: 16). The EU is certainly a place to which most people from BiH navigate toward in order to achieve personal and social safety: "But if I look at it as a future social worker, the EU means social peace and security" (Focus group 6 2019).

The notion of stability extends into the EU's symbolic identity as a *provider* of stability in BiH in the years following the war. The stability which the EU supposedly brings can be seen in various EU initiatives, programs and EU-funded projects. These projects and initiatives are intended to address different domains, such as a security sector reform, professionalizing judiciary system and empowering civil society. One of the best examples for this is the Althea Operation, formally known as the EU Force Bosnia and Herzegovina. It is a military operation in BiH designated to ensure proper military implementation of the Dayton Peace Agreement. Even though the operation started in 2004, its mandate and functions have been adjusted throughout the program's life-time, making it still relevant in BiH for peace maintenance and safety (IECEU 2017: 48).

However, the EU is not the only actor that builds up its own image as a symbol of stability in BiH. Constant bilateral engagement between BiH and the EU *member states* also contributes to enhancing the EU's reputation as a symbol of stability. Countries, such as Austria, Germany and Sweden have been actively engaged in BiH since the end of war and have also become places where Bosnian-Herzegovinians seek better life opportunities. Germany, for example, has been providing BiH with funding for conflict prevention projects through the Regional Cooperation Council (Foreign Federal Office 2020). Aside from that, Germany's economic partnership with BiH made grand contributions to the country's stability and even cultural development. Similarly, Sweden has been assisting BiH since 1992, providing support for post-war reconstruction and democratic processes (BiH Ambasada 2016). As individual member states show their power and support to BiH, it only amplifies the EU's perceived collective power and its ability to instill order beyond its borders.

The EU's efforts toward establishing a supra-ethnic, civic (all-Bosnian) identity in BiH can be considered a strategy of maintaining its role as a stability provider. In the interviews, many Bosnian-Herzegovinians commented on the idea of establishing a united, civic identity in BiH. In one of the interviews, the participant stated: "When it comes to the idea of the EU creating a unified Bosnian identity going beyond the three nations here, if that means unison and creating some shared opinions, then I support it. I think it would be nice to have a unified nation, and we should work for it" (BA_F_T_6 2018).

Correspondingly, another interviewee provides similar viewpoints: "When I hear that the EU is promoting the projects that work on going beyond national division and unity, I am glad.... I find that dialogue phenomenal, however, I doubt that it will ever succeed in the near future here" (BA_F_T_9 2018).

However, we have to note that such statements come mostly from Bosniaks, for which BiH is the only state they have, contrary to Bosnian Serbs and Bosnian Croats in BiH, who have their kin states and are, generally speaking, more reluctant regarding the attempts to establish all-Bosnian civic identity.

In this section on the EU, we should also mention the EU political initiatives launched by the European Parliament. This institution attempts to become an important actor in constructing the EU memory framework, which could have paved the way toward the stability through transitional justice. In line with this, the 2005 and 2009 Declaration on Srebrenica and 2015 Srebrenica commemoration Resolution became an important referential framework for recognizing the mass atrocities that are today understood as the 'symbols of the Bosnian war' (Milošević and Touquet, pp. 384–387). The latter fits well with the Bosniak narrative and is also vivid in the surveys conducted by the Directorate for European Integration (2019), where the support of BiH's integration in the EU in the Federation of BiH was 86.5 %, while the support in Republika Srpska was significantly lower (58.9 %).

The EU as a symbol of freedom

In this section, by freedom we mean the meanings assigned to this concept by Bosnian-Herzegovinians. The majority of our interlocutors had in mind, when referring to freedom the EU enables, the following ideas: safe haven during the war; and later, in the post-war period, possibility of mobility and travel, education opportunities outside of the home country and even cultural diversity, which allows someone to express her- or himself freely.

The foundation for EU's becoming the symbol of freedom happened already during the Bosnian war. Especially with the siege of Sarajevo, most people fled to EU member states; Germany, for example, received the most Bosnian refugees throughout the war out of all EU member states, around 320,000 (Valenta and Ramet 2011: 4). To this is linked also the economic freedom these countries offered, to some extent already discussed in the earlier section. Namely, most of Bosnian-Herzegovinians who fled BiH and migrated to the EU countries were often able to find there not only peaceful societies, but also better economic opportunities, comparing to the compatriots who stayed in BiH. The EU as a symbol of economic power was only reinforced, as the overall state of BiH has not improved after the war. As the discrepancies between the EU member states and BiH increased with time, the established perceptions of the EU became more rooted into the people's mentality.

Since BiH is not an EU member, BiH passport has long been limited in terms of visa-free and bureaucracy-free travel. Hence, for many, the limited mobility has been one of the dominant downsides of not being in the EU until 2010, when the EU finally backed visa liberalization for Bosnian-Herzegovinians and enabled visa-free travel to the EU. To support the claim that EU is considered as a symbol of free movement, Akmedir (2018: 11) showed that even after the visa-free regime was granted to Bosnian-Herzegovinians, 82 % of the study participants consider the EU to promote the freedom of travel. In our project, we also asked interlocutors whether they are prepared to exchange their Bosnian-Herzegovinian passport for the European one. Many participants said that they would do it only for the sake of the freedom of travel: "It's not something I've thought about, but now when I think about it, I might go for having more opportunities" (Focus group 7 2019).

Nevertheless, the opportunity to travel, for most, is closely related to work opportunities and better education opportunities. In the UNDP study, roughly 80 % of the participants thought that the EU meant better education opportunities (2017: 51). This is a clear indicator that the EU persists as a symbol of freedom, and a reason behind the continually increasing number of people leaving Western Balkans, BiH especially, to seek better opportunities. In the words of our interviewee: "There are young people and children who wanted to go somewhere else and get educated and so on, because they know that somewhere else is better than here, in our country" (BA_F_T_6 2018).

The notion of freedom, as stated earlier, reaches beyond mobility and education only. One of the important aspects of perceived freedom for Bosnian-Herzegovinian people is cultural diversity. As a country that had been known as the 'small Yugoslavia' because of its cultural diversity, Bosnia-Herzegovina's multi-ethnicity is one of the things that makes it unique. Before the Bosnian war, the country's cultural diversity was a point of pride and harmony, whereas the war had made it the foundation of conflict and intolerance. Consequentially, people in BiH live in a constant state of inter-ethnic and intercultural tensions among the three constituent peoples, (at least) three different religions and (at least) three different cultural narratives, which perpetuate the division between 'us' and 'them.'

For these reasons, EU's power to bring so many different countries, nations and cultures together into one alliance across a continent resonates with quite a lot of Bosnian-Herzegovinians. Akmedir (2018: 17) found that 63 % of the participants believe how the EU stands for cultural diversity. The EU as a symbol of freedom in regards to cultural diversity also intertwines with the notion of social security discussed previously. The relative lack of the interethnic tensions within the EU means that individuals would be able to gain more freedom in their personal lives, and more freedom to realize their ambitions and potentials without the added pressures of social instabilities. Furthermore, in one of the focus groups, participants expressed that "European means to accept the differences and be tolerant" (Focus group 6 2019). This notion of tolerance has been a widely used term to express the meaning of 'Europe' or 'European identity,' as claimed by another interviewee, being European means "etiquette, sophistication, acceptance of others and different, tolerance in any way possible" (BA_M_T_2).

The symbolic power of the EU in this sense is very important. Creating a sense of freedom of any kind certainly strengthens one's perception of power, especially when it comes to groups of people who do not have such conditions at hand. As a continually present external power in BiH, the EU became the symbol of freedom in many ways, where freedom of travel and education abroad take priority. With the global increase in travel and migration, being limited due to bureaucratic or political reasons (e.g. non-EU membership) can have immense impact on one's opportunities. The lack of one aspect is usually connected to a much wider spectre of conditions, which people will associate with it – like easy travel for EU citizens is also related to other opportunities for personal and professional growth among the people in BiH.

The EU as a symbol of hypocrisy and injustice

Given the fact that the engagement of the EU in BiH is almost three decades old, it is not surprising there are quite a few negative impressions regarding the EU's symbolic power in this country. One of the most prominent is perceiving the EU as a hypocritical actor. For many, this hypocrisy started with the EU's role in the Bosnian war. To understand what the EU has (not) done between 1992 and 1995, when war ravaged the country, and to understand why such opinions are prevalent, we briefly outline the EU's strategic approach towards BiH in the early 1990s.

The origin of the collective failure to intervene by the EU comes from its reluctance to recognize that the Bosnian war had an *international* character, and its reliance on negotiations instead of military intervention. The prior means that the Bosnian war had been identified as a *civil* conflict, justifying the EU's decision of non-interference (Cohen 1993). This decision has defined the rest of the course of the war, which culminated with the Srebrenica geno-cide, where, once again, the EU's lack of intervention and UNPROFOR's unpre-paredness allowed for over eight thousand people to be killed in a matter of days. Throughout the war, the EU and the UN were understood as virtually one entity – "the international community." To the people in BiH, each had failed to fulfil their expected roles, hence prolonging the Bosnian war and ignoring the constant atrocities happening in BiH.

Majority of our interlocutors had expressed a similar opinion – that the EU's failure to act and help BiH during the war showed its incapability to exercise its power. For instance, a participant from our study stated (BA_F_P_2 2018):

> That kind of distanced role of an observer was, in reality, horrifying. They came here and watched us, Balkan hordes, while we slain each other. . ... They constantly sold the story how worried they are and how innocent people are dying, and that it should be stopped, and what they'd done – they bombarded some locations, which counts as their involvement. I mean, the case of Srebrenica and the DUTCHBAT soldiers, who had watched the people being murdered, not even trying to at least save the children.

Although for the most part EU's hypocrisy is characterized by its ineffectiveness to stop the war, some of the reasons come from more contemporary issues, which are the EU's inability to bring positive change to BiH. One of the more vivid examples of this kind is the Office of the High Representative (OHR) in BiH. Initially, its primary role was to ensure civil implementation of the Dayton Agreement. The problematic aspect of this was that the OHR was also given the so-called Bonn powers, which enabled the OHR to impose laws, issue decisions or remove public officials who were not complying with the provisions of the Dayton Agreement. These powers were used often and became quite controversial both within and outside of BiH. According to Limantzakis (2014) and Majstorović and Vučkovac (2016: 151), "the OHR had dismissed a total of 119 officials, issued 757 decisions and imposed 286 laws until 2005 . . . sometimes along with freezing of their bank accounts. After the 2002 elections, the OHR also started scrutinizing all political candidates for major ministerial positions." Due to such frequent and rather drastic measures taken by the OHR, it was deemed as a semi-colonial institution misusing its power to instill disorder rather than stability. Such high engagement in local political affairs caused for the Parliamentary Assembly of the Council of Europe to seek ways to minimize the OHR's involvement in BiH and to transfer as much power as possible to domestic authorities (Limantzakis 2014). Ultimately, the Peace Implementation Council had set preliminary conditions for the closure of the OHR in BiH in February 2008, which also minimized OHR's use of powers in comparison to prior years. Since BiH authorities and institutions have yet to meet all the conditions a decade later, the OHR is still functioning in the country. As stated by the OHR (2015), "[w]hile progress has been made in some areas, chronic disagreement among the main political parties has produced gridlock that has prevented the full implementation of the agenda."

Exactly because the EU's symbolic power is at such a high level among the people in BiH, the expectations follow suit. However, for the most part, these expectations have not been met, which causes further dissatisfaction with the international community's power to help BiH get the push toward improvement that it needs. Hence, many have developed a certain degree of skepticism toward EU's power to bring positive change: "I don't think that something will happen anytime soon. I expect positive things, it's nice to hope for better things, but I think that other countries will enter the EU before us, that will progress before we do" (BA_F_T_6 2018). This skepticism also contributes to the sense of isolation, of being on the margins of EU's horizons: "There are barriers where you're clearly cut off and let know that you're not a part of it" (Focus group 6 2019). Another example of such attitude is stated below:

> Association to the EU should be the four basic freedoms – freedom of movement, freedom of product, freedom of capital and services. But for us, who are not in the EU, I can freely say that the U.S. is much more accessible and closer to us than the EU. It's good for those who are within it, to us who are not is a great barrier, and it sometimes even hurts us. (Focus group 6 2019).

In the study by Akmedir (2018: 20), the participants were asked whether they think that the EU is acting honestly toward BiH. The data showed how over 60 % of participants do not trust the EU, thinking that it does not act frankly toward the EU. What is more, Akmedir (2018: 20) adds how "/m/ixed signals from the EU, wrong approach or tough conditions without the necessary assistance could spoil the process of integration of Bosnia into the EU."

The EU as a threat to ethnic identity

The struggle to maintain ethnic identity of each constituent peoples has been very dominant in BiH. The overlapping histories and traditions of each of the BiH's nations make for a great challenge to establish separate historical narratives, as well as completely separate identities which would further their idea of sovereignty. Subsequently, the decades-, if not centuries-long struggle to establish and prove distinct historical paths of the nations in BiH had created a fear of potentially losing those 'hard-earned' identities to an international giant, the EU. Interestingly, while most people see Europe as a cradle of tolerance and cultural diversity, they simultaneously see the EU as a threating symbol to national identity: "I don't have a positive attitude toward the EU.

I think its goal is enrichment and loss of identity, so I definitely wouldn't like to be a part of it" (Focus group 7 2019).

Such positions are particularly prevalent in ethnic groups, which are in BiH in a minoritarian position: Bosnian Croats and Bosnian Serbs. In the words of our Bosnian Serb interlocutor: "Same as anyone abroad would ask me about my background, Serb is the primary identity, only later I am from Bosnia" (Focus group 7 2019).

It is important to emphasize that among the constituent peoples Bosnian Serbs hold most reservations toward BiH's accession to the EU due to the fear of identity loss. To compare, 86.5 % of Bosnian Muslim support the accession to the EU, while only 58.9 % of Bosnian Serbs stand behind the idea of BiH becoming a member state (Directorate for European integration 2019). Many Bosnian Serbs are following Milorad Dodik, the president of Republika Srpska's secessionist rhetoric and opposition to "intra-country negotiations and the work of state institutions and to question the territorial integrity of the country" (N1 2020). As already mentioned, the politics in BiH oftentimes have detrimental impact on other domains in the country, and such rhetoric has direct influence on the country's ability to improve, thus move closer to becoming an EU member state.

One way of understanding why Bosnian Serbs perceive the EU in such way is by understanding that the symbolization of the EU as a threat to ethnic identity is enabled through the well-established doxa that the EU relativizes (without necessarily supplanting) both ethnic and national identities (Bellier and Wilson 2000). This is possible, as argued by Borneman and Fowler (1997) and Schütze and Schöder-Wildhagen (2012), due to EU's self-representation as a (mental) space of "fundamentally reorganised territorialities and peoplehood," the two principles of group identification that have shaped the modern European order (Harmsen and Wilson 2000). In line with this, the presence of the EU in socio-cultural sense symbolises a threat to the 'imagined and performed statehood' of Republika Srbska that is, through Dodik's ethno-nationalist narrative, reaffirmed as the area of exclusively (Bosnian-)Serb ethnic space (Björkdahl 2018; Stjepanović 2015).

EU's *raison d'être* in BiH through doxic relationships

As already showed in the previous chapters, symbolic power is mediated through the careful use or selection of language that clouds reality. This follows Diez's (2005) logic of importance of the so-called discursive dimension – what the EU *says*. In other words, the EU projects and programs in BiH did not just involve the promotion of universal norms, but at the same time established practices of domination and exclusion through disciplining procedures (Juncos 2011: 85). Indeed, the EU engagement in the Western Balkans began in the mid-1990s as a direct response to the war in BiH, which paved the way toward establishing political and economic conditionality for the entire region for the first time. This conditionality, which corresponds with the Copenhagen criteria (1993) and the Stabilization and Association Process (SAP) (1999), laid ground for a new doxa – a new 'common sense,' centered on the post-conflict candidate states with their right to seek their own national path of development, but within the process of European integration. This type of thinking is not only promoted through rhetoric, but also through re-creating the relationships between actors and assigning them new roles. Interestingly, even though the EU's role in the Bosnian war was limited and indecisive, the EU has anyway managed to re-create new relationship with BiH (Burg and Shoup 1999: 79; Juncos 2005).

In line with the Bourdieu(s)ian approach, which underlines the "need to develop symbolic power . . . because a large number of social practices could not be achieved if they were perceived as stemming from the pursuit of pure self-interest" (Eagelton-Pierce 2012: 41), the June 2008 decision to sign a Stabilization and Association Agreement (SAA) between BiH and the EU follows this logic. By signing the agreement, the EU officially – legally and politically – acknowledged the Bosnian future is 'European;' it is the SAA agreement that is, through both socio-economic and legal language, framing the EU's proactive approach in BiH and enabling the EU to discipline and 'normalize' BiH's social and political landscape while disavowing the alleged pursuit of self-interest. Here, it is important to note that symbols – and the SAA agreement is one of them – can be understood through the prism of order due to its socio-subjective manifestation that brings order and structure in people's lives (Manners 2010: 7).

As Juncos (2011: 90–91) pointed out, the EU's approach towards BiH is not attractive only due to the level of the potential prosperity, but also for what it symbolizes in terms of reconciliation, as the latter in BiH follows the same rationality as the French-German reconciliation – one of the best examples of rapprochement in the world and perhaps an inevitable step towards the greater integration of Europe. Furthermore, the integration of BiH into the EU would not just strive towards reconciliation but also provide both internal and external security.

The symbolic dimension within this argument should be found within the premise of ideological and physical domination, namely: a) ideological domination because the officials of the EU and the EU member states' representatives claim in their discourse that for BiH, there is 'no alternative' to European integration; b) physical domination due to economic conditionality and crisis management instruments (Belloni 2019; Juncos 2011). This corresponds with data collected in our fieldwork, and some other studies (e.g. Majstorović and Vučkovac 2016).

In the past years, however, the EU's doxic relationship with BiH and other Western Balkan countries was severely criticized (Merlingen and Ostraiskaite 2006; Rees 2005). This criticism went into the direction that the discretionary interpretation of EU's role by European politicians, bureaucrats and experts created the subordination of targeted societies, which in turn functioned as a cornerstone for reducing the capacity of locals to construct a future in their own vernacular image (Merlingen and Ostraiskaite 2006: 50). Based on that, the EU's rhetoric has changed in order to give the impression that the targeted country can only benefit from the EU model if its society is included. The latter, which is conceptualized under the term 'local ownership,' assumes responsibility and participation on an equal footing by moving away the focus exclusively on the policymakers or elites and establishing relations with the civil society (Donais 2012; Juncos 2018; Papakostas and Pasamitros 2014; Yong Lee and Özerdem 2015).

In line with this, the EU has often highlighted that BiH should build its own capacities in order to pursue the process of European integration autonomously. Furthermore, the EU's rhetoric emphasized the need for BiH's ownership over the agenda in order to adopt key reforms for meeting obligations laid down in the SAA. This approach has not always matched the reality, as also argued by Biddle (2010), Ejdus and Juncos (2018) and Kappler and Lemay-Hebert (2015).

Common critics of the contemporary academic debates are grounded on the argument that the EU took upon itself a prominent supervisory role that shaped indirectly key developments as the operationalization of the local ownership was done *via* paternalistic top-down practice. The latter, which was arguably disguised through a *language* of domestic (local) ownership, is manifested through techniques of governmentality and practices of domination in BiH (Chandler 2010; Ejdus 2017; Juncos 2018). Furthermore, as Belloni (2019: 39) argued, "the notion of local ownership turned into a technique of governing populations at a distance and a sort of maturity test for local authorities, whereby an authoritative judge – the EU – assessed the reliability and trustworthiness of local elites in implementing the EU model." The discrepancy between rhetoric and actions, which can be observed through the practice of domination, can be seen in a number of examples, namely: a) The EU High Representative has been criticized for imposing institutional reforms and bypassing BiH's institutions (Juncos 2011: 97); b) EU's programs followed the logic of institutional-building in order to comply with the acquis instead of funding the capacity-building projects for the BiH's civil society (Edmunds, Juncos and Algar-Faria 2018); c) EU's (failed) attempt to impose constitutional reforms in BiH between 2006 and 2010 (Belloni 2019).

Finally, the EU's doxic relationship with BiH, as argued here, can be interpreted through the prism of sophisticated indoctrination through domination, which can be defined as the collective instilling of 'knowledge' and values through formalized repetitive practices that unfold through the SAA. These practices, which are commonly understood as deceit, should be understood as a form of symbolic power that go 'undercover' in order to change status quo without confrontation, as argued by Vangeli (2018: 679).

Conclusion

Our analysis has shown that the EU is a versatile power-symbol in BiH to date. Using a *Bourdieusian* approach through Lukes' third dimension of power (shaping the preferences and behavior of others), we demonstrated that the EU, which remains a symbol of prosperity, freedom and better life opportunities for many Bosnian-Herzegovinians, constantly clash with the notion of the EU symbolizing hypocrisy and double standards – for good reasons, though (the EU's unforgotten ineffectiveness in halting the war in BiH; the dubious role of the Office of High Representative as an overseer of the Dayton Peace Accords; earlier attempts of the EU engagement, which did not consider the specifics of BiH as a recipient country and rather insisted on the policies not suitable for Bosnian context by imposing a top-down approach, which made BiH look more like an international protectorate than an independent sovereign country etc.).

The EU, in principle, believes that strong ethnic identities are strong drivers of ethno-nationalism, and consequently, shapes its policies accordingly. However, for a significant number of BiH citizens (Bosnian Serbs in particular), the EU and its member states represent a power-symbol, which aims at "reducing," or at least, softening the value of ethnic identities at the expense of building a civic (all-Bosnian) identity and 'European' identity. Interestingly, the majority of people who believe the EU is ideologically attacking their ethnic identity, traditions and 'way of life' does not reject the notion of the EU as a symbol of economic power, liberty and freedom; they tend to agree that the EU area is a political and economic environment that is to be emulated in order to achieve progress in BiH.

The EU symbolic power, though supported with a wide range of economic tools and incentives, apparently has a certain ability to shape the views of peoples in BiH, as *Bourdieusian* argumentation has it. In particular, through deliberate actions of the EU and its member states or even unintentionally, the EU for many Bosnian-Herzegovinians emerged as a symbol of the better future – be it from the aspect of BiH becoming a member of the EU or as a place of emigration, which promises the better future. Although BiH is a relatively democratic and open society, where access to information is available, people in BiH often become implicitly compliant and might not be fully aware of the essence of the (Europeanization) processes, and the extent the EU as a power-symbol has for them (some even believe that the EU exclusively offers a path to 'normality' for BiH). Such opinions are perhaps not much different in other post-conflict societies around the world, where people believe that their own country, often led by incompetent and corrupt political leadership – which is a widely-shared belief in BiH –, is not able to resolve its domestic issues efficiently. In such circumstances, perceiving external power-symbols as a means of prosperity does not come as a surprise.

Acknowledgment

This project has received funding from the European Union's Horizon 2020 research and innovation program under grant agreement No 769252 and the research programs "Obramboslovje" (P5-0206) and "Slovenija in njeni akterji v mednarodnih odnosih in evropskih integracijah" (P5-0177), funded by the Slovenian Research Agency.

References

Adler-Nissen, Rebecca. (2014) "Symbolic power in European diplomacy: the struggle between national and foreign services and the EU's External Action Service," *Review of International Studies* 40(4): 657–681.

Akdemir, Erhan (2018) "European Union Perception of Bosnia and Herzegovina's People," *Journal of Balkan Research Institute* 7(1): 1–30.

Available at https://www.thebalance.com/world-s-largest-economy-3306044 (accessed March 18, 2020).

Available at http://ba.n1info.com/English/NEWS/a412261/The-Quint-Dodik-s-politics-detrimental-to-Bosnia-s-EU-accession-development.html (accessed March 18, 2020).

Available at http://www.dei.gov.ba/dei/media_servis/vijesti/default. aspx?id=21927&langTag=en-US (accessed March 19, 2020).

Available at http://www.ohr.int/?page_id=1318 (accessed March 17, 2020).

Available at https://www.auswaertiges-amt.de/en/aussenpolitik/bosnia-and-herzegovina/228116 (accessed March 17, 2020).

Barnett, Clive (2001) "Culture, Geography, and the Arts of Government," *Environment and Planning D: Society and Space* 19(1): 7–24.

Bellier, Irene and Wilson, Thomas M. (2000) *An Anthropology of the European Union.* Oxford: Berg.

Belloni, Roberto (2009) "European integration and the Western Balkans: lessons, prospects and obstacles," *Journal of Balkan and Near Eastern Studies* 11(3): 313–331.

_____ (2019) *The Rise and Fall of Peacebuilding in the Balkans.* London: Palgrave Macmillan.

Biddle, Colin (2010) "International Failure in Bosnia and Herzegovina: The Problem with Local Ownership," (MA Thesis) *University of North Carolina, Chapel Hill.*

Bieler, Andreas (2005) "Class Struggle over the EU Model of Capitalism: Neo-Gramscian Perspectives and the Analysis of European Integration," *Critical Review of International Social and Political Philosophy* 8(4): 513–526.

_____ (2006) *The Struggle for Social Europe. Trade Unions and EMU in Times of Global Restructuring.* Manchester: Manchester UniversityPress.

Bieler, Andreas and Morton, Adam D. (eds.) (2001) *Social Forces in the Making of the New Europe: The Restructuring of European Social Relations in the Global Political Economy.* Basingstoke: Palgrave.

Björkdahl, Annika (2012) "Towards a reflexive study of norms, norm diffusion and identity (re)construction: The transformative power of the EU in the Western Balkans," *Canterbury Law Review* 18: 79–96.

_____ (2018) "Republika Srpska: Imaginary, performance and spatialization," *Political Geography* 66(1): 34–43.

Borneman, John and Fowler, Nick (1997) "Europeanization," *Annual Review of Anthropology* 26(3): 487–515.

Bourdieu, Pierre (1990) *The Logic of Practice.* Stanford: Stanford University Press.

_____ (2003) "Participant Objectivation," *Journal of the Royal Anthropological Institute* 9(2): 281–294.

Bouris, Dimitris (2011) "The Limits of Normative Power Europe: Evaluation the Third Pillar of the Euro-Mediterranean Partnership," *Political Perspectives* 5(2): 80–106.

Burg, Steven L. and Shoup, Paul S. (1999) *The War in Bosnia-Herzegovina: Ethnic Conflict and International Intervention*. London: M.E. Sharpe.

Chandler, David (2010) "The Paradox of the 'Responsibility to Protect'," *Cooperation and Conflict* 45(1): 128–134.

Cohen, Ben (1993) 'Why Europe failed to halt the genocide in Bosnia,' *Washington Report on Middle East Affairs*.

Cowles, Maria G. (2003) "Non-state actors and false dichotomies: reviewing IR/IPE approaches to European integration," *Journal of European Public Policy* 10(1): 102–120.

Diez, Thomas (2005) "Constructing the Self and Changing Others: Reconsidering 'Normative Power Europe'," *Millennium: Journal of International Studies* 33(3): 613–636.

Available at http://dei.gov.ba/dei/media_servis/infografike/default.aspx?id=21801&langTag=bs-BA (accessed March 19)

Donais, Timothy (2012) *Peacebuilding and Local Ownership: Post-Conflict Consensus-Building*. London: Routledge.

Eagelton-Pierce, Matthew (2012) *Symbolic Power in the World Trade Organization*. Oxford: Oxford University Press.

Edmunds, Timothy, Juncos, Ana E. and Algar-Faria, Gilberto (2018) "EU local agency capacity building: ownership, complexity and agency," *Global Affairs* 4(2/3): 227–239.

Ejdus, Filip (2017) "Here is your mission, now own it!" The rhetoric and practice of local ownership in EU interventions," *European Security* 26(4): 461–484.

Ejdus, Filip and Juncos, Ana E. (2018) "Reclaiming the local in EU peacebuilding: Effectiveness, ownership, and resistance," *Contemporary Security Policy* 39(1): 4–27.

Available at https://ec.europa.eu/neighbourhood-enlargement/sites/near/files/pdf/key_documents/2011/package/ba_rapport_2011_en.pdf (accessed March 17, 2020).

Available at https://ec.europa.eu/neighbourhood-enlargement/sites/near/files/20190529-bosnia-and-herzegovina-analytical-report.pdf (accessed March 18, 2020).

Available at https://ec.europa.eu/eurostat/databrowser/view/sdg_08_10/default/table?lang=en (accessed 17, 2020).

Available at https://ec.europa.eu/eurostat/tgm/table.do?tab=table&init=1&language=en&pcode=tps00203&plugin=1 (accessed March 17, 2020).

Available at https://ec.europa.eu/eurostat/statistics-explained/index.php/Social_protection_statistics (accessed March 17, 2020).

Gross, Eva and Juncos, Ana E. (2011) *Making sense of EU conflict prevention and crisis management: Institutions, policies and roles.* London: Routledge.

Gstöhl, Sieglinde and Schunz, Simon (2016) *Theorizing the European Neighbourhood Policy.* London: Routledge.

Harmsen Robert and Wilson Thomas M. (2000). "Approaches to Europeanization," *Yearbook of European Studies* 14(1): 13–26.

Juncos, Ana E. (2011) "Power Discourses and Power Practices: The EU's Role as a Normative Power in Bosnia" in Richard. G. Whitman (ed.), *Normative Power Europe: Empirical and Theoretical Perspectives,* pp. 83–99. London: Palgrave Macmillan.

_____(2005) "The EU's post-Conflict Intervention in Bosnia and Herzegovina: (re) Integrating the Balkans and/or (re)Inventing the EU?" *Southeast European Politics* 6: 88–108.

_____ (2018) "Resilience in peacebuilding: Contesting uncertainty, ambiguity and complexity," *Contemporary Security Policy,* 39: 559–574.

Kappler, Stefanie and Lemay-Hébert, Nicolas (2015) "Hybrid local ownership in Bosnia-Herzegovina and Kosovo: from discursive to material aspects of ownership" in Sung Yong Lee and Alpasian Özerdem (eds.), *Local ownership in International Peacebuilding: Key Theoretical and Practical Issues,* pp. 74–92. Oxon: Routledge.

Kuus, Merje (2015) "Symbolic power in diplomatic practice: Matters of style in Brussels," *Cooperation and Conflict* 50: 368–384.

Limantzakis, George (2014) "EU Policy and the Role of the OHR in Bosnia-Herzegovina: Resolving the Problem or Being Part of It?" *Interalia.*

Lukes, Steven (2005) *Power: A radical view. 2nd edition.* London: Palgrave Macmillan.

Majstorović, Danijela and Vučkovac, Zoran (2016) "Rethinking Bosnia and Herzegovina's post-coloniality: Challenges of European discourse," *Journal of Language and Politics* 15: 147–172.

Manners, Ian and Murray, Philomena (2016) "The End of a Noble Narrative? European Integration after the Nobel Peace Prize," *Journal of Common Market Studies* 54: 185–202.

Merlingen, Michael and Ostraiskaite, Rasa (2006) *European Union Peacebuilding and Policing.* London: Routledge.

Milošević, Ana and Touquet, Heleen (2018) "Unintended consequences: the EU memory framework and the politics of memory in Serbia and Croatia," *Southeast European and Black Sea Studies* 18: 381–399.

Noutcheva, Gergana (2009) "Fake, partial and imposed compliance the limits of the EU's normative power in the Western Balkans," *Journal of European Public Policy* 16: 1065–1084.

Papakostas, Nikolaos and Pasamitros, Nikolaos (2014) *An Agenda for the Western Balkans: From Elite Politics to Social Sustainability*. Columbia: Columbia University Press.

Patalakh, Artem (2017) "EU Soft Power in the Eastern Neighbourhood and the Western Balkans in the Context of Crises," *Baltic Journal of European Studies* 7: 148–167.

Pernicka, Susanne and Lahusen, Christian (2018) "Power and Counter Power in Europe. The Transnational Structuring of Social Spaces and Social Fields," *Österreichische Zeitschrift für Soziologie* 43: 1–11.

Prism Research Agency (2017) *Socio-economic Perceptions of Young People in Bosnia and Herzegovina*.

Rees, Wyn (2005) "The External Face of Internal Security" in Christopher Hill and Michael Smith (eds.), *International Relations and the European Union*, pp. 205–224. Oxford: Oxford University Press.

Risse, Thomas, Ropp, Stephen. C. and Sikkink, Kathryn (1999) *The Power of Human Rights: International Norms and Domestic Change*. Cambridge: Cambridge University Press.

Robinson, Nick (2006) *Learning from Lukes? The Three Faces of Power and the European Union. (ECPR Paper)*. School of Politics and International Studies, University of Leeds.

Rudloff, Bettina and Laurer, Moritz (2016) "The EU as global trade and investment actor – The times they are a-changin," (Working Paper RD EU/ Europe). Berlin: German Institute for International and Security Affairs.

Rumford, Chris and Murray, Philomena (2003) "Globalization and the Limitations of European Integration Studies: Interdisciplinary Considerations," *Journal of Common Market Studies* 11: 85–93.

Schütze, Fritz and Schröder-Wildhagen, Anja (2012) "European Mental Space and its Biographical Relevance" in Robert Miller and Graham Day (eds.), *The Evolution of European Identities. Identities and Modernities in Europe*, pp. 255–278. London: Palgrave Macmillan.

Schwarzer, Daniela (2017) "Europe, the End of the West and Global Power Shifts," *Global Policy* 8: 18–26.

Shepherd, Alistair J. (2009) "A Milestone in the History of the EU: Kosovo and the EU's International Role," *International Affairs* 85: 513–530.

Šlosarčik, Ivo (2015) "The Czech Republic and Its (Non)Accession to Schengen and Eurozone" in Annika Björkdahl, Natalia Chaban, John Leslie and

Annick Masselot (eds.), *Importing EU Norms: Conceptual Framework and Empirical Findings,* pp. 13–22. New York: Springer.

Stjepanović, Dejan (2015) "Territoriality and Citizenship: Membership and sub-state polities in post-Yugoslav space," *Europe-Asia Studies* 67: 1030–1055.

Strezhneva, Marina (2018) "The European Union as a Global Actor: The Case of the Financial Transaction Tax," *European Review* 26: 704–720.

Swartz, David L. (2013) *Symbolic Power, Politics, and Intellectuals.* Chicago: University of Chicago Press.

Tonra, Ben (2005) "The European Union as a Global Actor" in Michelle Cini and Angela K. Bourne (eds.), *Palgrave Advances in European Union Studies,* pp. 117–130. London: Palgrave Macmillan.

Valenta, Marko and Ramet Sabrina P. (2011) *The Bosnian Diaspora: Integration in Transnational Communities.* Farnham: Ashgate Publishing, Ltd.

Vangeli, Anastas (2018) "Global China and Symbolic Power: The Case of 16+1 Cooperation," *Journal of Contemporary China* 27: 674–687.

Wagnsson, Charlotte and Hellman, Maria (2018) "Normative Power Europe Caving In? EU under Pressure of Russian Information Warfare," *Journal of Common Market Studies* 56: 1161–1177.

Webber, Douglas (2016) "Declining Power Europe: The Evolution of the European Union's World Power in the Early 21st Century," *European Review of International Studies* 1: 31–52.

Williams, Michael C. (2015) "Securitization as political theory: The politics of the extraordinary," *International Relations* 29: 114–120.

Yong Lee, Sung and Özerdem, Alpasian (2015) *Local Ownership in International Peacebuilding: Key Theoretical and Practical Issues.* London: Routledge.

Zupančič, Rok and Pejič, Nina (2018) *Limits to the European Union's Normative Power in a Post-conflict society: EULEX and Peacebuilding in Kosovo.* Cham: Springer.

Contributors

Valentin Behr holds a PhD in political science from the University of Strasbourg (2017). He is currently a postdoctoral research fellow at the University of Strasbourg at the SAGE Research Center. His main research interests include the sociology of knowledge and ideas, the sociology of political elites, the sociology of intellectuals, the sociology of the state, and politics of memory. He has published in *French Politics, European Politics and Society, Genèses* and *Revue d'études comparatives Est-Ouest*, among others.

Paul Blokker is an Associate Professor in political sociology at the Department of Sociology and Business Law, University of Bologna, Italy. He is also research coordinator at the Institute of Sociological Studies, Charles University, Prague, Czechia. His research focusses on the sociology of constitutions, constitutional politics, democratic participation, and populism.

Elżbieta Hałas is Full Professor of Humanities and Sociology at the Faculty of Sociology, University of Warsaw, Poland. Her fields of interest include: cultural sociology, relational perspectives in social theory, symbolic interactionism, social symbolism and symbolic politics. Her research is focused on the problems of contemporary cultural and social transformations. She has published numerous articles in international journals, such as *Time and Society, Sign System Studies, Symbolic Interaction, Polish Sociological Review*, as well as several books including *Towards the World Culture Society: Florian Znaniecki's Culturalism* (Frankfurt am Main 2010); *Symbole i społeczeństwo* [Symbols and Society] (Warszawa 2007); edited books including *Life-World, Intersubjectivity and Culture: Contemporary Dilemmas* (Frankfurt am Main 2016), and multiple book chapters.

Ulf Hedetoft, Professor, dr. phil., University of Copenhagen, and Director, Center for the Study of Nationalism. Editor-in-chief, *Social Inclusion*. Research interests include nationalism; international migration; European history; cultural globalization; political cultures; transatlantic relations. Scholarly publications comprise about 230 items, amongst them the following: *Signs of Nations. A Political Semiotics of Self and Other in Contemporary European Nationalism* (Dartmouth 1995); The Nation-state Meets the World, *European Journal of Social Theory*, 2:1, 1999; *The Postnational Self: Belonging and Identity,*

University of Minnesota Press, 2002. *National Identities,* 2018; *Paradoxes of Populism*, Anthem Press, 2020.

Dick Houtman is a Professor of Sociology of Culture and Religion at KU Leuven, Belgium. His principal research interests are cultural conflict and cultural change in the West since the 1960s, particularly in and between the realms of politics, religion, consumption and (social) science itself. His latest book is titled *Science under Siege: Contesting the Secular Religion of Scientism* (co-edited with Stef Aupers and Rudi Laermans) and forthcoming with Palgrave Macmillan in 2021. His next book is provisionally titled *The Hunt for Real Reality: The West on the Wings of Imagination.*

Iris Ivaniš, MA, is a PhD candidate at the Faculty of Social Sciences, University of Ljubljana, Slovenia. Her PhD dissertation will focus on the role of educational reforms promoted by the EU in the framework of wider peacebuilding efforts in Bosnia-Herzegovina. She is currently employed as a project officer at the University of Ljubljana, working on an EU-funded project EUTOPIA, which promotes a connected and inclusive academic community of the future.

Luba Jurgenson, born in Moscow in 1958, is currently Full Professor at the Department of Slavic Studies of Sorbonne University and director of the research center Eur'ORBEM, "Cultures and Societies of Eastern, Balkan and Central Europe" (CNRS/Sorbonne). Her main research areas are: witness literature on Nazi camps and Gulag, representations and memory of mass violence in Eastern and Central Europe (20th century). Her most recent book publications include: *Lo Speccio del Gulag in Francia e in Italia,* Pisa University Press, 2019, with Claudia Pieralli; *Le Goulag, témoignages et archives*, Paris, Laffont, 2017, with Nicolas Werth; *Muséographie des violences en Europe centrale et orientale*, Paris, Kimé, 2016, with Delphine Bechtel. She is an editorial board member of the journal *Memories at stake.* She directed a dossier on landscape and memory: *Does Memory Blend into the Landscape? (Memories at Stake, n° 7, Autumn 2018).*

Hubert Knoblauch is Professor of General Sociology at the Technical University of Berlin. His areas of research are sociological theory, sociology of knowledge, religion and communication, qualitative methods, particularly videography and ethnography. Recent Publications include *Powerpoint, Communication, and the Knowledge Society* (Cambridge University Press 2013), *Videography. Introduction to Interpretive Videoanalysis of Social Situations* (Springer 2014), and *The Communicative Construction of Reality* (Routledge 2020).

Faris Kočan, MA, is a Young Researcher and Teaching Assistant at the Faculty of Social Sciences, University of Ljubljana, Slovenia. In his PhD dissertation, he tackles questions regarding ontological security and securitisation of identities in the context of Europeanization, focusing on the case of Republika Srpska. Before becoming Young Researcher, Faris Kočan worked on a H2020 project "RePAST", where he was focusing on the troubled past of Bosnia-Herzegovina within the field of arts and culture, history, media, politics and European integration.

Nicolas Maslowski, PhD, is a political scientist and sociologist. His interests include historical sociology, Central Europe, problems of memory, international relations, protests. He is currently working at the University of Warsaw, as the director of the CCFEF, a French Polish center in social sciences created by Michel Foucault in 1958.

Laure Neumayer is Assistant Professor of Political Science at the University Paris 1 Panthéon Sorbonne. Her research focuses on transnational memory politics in Europe, with a special interest for the memory of Communism. Her publications include *Criminalising Communism in the European Political Space after the Cold War* (Routledge, 2019); "Advocating for the cause of the victims of Communism in the European political space: memory entrepreneurs in interstitial fields," *Nationalities Papers*, 45(6), 2017; "Integrating the Central European Past into a Common Narrative: the Mobilizations around the Crimes of Communism in the European Parliament," *Journal of Contemporary European Studies*, 23(3), 2015; *History, Memory and Politics in Central and Eastern Europe* (co-editor with Georges Mink, Palgrave Macmillan, 2013). She recentley co-edited (with Sophie Baby and Frédéric Zalewski) the digital textbook *Condamner le passé? Mémoires des passes autoritaires en Europe et en Amérique latine* (Presses Universitaires de Paris Nanterre, 2019).

Joanna Nowicki is Professor at CY Cergy Paris University where she is Deputy Vice President RI Mid Europe and Director of the Master in Publishing Studies. She is a member of the LT2DI Laboratory (Lexicons, Texts, Speeches, Dictionaries) and the Editor-in-Chief of the journal Hermès, CNRS (French National Center for Scientific Research). Her work and publications focus on East/West communication, the European collective imagination, the circulation of ideas in Europe and Francophonie. Her latest publications include: *Rêve d'Europe*, (with Luciana Radut-Gaghi, Honoré Champion, 2017), *Incommunications européennes* (Hermès, Editions du CNRS, 2017), *A quoi sert* *la littérature* (with Axel Boursier, Éditions du Cerf, 2018), *La vie de l'esprit. Dictionnaire encyclopédique de la pensée et des penseurs de l'Europe du centre-est depuis 1945* (with Chantal Delsol, Robert Laffont, Éditions du Cerf, 2021).

Anna Pless (Kulkova) is a doctoral researcher at the Center for Sociological Research (CeSO), KU Leuven, Belgium. Her PhD project addresses the consequences of secularization for cleavage-based politics and voting behavior in Europe. Her publications include articles with Paul Tromp and Dick Houtman titled "The 'New' Cultural Cleavage in Western Europe: A Coalescence of Religious and Secular Value Divides?" *Politics and Religion* 13(3), (2020) and *'Religious and Secular Value Divides in Western Europe: A Cross-National Comparison (1981-2008)'* (2021).

Peeter Selg, PhD, is Professor of Political Theory in the School of Governance, Law and Society at Tallinn University, Tallinn, Estonia. His main research interests are related to social science methodology (especially the "relational turn" in political analysis), theories of power, governance and democracy, and studying and governing wicked problems. His work has been published among other outlets in *Sociological Theory, PS: Political Science & Politics, International Relations, Journal of Political Power, Journal of Language and Politics, Semiotica, Sign Systems Studies* and *The Palgrave Handbook of Relational Sociology.* His book (with Andreas Ventsel) is titled *Introducing Relational Political Analysis: Political Semiotics as a Theory and Method* (Palgrave Macmillan, 2020). He is the editor (with Nick Crossley) of the book series "Palgrave Studies in Relational Sociology."

Rok Zupančič is Associate Professor at the Faculty of Social Sciences, University of Ljubljana, Slovenia. His main research interest is peacebuilding in Southeast Europe, in particular the receptiveness of international and local peacebuilding endeavours in post-conflict societies. He leads research on Bosnia-Herzegovina in the framework of a H2020 project *RePAST – Revisiting the Past, Anticipating the Future*, which analyzes the troubled past in eight European countries.

Index

List of Figures

List of Tables

Studies in Sociology:
Symbols, Theory and Society

Book Series

The series has been created by Elżbieta Hałas (Poland) and Risto Heiskala (Finland) in order to stimulate and develop cooperation in research on the meaning, forms and functions of symbolism in society. The series is open to various theoretical and methodological orientations in the studies of social symbolism. The aim of the series is to show the central place of the problems of symbolization and symbolism in sociology – processes of symbolization in everyday life, in collective actions, social movements, organizations, in the public sphere of institutions, as well as in the construction of collective memories and identities, in the construction of the state and the nation, in international relations and in globalization processes.

The series presents theoretical and empirical questions of symbolic power, symbolic hegemony, symbolic control and symbolic politics; integrating as well as transforming and liberating functions of social symbolism in the processes of interactions and communication which shape knowledge, values and social sentiments.

For submission of manuscripts or further information please contact the editors:

Elżbieta Hałas
Faculty of Sociology
University of Warsaw
Karowa 18
00-927 Warsaw
Poland
ehalas@uw.edu.pl

Paolo Terenzi
Department of Political and Social Sciences
University of Bologna
Strada Maggiore 45
40-125 Bologna
Italy
paolo.terenzi@unibo.it

Studies in Sociology:
Symbols, Theory and Society

Edited by Elżbieta Hałas and Paolo Terenzi

www.peterlang.com

Printed by
CPI books GmbH, Leck